t
he

Also by Dennis Sewell

CATHOLICS – BRITAIN'S LARGEST MINORITY

# DENNIS SEWELL

# THE POLITICAL GENE

*How Darwin's Ideas Changed Politics*

PICADOR

First published 2009 by Picador

First published in paperback in 2010 by Picador
an imprint of Pan Macmillan, a division of Macmillan Publishers Limited
Pan Macmillan, 20 New Wharf Road, London N1 9RR
Basingstoke and Oxford
Associated companies throughout the world
www.panmacmillan.com

ISBN 978-0-330-42745-6

1 3 5 7 9 8 6 4 2

A CIP catalogue record for this book is available from
the British Library.

Typeset by Ellipsis Books Limited, Glasgow
Printed by in the UK by CPI Mackays, Chatham ME5 8TD

Visit **www.picador.com** to read more about all our books
and to buy them. You will also find features, author interviews and
news of any author events, and you can sign up for e-newsletters
so that you're always first to hear about our new releases.

*For Laura, Hilla & Thea*

*– who daily provide empirical evidence of meaning
and significance in life.*

# ACKNOWLEDGEMENTS

First and foremost I thank my beloved wife, Laura Cumming, for the immense efforts made and inconveniences suffered over many years while this book was being written and for being the perfect first reader. During the germination of this book Laura managed to produce twin daughters, cherish them through the early years of life and write her own (somewhat longer) book as well as allowing me the time to write mine. She made invaluable improvements to the initial draft and her powerful sense of moral indignation stiffened my resolve not to let the guilty men off too lightly.

I thank also my agent, David Miller at Rogers, Coleridge & White, and Charlotte Greig, Richard Milner, Paul Baggaley, Nicholas Blake and all the team at Picador for all their painstaking and improving work. I am grateful too to Andrew Kidd (late of Picador), who commissioned the book in the first place; and to Peter Ainsworth, Roderick Blyth, Robert Silver and Francis Wheen for the loan of helpful books and for suggestions and advice, and to the staff of the London Library for their patience and assistance.

Through various acts of kindness and indulgence Gwyneth Williams, Matthew D'Ancona, Elaine Thomas and Elizabeth Cumming all helped provide the circumstances in which this book could be written.

I acknowledge a tremendous debt to all those who have contributed to an explosion of recent scholarship in this field, including: Paul A. Lombardo, Michael G. Kenny, John G. West, William H. Tucker, Diane B. Paul, Jonathan Peter Spiro, Robert N. Proctor, Richard Weikart, Stefan Kühl and Daniel J. Kevles and many others whose names may be found in the chapter notes and bibliography.

I have attempted where appropriate to clear copyright permission for quotations, and thank all those who have granted permission, but in a few cases I have not been able to trace the present copyright owners in the standard databases and have found the original publishers are no longer trading. I invite any copyright owners I have not traced to contact me via Picador so that any issues may be resolved before future editions are published.

The quotations from the House of Lords debate in the Introduction are from Hansard, House of Lords, Thursday 19 March 2009 Cols. 368–386. This and other Parliamentary material is reproduced with the permission of the Controller of HMSO on behalf of Parliament.

*London, July 2009*

# Contents

# Introduction

On 19 March 2009, as a gesture by Parliament to mark the bicentenary of his birth, the House of Lords debated Charles Darwin's legacy. A Conservative, Baroness Hooper, had put down the subject for debate the previous year, concerned that the double anniversary (2009 also marked 150 years since the publication of Darwin's *On the Origin of Species*) might pass without the nation paying due respect to one of its greatest scientists. She need not have worried. All kinds of hoopla had already been planned. Under the rubric of Darwin 200, a festival of events – talks, exhibitions, and performances – was scheduled all across Britain. Wreaths were laid at Westminster Abbey; the Royal Mail issued commemorative stamps; the BBC broadcast a season of programmes exploring almost every aspect of the Darwin story; the artist Damien Hirst designed the dust jacket for a special edition of Darwin's masterpiece; Bristol Zoo offered free admission to men with beards; and the Natural History Museum served pea soup made from a recipe devised by Darwin's wife Emma.

Nevertheless, Parliament also wanted to have its say. Lady Hooper opened the debate with a tribute to the great naturalist's meticulous observation and diligent collection of evidence. His theory of evolution by natural selection, she declared, had 'dramatically influenced the society in which we live'. If only the Life Peerages Act had been in force in his day, Lady Hooper said, then Darwin would have become a distinguished member of the House of Lords.

On this latter point, the baroness was probably wrong. Charles Darwin was too committed to his work and too personally diffident ever to have accepted a peerage. He was extremely wary of the meta-scientific controversies he knew his theory provoked, and this led him to adopt a studied ambiguity, amounting sometimes to evasiveness on what he considered sensitive topics, that still has scholars squabbling over quite where he stood on one issue or another.

Debates in the Lords are quite different in tone from those in the Commons. Their lordships are civil to one another, and remarkably tolerant of bores. Peers never need fear the jeers, catcalls and smart-alec interventions that characterize exchanges in the lower house. Their proceedings may seem stuffy and tame to those who prefer their politics bareknuckle; but in their slow and stately way their lordships do eventually get round to addressing the important questions.

Only in a Lords debate on Darwin would you find speaker after speaker who had actually been to the Galapagos Islands, or could boast some family connection to Darwin's circle. Lord Lyell told the House how his great-great-great-uncle, the eminent geologist Sir Charles Lyell, had been one of Darwin's closest friends, but was considered by Emma Darwin 'quite enough to flatten a dinner party'. Lord Jenkin of Roding (Patrick Jenkin, Environment Secretary under Margaret Thatcher) turned out to be the great-grandson of Professor Fleeming Jenkin FRS, one of the few scientist critics of Darwin's theory to persuade him to change his mind and revise the text of

*On the Origin of Species.* In general, those who spoke in the debate were agreed that Darwin's theory was one of 'vast explanatory power'; that it had 'ignited a revolution not just in biology, but also in society'; and that Charles Darwin himself was altogether a good egg: modest, courteous and mild.

The Labour peer Lord Haskel, however, introduced a welcome counterpoint to the celebratory theme. 'Darwin made a wonderful discovery,' he said, 'but it is also a powerful idea that when removed from the subtlety of science to the bluntness of politics becomes a pretty blunt political instrument.' Haskel urged his fellow peers to remember all the millions who have suffered by the application of Darwinian theory to human society, citing racialism, social Darwinism, and eugenics. 'As we know, those ideas reached a climax in Germany with the ideas of the master race and the elimination of the Untermenschen. All that was justified by Darwin's theory of natural selection, the survival of the fittest and the use of Darwin's theory as a means to view other people as fundamentally inferior.' This was not, Lord Haskel warned, a problem safely confined to history. 'Sadly those ideas are still around,' he said, calling for an ethical and moral watch to be kept on the social applications of science.

This book is about precisely this: the political uses and abuses of Darwin's ideas in recent history, and their persistence in the present day. As far as possible, I have tried to maintain the focus of the narrative at the practical and political, rather than the theoretical, level. In dealing with eugenics, for instance, what interested me was not so much the phenomenon itself, considered in the abstract, but finding out how a tightly knit group of scientists (and most of the main actors in this story were scientists – biologists, zoologists, psychologists and doctors) went about trying to sell an esoteric idea to the general public; how they organized, mobilized, and influenced politicians; and how they succeeded in getting laws enacted to suit their ideological purposes.

By approaching the subject at the level of individual political actors, I have also tried to connect what might otherwise seem quite disparate and discrete episodes, but which are actually parts of a continuum. The common factors between, say, the sterilization of a teenager in Virginia in the 1920s, crimes against humanity perpetrated by Nazi physicians, and the funding of research into racial differences in IQ, are very far from obvious. Yet I hope they will become swiftly apparent when the same face can be identified at each scene.

A second line of my enquiry has been to seek to establish how robust the links really were between what Charles Darwin actually wrote or said, and what others, claiming to sail under Darwin's flag, carried into the social and political domain. I have been surprised, sometimes even shocked, to discover that in some sensitive areas the connections are rather stronger than I had expected them to be. When I began writing this book I was aware that many people regarded scientific racialism and eugenics as wholly unwarranted extrapolations from Darwin's thought, and effectively nothing to do with Darwin. I had intended to take an impartial approach, holding that view in balance with its opposite. I have come to the conclusion, however, that it is a false view, as absurd as claiming that the Russian Revolution had nothing to do with Karl Marx, or the attack on the Twin Towers had nothing to do with Islam. Provenance, though, does not necessarily imply culpability. Whether there is any moral fault, I leave the reader to judge.

Darwin was, on the whole, a very honest writer indeed.

When he was unsure of something he would surround his tentative speculations with abundant qualifications or caveats. From time to time, however, some of these have struck me as being insincere. On such occasions I have tried to find out whether Darwin was saying one thing on the record in his published work, and something quite other in his private correspondence or conversation. Sometimes this does indeed appear to have been the case. I am aware that because I have searched out instances of this kind, and selected quotations to suit my rather tightly defined purpose, Charles Darwin may emerge from this story looking a more venal individual than is either warranted, or would be found in a fuller and more rounded portrait. But this book is not a portrait and does not pretend to offer any kind of fair or substantial biographical treatment of Darwin himself.

Although I have not set out to indict Darwin for any crime, I am acutely aware of the vast corpus of creationist writing that seeks to lay at his door responsibility for almost every outrage committed by extremists of left and right throughout the past one and a half centuries. The authors hope by so doing not only to smear Darwin the man, but also to undermine belief in the theory of evolution. Perforce I find myself traversing some of the same thematic territory. Though I hope the following declarations will be unnecessary, for the sake of absolute clarity I am going to make them anyway: I am not and never have been a creationist and have no quarrel whatsoever with the orthodox account of evolution as taught in English schools under guidelines established by the government.

In any case, this book is concerned with the intersection of evolutionary science and politics; it is not about religion. Except in a chapter devoted to an account of the Scopes monkey trial and the subsequent battles to influence the content of the science curriculum of American schools, and a discussion in the final chapter of the clash of science and faith in the public square, religious questions barely figure in this story at all.

Nor is this a science book. To ensure it is readily accessible to the general reader, I have tried to cut out as much scientific jargon as possible and to avoid lengthy digressions examining scientific disputes or innovations, except where they are essential to an understanding of the story. In a few instances, where the elaboration of technical detail would be helpful, but might obstruct the flow of the narrative, I have provided it in the notes at the end of the book.

The application of Darwin's ideas to society is something that has been attempted in many ways in many countries during the past hundred and fifty years. To give a definitive account of them all would be way beyond the scope of this slim volume. I have therefore selected a series of snapshots which seem to me to capture the essence of the project, such that each chapter tells a different story but all are in some way connected. I invite the reader to follow the thematic threads and the footprints of a cast of core characters. I have also limited the geographical range to the United States, Britain and Germany.

For the sake of clarity, while moving from country to country, I have sometimes imposed a consistency of terminology where, in fact, none existed. For instance, practitioners of eugenics in Britain called themselves 'eugenists', while in America they called themselves 'eugenicists'. I have plumped for the American word, partly because 'eugenist' seems rather twee and partly because 'eugenicist' makes more etymological sense. I have adapted quotations to conform to this scheme.

Although I have generally tried to avoid doing so, there are occasions when I use the word 'Darwinist' because in the specific context it seems to me the mot juste. Once again, I feel the need to issue a disclaimer because this word (and the related 'Darwinism') has been appropriated by creationists to imply that believers in evolution have turned themselves into something approaching a religion. Just because creationists have seized upon a word does not mean the rest of us should be robbed of its convenience and utility. When I employ the term it is to recognize the distinction between Darwin's scientific ideas (which are 'Darwinian') and the use of his thought to form the basis of an ideology or outlook pertaining to politics and society. Again, this is something I expand upon in the notes where appropriate.

Darwin's 1859 book was published under the title *On the Origin of Species by Means of Natural Selection, or the Preservation of Favoured Races in the Struggle for Life*. Later editions appeared with the shorter and more familiar title *The Origin of Species*. So as not to congest the text, I will from now on refer to this book as the *Origin*. The word 'evolution' does not itself appear in the 1859 edition and the book did not explicitly discuss the evolution of our species or make specific reference to our common ancestry with apes. Indeed, all Darwin had to say on the matter was this passing observation: 'In the distant future I see open fields for far more important researches. Psychology will be based on a new foundation, that of the necessary acquirement of each mental power and capacity by gradation. Light will be thrown on the origin of man and his history.'

The public, however, was extremely quick on the uptake. While intellectuals such as T. H. Huxley were chiefly struck by the fact that Darwin's book did away with teleology in nature, most people understood (or misunderstood) it to mean that men were descended from familiar apes. Magazines throughout 1860 were filled with cartoons featuring Darwin and monkeys. Laughing at the very notion was perhaps the way Victorian England found for coming to terms with its anxieties about the subject. If the common ancestry of all life forms was too much to accept in one gulp, focusing on our nearer evolutionary forebears was a stage along the way. The idea that human beings, previously regarded as sui generis, were just another part of the animal kingdom was an unsettling one for politicians as well as for ordinary people. 'What is the question?' Benjamin Disraeli asked rhetorically in 1864. 'It is now placed before society with, I might say, a glib assurance which to me is astonishing. The question is, "Is man an ape or an angel?" Now I am on the side of the angels.'

Charles Darwin was relatively quick to take the matter further. In 1871, he published his second important book on evolutionary theory, *The Descent of Man, and Selection in Relation to Sex* (henceforth the *Descent*). This book explicitly addressed the evolution of man, his close relationship with apes, and ventured theories about the evolution of man's mental powers and even his moral and ethical faculties. In this book, Darwin also considered the sensitive question of whether the various races of man were all members of the same species. Although it will doubtless be for the *Origin* that Darwin will always be best remembered, it was the *Descent* that was chiefly responsible for generating the controversies examined in this book.

Our story begins in New York City, in the early years of the twentieth century, when the idea that apes were our evolutionary cousins became the talk of the town.

# CHAPTER ONE

If evolution is true, why are there still monkeys?

Larry King, CNN

In the autumn of 1906, one of the panjandrums of the American scientific Establishment decided to give the New York public an object lesson in human evolution. William Temple Hornaday, formerly of the Smithsonian Institution, and now installed as the director of the Bronx Zoo, put a twenty-three-year-old Congolese pygmy on public display in his monkey house. The pygmy's name was Ota Benga, and he shared his cage with an orang-utan called Dohung. Dinah the gorilla lived next door.

The spectacle attracted enormous crowds. On its second day, more than 40,000 visitors pressed to take a peek at the attraction. Before long, the excited throng were asking precisely the questions the exhibitors hoped they would: Was Ota Benga a monkey or a man? Or, as the zookeeper himself speculated, was this perhaps a transitional form between the two, the famously elusive missing link? In order to come to an informed judgement, a reporter from the *New York Times* made a dutiful study, switching his gaze from Ota Benga to Dohung and back again. 'The pygmy was not much taller than the orang-utan,' he observed, 'and one had a good opportunity to study their points of resemblance. Their heads are much alike, and both grin in the same way when pleased.'[1]

For those among the gathering already familiar with the writings of Charles Darwin and his supporters, the moot issue of Ota Benga's humanity was, in fact, only a question of degree. There was at that time a broad consensus among men of science that the several races of mankind had travelled different distances down the evolutionary highway, and at the rear of the caravan there was a certain amount of overlap between the laggards and members of other mammalian species – in terms of talents, abilities and, consequently, worth.

Hornaday, in particular, believed that some of his simian charges could often be more than a match for their human cousins. '. . . I would try to teach orang-utans and chimpanzees the properties of fire, and how to make and tend fires. I would try to teach them the seed-planting idea, and the meaning of seedtime and harvest,' he wrote, describing an ideal experiment into animal intelligence. 'I would teach my apes to wash dishes and to cook, and I am sure that some of them would do no worse than some human members of the profession who now receive $50 per month, or more, for spoiling food.'[2]

It may have been a more generally misanthropic Hornaday who wrote those words over a decade afterwards, at a time when good domestic help was apparently hard to find, and when the experience of the First World War made it seem, as he put it himself in the pessimistic language of race-suicide theory, 'as if the Caucasian really is played out'.[3] Nevertheless, there is no reason to suppose that Hornaday's views on what measure of respect is owed to an individual by virtue of his humanity was greatly different back in 1906, when he chose to put a black man in a cage.

Hornaday was not, however, hostile to the notion of rights. On the contrary, he once drafted a bill of rights himself. It was a generous-hearted charter of animal rights in which he condemned hunting for sport; described bullfighting as 'disgustingly cruel'; deprecated the use of monkeys by organ-grinders, and demanded that 'the sale and use of chained live chameleons as ornaments and playthings for idiotic or vicious men and children' should be prohibited by law.[4] Nevertheless, when a group of Baptist pastors – drawn mainly from African American-led churches – objected to the zoo putting a human being on show, Hornaday could not see what the fuss was about and resisted them at every turn.

Standing shoulder to shoulder with Hornaday throughout the ensuing controversy was another of the instigators of the exhibit, the secretary of the New York Zoological Society, Madison Grant. A politically well-connected lawyer and pas-sionate conservationist, Grant would subsequently emerge as one of the leading theoreticians of scientific racialism and an enthusiastic champion of eugenics. But the presence of such an infamous figure so close to the action should not mislead us into supposing that the indignity inflicted upon Ota Benga represented merely one more in a long series of casual and only-to-be-expected racist outrages, familiar enough in the American social landscape before Dr Martin Luther King, Rosa Parks and the civil rights movement brought matters to a resolution. This was, after all, New York not Mississippi. Jim Crow laws did not apply in the Bronx. Besides, right across the nation African Americans had been making noticeable social progress. Booker T. Washington had already been the guest of

President Theodore Roosevelt in the White House; W. E. DuBois had already earned his doctorate at Harvard; and African Americans in the Empire State had been able to vote in local and national elections for well over a hundred years (even if, at times, they may have believed they had nothing for which to vote) by the time that Ota Benga was placed on such humiliating display.

Under normal circumstances one might have expected social and ethical constraints – and maybe even legal and constitutional ones too – to prevent such an outrage against human dignity from taking place. But these were not normal circumstances. The authority of science had been invoked, and in a self-consciously progressive era, this consideration trumped all others. Two years previously, Harpers in New York had published an English edition of Ernst Haeckel's *The Wonders of Life*, in which the German evolutionist had posed a radical challenge to a truth about universal human equality that the founding fathers of the United States had held to be self-evident. 'These lower races', Haeckel argued, citing as examples the Veddahs of Ceylon and Australian aborigines, 'are psychologically nearer to apes and dogs than to civilized Europeans; we must, therefore, assign a totally different value to their lives.'[5]

Charles Darwin too had pondered the anomalous situation in which sophisticated Europeans shared the world not only with apes, but also with other somewhat embarrassing reminders of their evolutionary journey. But the great naturalist had seen the future, and found it reassuringly lethal. 'The civilized races of man will almost certainly exterminate, and replace, the savage races throughout the world,' Darwin predicted in the *Descent*. 'At the same time, the anthropomorphous apes ... will no doubt be exterminated. The break between man and his nearest allies will then be wider, for it will intervene between man in a more civilized state, as we may hope, even than the Caucasian, and some ape as low as a baboon; instead of as now between the Negro ... and the gorilla.'[6]

In the case of the pygmies of the Congo, the Force Publique (a brutal militia that enforced rubber quotas in the territory and pilfered ivory on the side) had already made a start towards their extermination at around the turn of the twentieth century. The Congo Free State was run at this time not as a conventional colony of Belgium, but as the private ranch of King Leopold II himself, and was registered as a corporation, with Leopold as sole shareholder. The Batwa tribe of pygmies, to which Ota Benga belonged, contributed little or nothing to Leopold's profits and were competitors in the ivory trade. During a campaign of genocide perpetrated by the King's militia, Ota Benga's family were killed and he found himself put up for sale in a slave market, where he was purchased by Phillips Verner, an explorer from South Carolina, and a keen Darwinist, who was scouring Africa for anthropological curiosities to take to the 1904 St Louis World Fair. There the pygmy struck up a friendship with the Apache warrior Geronimo, with whom he appeared in an ethnographic vignette.

Two years later the explorer and his pygmy wound up flat broke in New York City. Verner looked for somewhere for Ota Benga to stay while he went home to the South to raise some money. He tried the Salvation Army first, and then the New York Police Department. Neither could accommodate Ota. But Herman Bumpus, the director of the Natural History Museum, gave the young African visitor a room, bought him a suit and generally treated him in a kindly fashion. The only requirement made of him was that he should from time to time amuse some of the rich socialites whose philanthropy Dr Bumpus wished to cultivate. But Ota Benga took against the ladies who lunch, and disgraced himself by shouting, screaming and finally hurling a chair at Florence Guggenheim. So the pygmy's next stop was the zoo.

There were two main strands of objection to the public display of a human being in a zoo. The Reverend J. H. Gordon of the Colored Baptist Ministers' Conference voiced both of them. 'We do not like this exhibition of one of our race with the monkeys,' he said after visiting Ota Benga at the monkey house. 'Our race, we think, is depressed enough without exhibiting one of us with the apes.'[7] Calling upon New York's mayor, George Brinton McClellan Jr., to intervene, Gordon insisted that 'the Darwinian theory is absolutely opposed to Christianity, and a public demonstration in its favour should not be permitted.'[8] The following day's *New York Times* carried a riposte from the Darwinist camp. 'It is most amusing to note that one reverend colored brother objects to the curious exhibition on the grounds that it is an impious effort to lend credibility to Darwin's dreadful theories,' observed the newspaper's Topics of the Times columnist. '...The reverend colored brother should be told that evolution, in one form or another, is now taught in the textbooks of all the schools, and that it is no more debatable than the multiplication table.'[9]

The terms of that exchange are very familiar to us today. A little over a hundred years later, the champions of science and Evangelical Christianity still bark at one another across the public square. Sarah Palin's alleged creationism, and support for discussing the theories of the intelligent design movement in class, though not an issue of decisive salience during the 2008 US Presidential Election campaign, was nevertheless significant in determining the way the media represented her. Many liberal voters were at a loss to understand how it could possibly be that almost a decade into the twenty-first century there was any chance at all that someone who questioned the theory of evolution could be elected to the vice-presidency of the United States, where she would be only a heartbeat away from having her finger on the nuclear button. Which only goes to show how remote those liberal voters were from the beliefs and sentiments of what Governor Palin liked to call 'real America'.

Earlier in the year there had been moments where it looked as if Darwin's theory would be used as a litmus test in the Republican primaries. During a debate on 3 May 2008, the candidates were asked whether there was anyone on stage who did not believe in evolution. Three of them – Senator Sam Brownback of Kansas, Representative Tom Tancredo of Colorado, and former Arkansas governor Mike Huckabee – were prepared to proclaim their disbelief proudly and unambiguously. The man who would go on to win the nomination, John McCain, preferred to have it both ways. Though he did believe in evolution, the Arizona senator said, when he hiked the Grand Canyon, he liked to believe the hand of God was there also.

If one were to take the cynical view that unprincipled opportunism actuates all politicians in all circumstances, these answers could be used as evidence that these Grand Old Party hopefuls really did have their fingers on the national pulse and had made the appropriate political calculation. Astonishing as it may be to urban sophisticates, a survey by the Pew Forum on Religion and Public Life, carried out as recently as August 2006, discovered that only 26 per cent of adult Americans accept Charles Darwin's theory of evolution by natural selection as it is understood by scientists and taught in public schools.[10]

How could it be that after 150 years, evolutionary scientists have managed to persuade only a little over a quarter of Americans of the veracity of their theory? The reluctance of the majority to embrace Darwin cannot plausibly be attributed to stupidity. Americans are not stupid, nor are they resistant to new ideas. During the twentieth century, the United States established itself as the most economically successful and technologically advanced society on earth, leading the world in innovation and achievement. Americans are the very last people one should expect to deny a scientific truth.

Perhaps it is not Darwin's theory itself that so many Americans find off-putting, but the foul dust that follows in its wake. Even from the off, large and elaborate claims have been made about multiple philosophical, social and political implications of evolution. During the intervening years the theory has metastasized. From a neat explanation of variation within species and a plausible hypothesis for the origin of species, it quickly became an account of the origins of all life, then a general explanatory theory of the development and survival of everything, a grand narrative to end all grand narratives. It has been presented to us by Professor Daniel Dennett as a 'universal acid'[11] that dissolves every ethical and moral system it encounters, and by Professor Richard Dawkins as a compelling argument against the existence of God and a slam-dunk case for giving up any search for meaning, purpose or direction in human affairs.

Just as we were struggling to adjust to the death of the afterlife, the dissolution of decency and the end of teleology, along came a fresh wave of evolutionary psychologists and sociobiologists, to tell us that evolution explains almost every aspect of our behaviour: a man's propensity to rape, a woman's preference for pink, and why even a *New York Times* reporter might grin in the same way as an ape when pleased. Nothing is sacred. Even the love parents feel for their children is fed into the reductionist mill. A long time ago, when we were all hunter-gatherers, so we're told, there lived large numbers of unappealing infants who, subjected to some unknown selection pressure, perished, leaving only those whose winsome ways could secure maternal or paternal protection. The survival of the cutest.

As if all this were not sufficiently unsettling, the Black Book of Darwinism contains some real horrors. As we shall see, evolution has been used in the relatively recent past to justify all manner of moral outrages from sterilization to mass-murder. In the imminent future, advances in genetic science will open up a whole new world of possibilities to do unimaginable good, or irrevocable harm. In this context, the reluctance of so many – and not just in the United States – to give Charles Darwin and his ideas an unqualified thumbs-up starts to look less like the ignorant prejudice of the stereotypical redneck, but rather an understandable reluctance to endorse a system of thought that appears subversive of so many cherished values.

When we are asked about our belief in evolution, some of us will find it important to discover the real truth; others will choose to believe what it seems to them good to believe. What, in any case, is the pollster really asking when he asks if you believe in evolution? Will he get one answer if he asks whether you accept that you share a common ancestor with the apes, but a different answer if he asks you to acknowledge common descent with the cauliflower? Is he just wanting to confirm that you concur that creatures change in small ways over long periods of time, and those whose constitutions are best adapted to their environments tend to survive and multiply, while those poorly suited to their circumstances are more likely to die off? Or is he inviting you to assent to a darker and more worrying proposition: that our lives have no special meaning or significance; that all there is and has been in this world came about through a series of astonishing flukes, and that the idea of a loving God is something we have invented for our consolation in the face of the pitiless indifference of Nature?

Depending on which way the question is framed, one would expect to get a different result each time. The issue of evolution provides plenty of opportunities for unscrupulous push-polling, and we need to be thoughtful in our analysis of survey results. The scientist may assume that if a majority of people explicitly assent to a particular proposition, then they assent implicitly to all that logically follows on from that proposition. But the politician knows that that is very rarely the case. Opinion polls frequently record that what we really want is higher spending at the same time as lower taxes; jam today and sound money too; peace in our time as well as decisive interdiction against evil tyrants; civil liberty together with the smack of firm government. The attitudes we strike when faced with a pollster's questionnaire are not the product of ratiocination, so much as the expression of sometimes contradictory impulses and yearnings. But that should not in any way diminish the importance of polling data. Democratic politicians need to understand what excites or alarms us, what we admire or find absurd, what we believe with all our heart, and what we only reluctantly go along with.

Yet even our idea of what seems ridiculous or incredible will depend upon where we start. Some decided atheists, for instance, resent social pressure to describe themselves as 'agnostic' about the existence or otherwise of a deity. They profess themselves unable to understand why they should have to be even-handed in their consideration of that particular possibility, when no one would expect them to be fence-sitters on the question whether or not there is a teapot in orbit near Mars.[12] On the other hand, US Supreme Court Justice Antonin Scalia has pointed out how a refusal to believe in Christ's resurrection might be construed as equally ridiculous, since to deny it implies that 'everything from the Easter morning to the Ascension had to be made up by the grovelling enthusiasts as part of their plan to get themselves martyred.'[13] No meeting along the road to Emmaeus, no Doubting Thomas, no fishing trip to Tiberias. If Christ's followers were indeed fabricators of evidence, why would they make up these stories, in all their puzzling complexity and, let's face it, intimacy of scale? By setting out the case in this way, Justice Scalia invites us to find it much easier to accept that Jesus rose from the dead than that an elaborate and unlikely conspiracy was concocted among his disciples – a train of thought unquestionably worth pursuing further than any fruitless speculation about Bertrand Russell's celestial teapot.

In the supreme court of public opinion, convened back in 1906, to decide the case of the pygmy in the zoo, many of the vital issues were not very different from those we still struggle to resolve in our debates today. The story of Ota Benga can be seen as raising a range of questions to which, as a society, we have yet to work out all the answers. Much, of course has altered during the intervening years, particularly in the fields of race relations and civil rights. But though the United States has elected its first African American president, and the idea of displaying a human being in a zoo ought to be altogether unthinkable, it would be a mistake to conclude that all the ideas and attitudes that put Ota Benga in his cage have ceased to have any traction.

In August 2005, ninety-nine years after Ota Benga appeared side by side with Dohung, London Zoo opened an exhibit called 'Human Zoo', in which three men and five women frolicked on some rocks clad in pinned-on fig leaves and bathing suits. The style of presentation was modelled on that of the neighbouring apes, with the usual flannel-panel detailing the geographical distribution, habitat and diet of *Homo sapiens*. This time, owing to the proliferation of liability insurance and health and safety legislation, the humans were kept separated from the apes by an electric fence. The zoo said that the purpose of the exhibit was 'to demonstrate the basic nature of man as an animal'.[14] A spokesman added that 'Seeing people in a different environment, among other animals . . . teaches members of the public that the human is just another primate.' This theme was taken further by Tom Mahoney, who had been one of those on show. 'A lot of people think humans are above other animals,' he said. 'When they see humans as animals here, it reminds them that we're not that special.'[15]

Politically, a society that holds human life to be sacred and one that thinks we're 'not that special' are a world apart. The difference between Tom Mahoney and Ota Benga, of course, was that Mr Mahoney volunteered to perform before the zoo-going public, while the poor pygmy had no say whatsoever about being placed on display. But is that a distinction of any real value, if the zoo's central claim is correct? If Ota Benga was not that special, being rather 'just another primate', then Director Hornaday was under hardly any more of an obligation to seek his informed consent before ushering him into his cage than he was to secure the agreement of Dohung the orang-utan and Dinah the gorilla to their captivity and exhibition.

In their forthright rejection of Darwinism, one imagines that the Baptist ministers who came to Ota Benga's aid understood that evolution posed a threat not only to the authority of scripture and the place of religion, but also to the principles enshrined in the American Founding. Like the Baptist minister who would follow them to describe his dream at Washington's Lincoln Memorial in August 1963, they too would have read the magnificent words of the Constitution and the Declaration of Independence as a promissory note that all men, black as well as white, would be heir to. Whether you take the words 'all men are created equal' or 'endowed by their Creator with certain unalienable Rights' literally; or understand them in a metaphorical sense – either way, natural rights – what John F. Kennedy described as 'the belief that the rights of man come not from the generosity of the state, but from the hand of God'[16] – would be utterly undermined if Darwin's wholly materialistic explanation of man's origin were true.

Imagine we declared a Year Zero, dispensing with all those rights and freedoms that stem from the idea of natural rights and Western values with a Judaeo-Christian root: would we be able, from a blank slate, to reason ourselves back to where we are now? Or would the icy logic of Darwinism begin the slow undoing of human rights? Charles Darwin, himself, was confident that reason alone would see us through: 'As man advances in civilization, and small tribes are united into larger communities,' he wrote, 'the simplest reason would tell each individual that he ought to extend his social instincts and sympathies to all the members of the same nation, though personally unknown to him. This point being once reached, there is only an artificial barrier to prevent his sympathies extending to the men of all nations and races.'[17]

Yet the very existence of democratic politics with its debating chambers and whipped votes can be seen as a vivid demonstration of the limits of pure reason. Each party to any political argument will, of course, claim to have reason on its side. Each will deploy reasoned arguments to advance its case. But politicians are seldom persuaded by the logic of their opponents; and when they are, they do not admit it. Reason may be indispensable to the political process, but reason is not enough. The most striking examples of political rhetoric are those that make appeals to the transcendent.

Vaclav Havel, the then president of the Czech Republic, went further, making mankind's need for transcendence the actual subject of a speech in Philadelphia in 1994. 'Classical modern science', Havel said, 'described only the surface of things, a single dimension of reality. And the more dogmatically science treated it as the only dimension, as the very essence of reality, the more misleading it became.' Havel was speaking in Philadelphia's Independence Hall, so it was only natural that he too should cite the same text as the Reverend Martin Luther King and President Kennedy had before him: 'The Declaration of Independence states that the Creator gave man the right to liberty. It seems man can realize that liberty only if he does not forget the One who endowed him with it."[18]

As well as the big questions of public morality – how the *New York Times* or Mayor George Brinton McClellan Jr. should have addressed the issue of the pygmy in the zoo – the Ota Benga case also illustrates how Darwinism might inflect individual ethical decisions. Did William Hornaday and Madison Grant's enthusiasm for evolution in any sense lead them to make the wrong call? The debate about whether it is possible to have a godless morality is still to be definitively settled. Our moral concepts do tend to be rooted in religious teaching and expressed in religious terms and though every believer can number among their own friends atheists who behave as well, if not better, than religious folk, it could be that the non-believers are living off ethical capital built up in a more pious age. The humanist counter to that is that the Ten Commandments – or at least those of them that deal with how we behave towards one another – did not need to be brought down from Sinai on tablets of stone since they are pretty self-evident, and appear in much the same form across most cultures. But the specifically Darwinist counter is that ethics are rooted not in religion, nor in culture, but in biology. Its advocates argue that, just as Noam Chomsky has shown how we are genetically equipped to acquire language, our brains may be similarly endowed with neural circuitry that leads us to develop moral sentiments. Though these are fairly basic to begin with, little more than gut-feelings or vague intuitions, they are capable of astonishing development and refinement through our interaction with our environment, in much the same way as happens with language.

Though it might be cheering to discover that Ivan

Karamazov was wrong to conclude that without God, every-thing is permissible; we should perhaps remind ourselves that William Hornaday and Madison Grant did decide in the end that the sacrifice of Ota Benga's rights and dignity was fully justified by the educational benefits they expected would accrue from the exhibit. This example of crude, utilitarian moral reasoning should make us somewhat less sanguine about how any educated, rational being, equipped with a moral system designed by natural selection, is likely to behave when confronted with an ethical dilemma.

In his inauguration speech in January 2009, President Barack Obama promised 'to restore Science to its proper place'.[19] Quite what he meant by this resounding phrase has been the subject of speculation. Perhaps he intended to signal that he would remove the limitations on the use of federal funding for stem-cell research imposed by his predecessor. Perhaps he was giving a broader signal that his administration would take a more active approach to the challenge of reduc-ing carbon emissions. Or maybe the new president wanted to indicate that he did not share George W. Bush's view that intelligent design should be taught alongside evolution in America's public schools.

This part of the inaugural address was understandably met with cheers and whoops of delight on campuses across the United States. But some more thoughtful scientists tempered their euphoria with one cautious misgiving. They recognized a danger in science pushing itself forward in the public square as a strident voice insisting that it, and it alone, is the bearer of truth. The previous eight years of the Bush administration had seen the science establishment relapse into the old, bad habit of trying to present itself as an authority. Moreover, to shore up that authority, it had increasingly become reliant upon claiming, and parading, a consensus.

It was perfectly understandable why it did so. On two major issues of public importance, anthropogenic global warming and evolution, the scientific mainstream found itself challenged – in the media and in politics – by campaigners who denied what most scientists thought were fundamentally proven and settled facts. The various scientific bodies discerned that they were up against what were effectively very well-funded propaganda operations. The truth, as they saw it, was under siege by the practitioners of the black arts of news manipulation. And as the debate on embryonic stem-cell research was added to the list, it began to look to some as if the political Right had launched a full-scale war on science.

In 2001, the Discovery Institute, a think tank and research organization that represents the more intellectually respectable end of the intelligent design movement, took out an advertisement under the headline 'A Scientific Dissent from Darwinism', which appeared in two prestigious political magazines, the *New Republic* and the *Weekly Standard*, and in the *New York Review of Books*. The text noted that the media and educationalists tended to assert that Darwinian evolution offered a sufficient explanation of living things and that PBS had recently claimed that 'all known scientific evidence supports [Darwinian] evolution' and that 'virtually every reputable scientist in the world' concurred.

'The following scientists,' the advertisement continued, 'dispute the first claim and stand as living testimony in contradiction to the second. There is scientific dissent to Darwinism.'[20]

Underneath appeared the names of the signatories

alongside details of the universities where they worked or gained their doctoral qualifications.

To many scientists this looked like a familiar tactic, one pioneered by Big Tobacco when the medical dangers of smoking first became apparent. 'Doubt is our product,' read an internal memo of the tobacco company Brown & Williamson in 1969, 'since it is the best means of competing with the "body of fact" that exists in the mind of the general public. It is also the means of establishing a controversy.'[21]

However, as each of the scientists was contacted and prompted to expand further on his or her views, it became apparent that there were those who genuinely were not prepared to go the whole hog with Darwin, and not because they were being funded by some interest group. It was, in most cases, not so much that they disputed evolution as such, but they disputed standard Darwinian teaching on the origins of life, or were not prepared to buy into the social and philosophical implications of the theory that Darwinists insisted were part of the package.

The National Centre for Science Education came up with an amusing response. They drafted their own statement endorsing evolution as 'a vital, well-supported, unifying principle of the biological sciences',[22] but reserved the right to sign it only to people called Stephen (or Stephanie) or some variant thereof. Very soon they had collected more than five hundred signatures for Project Steve. Though it had its charm, the problem with this approach was that, in the end, it was merely another variant of wielding consensus like a club in the public square while loudly asserting one's authority.

In theory, notions of authority and consensus should be repugnant to the scientific mind. Science has always progressed by challenging accepted beliefs, defying prevailing wisdoms. A good scientist should be just as keen to falsify the findings of other scientists as to confirm them. Restoring science to its rightful place should be about listening to the empirical evidence science offers about matters within its sphere, not about setting bodies of scientists up as authorities. We can be fairly confident that whatever is the consensus among scientists today will have been superseded in a generation's time. Scientific knowledge is, of its nature, provisional; and science is most truthful when it acknowledges its own uncertainties.

The scientific consensus that prevailed in Ota Benga's time held that the 'lower' races were less evolved than Caucasians. Henry Fairfield Osborn, one of the most esteemed American anthropologists of the first half of the twentieth century, seemingly could not bring himself to include the African as a member of the human race at all. 'The standard of intelligence of the average adult Negro is similar to that of the eleven-year-old youth of the species *Homo sapiens*,' he famously observed.[23]

As recently as 2007, the geneticist James Watson explained his gloomy prognosis for Africa's social and economic development in these terms: '. . . there is no firm reason to anticipate that the intellectual capacities of peoples geographically separated in their evolution should prove to have evolved identically'. And: 'Our wanting to reserve equal powers of reason as some universal heritage of humanity will not be enough to make it so.' Watson has form. In 1962 he won the Nobel Prize for his work as one of the team that discovered the structure of DNA.[24]

Yet *pace* the occasional maverick, the consensus has changed since Grant and Hornaday summoned all the pompous authority of science to put Ota Benga in his cage. The doctrine of scientific racialism that, in the interim, led to appalling suffering across the world was later utterly discredited. For many years scientists preferred to emphasize the things that all races share. Studies were carried out to identify the genes that have been subject to evolutionary change since the various races began to come into being. Reportedly, they tended to be those to do with skin pigmentation and hair type, or those associated with adjusting to a different diet. Under the skin, and away from the dinner table, we were reassured, we are all much the same and no one is more highly evolved than another. The idea that black people were closer in the evolutionary scale to apes than white people is seen by scientists today as a ghastly mistake, but they are not taking any responsibility for it. Yesterday's scientific consensus is regarded as highly unscientific, as if really nothing to do with science at all. Yet its traces linger in the minds of millions, inflecting attitudes to race everywhere. Moreover, the latest developments in genetics seem to point to there being more biological differences between races than it has been fashionable to believe in recent years, so we should anticipate that a fresh set of pernicious social inferences will be drawn from evolutionary science in the future.

Ota Benga left the zoo after a short time and went to stay with one of the pastors who had taken up his cause. After living for a while in Brooklyn, where he learned to read and was baptized a Christian, he moved to rural Virginia and took a job in a tobacco factory. On 20 March 1916, after enquiring about the price of a steamer ticket back to Africa, he shot himself through the heart.

# CHAPTER TWO

Politics is applied biology.

Ernest Haeckel

Charles Darwin could trace his descent from Charlemagne and an ape; and his political legacy has turned out to be no less startling than his lineage.

Immediately after the publication of the *Origin* in 1859, Darwinian evolution began to play a variety of roles in advancing political arguments: as a backbone or a backstop; a cause or a catalyst; or simply the camouflage for prejudice. Various ideas of evolution had existed for a long time before Darwin, but by discovering the mechanism of natural selection, he had invested the concept with a powerful authority that others quickly sought to yoke to their own ideas and projects.

It should not be surprising that Darwin's theory was so readily translated into the domain of social and political thought, for much of what is most striking in the *Origin* was drawn from political and economic writing in the first place. Darwin had made his voyage aboard the *Beagle*, had collected specimens, scribbled down observations, followed hunches and intuitions, formed and discarded conjectures.

But something was still missing. While groping towards his theory of natural selection, Darwin scoured the social and political shelves of his library for something to jog his mind, to bring his inchoate ideas to term, to complete the conceptual circle. We know that the Scottish Enlightenment philosopher Dugald Stewart's *On the Life and Writing of Adam Smith* was fresh in Darwin's mind and that the penny finally dropped while he was reading Thomas Malthus's grim prognostications in *An Essay on the Principle of Population* – a text Darwin reported, without evident irony, he had picked up in October 1838 'for amusement'. It was while contemplating Malthus's account of the universal struggle for existence, Darwin said, that '. . . it at once struck me that under these circumstances favourable variations would tend to be preserved, and unfavourable ones to be destroyed. The result of this would be the formation of new species.'[1]

Malthus had argued that population increases would always undercut any attempt to improve the conditions of the poor, which meant that schemes to eradicate poverty were largely a waste of time. This ensured that his name would forever excite virulent antipathy among the political left, probably as much for his dismissing them as irrelevant as for his hard-heartedness towards the poor themselves. Yet despite Darwin's debt to Malthus, Karl Marx was quick to proclaim affinities between Darwin's work and his own. 'Darwin's book is very important,' Marx wrote to the German socialist Ferdinand Lassalle shortly after reading the *Origin*, 'and serves me as a basis in natural science for the class struggle in history.'[2] Friedrich Engels took the same view, slipping a brief credit for Darwin into his preface for the 1888 edition of *The Communist Manifesto*. 'Just as Darwin discovered the law of evolution in organic nature,' Engels later declared in his graveside eulogy at Marx's funeral, 'so Marx discovered the law of evolution in human history.'[3]

Although this was to a large extent a shameless bid to gain credit by association with Darwin's popular and clearly world-changing theory, there was some genuine overlap. Darwin offered a materialist explanation of nature's history, dispensing with supernatural and metaphysical considerations. Marx could regard this as congenial in terms of clearing the ground. Moreover there were conceptual similarities between the way natural selection wrought changes in the natural world and Marx's own ideas about how changes in the means of production (new inventions, for instance) displaced older, less efficient forms, creating a new social reality. 'Both theories', wrote A. D. Lindsay in his introduction to Marx's *Capital*, 'purport to show how a struggle which is in itself blind and haphazard produces results which seem purposive because in the process the unfit variations are cut out.'[4]

The still widely reported story that Marx offered to dedicate *Capital* to Charles Darwin is, however, untrue. Darwin had written to Edward Aveling, a member of the National Secular Society, in 1880 politely declining the young man's offer to dedicate to him a slim volume entitled *The Student's Darwin*. The publication was to be one in a series under the general title 'The International Library of Science and Freethought', edited by the notorious atheists Annie Besant and Charles Bradlaugh. Having been careful to understate his hostility to religion, even disguising his abandonment of religious faith, Darwin did not want to blow his cover. Some years later, Aveling became the lover of Karl Marx's daughter Eleanor. During the time the couple lived together, Darwin's letter, which began 'Dear Sir' and gave no other clue as to the identity of its addressee, was filed alongside papers relating to Eleanor's father, and researchers subsequently drew the understandable, but mistaken, conclusion that one Titan of nineteenth-century thought had coolly rebuffed another. An American graduate student, Margaret Fay, discovered the truth as long ago as the late 1970s, and the whole story was definitively disposed of by Francis Wheen in his 1999 biography of Karl Marx.[5] Nevertheless, the myth that Marx dedicated *Capital* to Darwin is still endlessly repeated as fact on creationist websites, presumably with the aim of painting Darwin as a closet Red.

Similar suggestions used to irritate Darwin during his lifetime. 'What a foolish idea seems to prevail in Germany on the connection between Socialism and Evolution through Natural Selection,' he complained to the Austrian explorer and scientist Karl von Scherzer in 1879.[6] Evolution had been enthusiastically received in Germany, the German translation of Darwin's *Origin* appearing only months after its London publication. The idea appealed to continental liberals, who were still engaged during the middle part of the century in fully emancipating themselves from reactionary, aristocratic power. It was also attractive to socialists, who felt part of an emerging modernity, eager to remake the world according to secular, scientific systems of thought. Squabbling over who had bragging rights for Darwin became part of the political struggle.

'I ask myself in surprise what in the world has the doctrine of descent got to do with socialism?' responded Darwin's chief German popularizer Ernst Haeckel. Socialism, he insisted, 'demands equal rights, equal duties, equal possessions' while evolution showed that 'the realization of the demand is a pure impossibility'. The two theories, Haeckel said, were as much alike 'as fire and water'.[7] Haeckel would lead German evolutionists in the direction of a social Darwinism that was racialist, imperialist, and militarist. He rejected the idea that matter and spirit were separate, preaching a cranky worldview that he called Monism – a volatile compound of pantheism, philosophical materialism and determinism, which held that matter was imbued with psychic sensitivity. Haeckel's ideas provided the model for the pseudo-spiritual, pseudo-scientific system of ideas later adopted by the Nazis, and by some French and Italian fascists too.

Charles Darwin and Ernst Haeckel enjoyed a close relationship. They exchanged news and ideas, and in 1866 Haeckel visited Darwin at his home, Down House in Kent. The visit was a success, and Darwin asked him back the following year. He also arranged for Haeckel to meet a number of his friends, including T. H. Huxley. Although significant scientific differences between them would emerge, Darwin would nonetheless offer to help fund Haeckel's research. The relationship revealed in their exchanges is not merely cordial but collaborative. Darwin writes of 'our work' and 'our subject' and it is clear that Haeckel was keen to promote evolution as widely as possible, and just as keen to savage its critics. If, in Britain, Huxley was 'Darwin's Bulldog', Haeckel was his Rottweiler.

Although much of the appeal of science at this time lay in its sweeping away the superstitions of the past, with Haeckel's help evolutionary science was acquiring fresh superstitions of its own. At about the time Haeckel visited Darwin at Down House, he began to promote the idea that each developing embryo relives the evolutionary story of its species, resembling in sequence the adult forms of its ancestors. The human embryo, for instance, would pass from a fish-like stage, where it would have gills, via reptilian and early mammalian stages, to taking on a decidedly simian look before becoming human. Haeckel supported his theory with drawings of embryos from a range of different species at their various points of development.

Haeckel's Biogenetic Law proved to be an immensely powerful idea, a trump card in many a dinner table argument about the truth of evolution. Rather like the crystalline structure of a snowflake, the idea is wondrous yet credible, one of nature's little miracles. Moreover, it would be inexplicably odd if our embryos went through this particular sequence of morphological changes and evolution were not to be true after all. Haeckel's law, sometimes known as 'recapitulation theory' and summarized in the pithy phrase 'ontogeny recapitulates phylogeny' was enthusiastically taken up within the scientific community and the wider world. It was adopted and endorsed by Sigmund Freud, and by generations of scientists and physicians after him.

Unfortunately, the Biogenetic Law had been comprehensively refuted by one of Haeckel's contemporaries, Wilhelm His, who had taken the trouble to actually look at human embryos under a microscope. At the beginning of the twentieth century, Haeckel admitted the fraud, confessing that his embryo drawings were fakes. Amazingly, the myth persisted for a further hundred years and more. In 1981, this phoney account of the embryo's procession through man's evolutionary past was included in the expert scientific evidence provided by a leading geneticist to the United States Congress during an enquiry into abortion law; it continued to feature in some school biology textbooks in North America as late as 1999; and in 2005 was still part of the standard patter provided to pregnant women during their ultrasound scans at a major London teaching hospital. Like the long discredited story of Marx's dedication of *Capital*, the legend of the Biogenetic Law lives on in the minds of millions.

Although caught out in this particular deception, Haeckel found that he could get away with all manner of other intellectual impostures and hare-brained theories in his capacity as one of Germany's scientific eminences and an intimate of Charles Darwin. One of his wheezes, as silly as it was noxious, was that members of 'woolly-haired' races are across the board inferior to straight-haired people, irrespective of the culture in which they grew up. However, before we laugh too hard at this quaint example of nineteenth-century simple-minded racism, we should perhaps remember that even today there is at least one well-known scientist who, while also sporting the colours of Charles Darwin, compares the measurements of black men's penises in the hope of finding some correlation (perhaps inverse) with IQ.

Karl Marx, meanwhile, had revisited Darwin's work, this time finding the Malthusian references niggling and fancying he spotted a shadow play of capitalist ideology between the lines of the text. 'It is remarkable how Darwin rediscovers, among the beasts and plants, the society of England with its division of labour, competition, opening up of new markets, "inventions" and Malthusian "struggle for existence",' Marx wrote to Engels in June 1862. 'It is Hobbes's *bellum omnium contra omnes* and is reminiscent of Hegel's Phenomenology, in which civil society figures as an "intellectual animal kingdom", whereas, in Darwin, the animal kingdom figures as civil society.'[8]

Marx was not alone in finding that Darwin's *Origin* reflected the ideology of laissez-faire capitalism. The book presented the natural world as one characterized by intense competition between individuals for survival, all were locked in a never-ending struggle for existence, in which only the fittest would survive. We can speculate that it might all have been very different. Imagine if Darwin had never paid much attention to Adam Smith and had been too busy with his work to take time off to amuse himself with Malthus. The first question is whether he would have made his breakthrough at all? The evidence of his notebooks suggests he probably would. So, imagine that Darwin had his eureka moment while listening to Mozart or reading Shakespeare's sonnets instead of while occupied with the gruesome topics of overpopulation and poverty. Would the hard science of Darwin's theory have been any different, shorn of its emotive Malthusian imagery? 'I should premise that I use the term Struggle for Existence in a large and metaphorical sense', Darwin wrote in Chapter Three of the *Origin*, and we should perhaps take him at his word. After all, scientists nowadays do not generally discuss evolution by natural selection in bloodcurdling language. They talk of changes in allele frequency within populations that are brought about in response to selection pressure.[9] All very tame.

One can never be sure about a historical *what if . . . ?* Nevertheless, it seems likely that the scientific core of Darwin's theory would have remained intact even if the cultural context of its conception had been somewhat different. Political reactions to the theory, however, would have been utterly changed. It has been the metaphorical content of the evolution story that has had the greatest effect on the minds of the non-scientist. The key idea that people associate with the

*Origin* is the 'survival of the fittest' – a phrase that was not Darwin's own, and which did not even appear in the first four editions of the book.

Walter Bagehot, the British constitutional writer and editor of *The Economist* magazine, published in 1867 a work entitled *Physics and Politics: Thoughts on the Principles of Natural Selection and Inheritance to Political Society*. Bagehot's account of the origin of society roots it in the application of strict law. Natural selection really only enters into his system when it selects between organized groups – tribes, societies and so on. Passages in Bagehot's book foreshadow some of what 'social Darwinism' would subsequently be understood to mean. 'In every particular state of the world, those nations which are strongest tend to prevail over the others,' Bagehot observed, 'and in certain marked peculiarities, the strongest tend to be the best.'[10] This looks like a bald assertion that might equals right, but that was not quite what Bagehot was arguing. He believed that where nations were unequally matched the strongest would win out; where they were equally matched, the noblest would have the edge. Bagehot's focus on social evolution operating at the group level meant that, in early societies at least, the individual was subordinated to the collective. Only those groups made up of team players would survive and prosper. However, those that succeeded in establishing themselves could permit a measure of individual liberty and democratic government within an evolutionary stage Bagehot called 'The Age of Discussion'.

Ramsay MacDonald, later to become Britain's first Labour prime minister, made an attempt to unite Darwinian theory with left of centre thinking with his *Socialism and Society* (1905). MacDonald accepted the overall framework of evolution as a historical and scientific fact (he had a scientific background himself), but rejected the view that humans were just like any other animal. Mankind's intelligence and development within culture and civilization, MacDonald thought, put him in a special position where the rule of the survival of the fittest need not apply to him. Man could construct his own world on the basis of cooperation rather than competition. This approach, emphasizing human exceptionalism and taking a somewhat pick'n'mix approach to Darwin's ideas (which by this time included the *Descent*) became common on the left. It was easy enough, of course, for non-scientists to ignore any inconvenient aspects of Darwin's work, but professional scientists faced a stiffer challenge. Prince Peter Kropotkin in *Mutual Aid*, published in 1902, argued that the move from selfish competition to social cooperation was a part of evolutionary development itself. He emphasized the way in which animals of the same species very often supported and assisted one another in finding food and surviving. He wrote:

> In the animal world we have seen that the vast majority of species live in societies, and that they find in association the best arms for the struggle for life: understood, of course, in its wide Darwinian sense – not as a struggle for the sheer means of existence, but as a struggle against all natural conditions unfavourable to the species. The animal species, in which individual struggle has been reduced to its narrowest limits, and the practice of mutual aid has attained the greatest development, are invariably the most numerous, the most prosperous, and the most open to further progress.[11]

With this elegant argument Kropotkin was able to class man as an animal just like all the others, but at the same time exempt him from the Malthusian struggle, in all but its weakest metaphorical sense. Man's tendency to cooperate, Kropotkin believed, had developed during his evolutionary journey and as he had evolved even further, he added more and more layers of ethical and social sophistication, enabling him to leave the competitive struggle way behind in history.

The label 'social Darwinist', though it can be applied to the advocates of imperialism, scientific racialism and eugenics, is normally reserved for those who drew inspiration from Darwin's works for their theories about competition as the driving force in economics, politics and social class. These people did not call themselves 'social Darwinists' as such. Historically, there was never a banner of social Darwinism behind which political activists or social theorists marched. Trying to track down an avowed social Darwinist of laissez-faire capitalist stripe is like hunting the Snark. However, there is a view of history that holds that in the second half of the nineteenth century a Briton, Herbert Spencer, and an American, William Graham Sumner, were the leading ideologues of a movement to justify a rapacious, red-in-tooth-and-claw capitalism by importing Charles Darwin's ideas into social theory and that this movement was encouraged, and to some extent subsidized, by its chief beneficiaries – the Robber Baron capitalists of the age.

This interpretation of events was first popularized by the social historian Richard Hofstadter, writing in the 1940s. Before Hofstadter, hardly anyone had ever used the term social Darwinist, even though it was coined as far back as 1879, and the few times it had been used it was not by those to whom Hofstadter applied it, but always by their critics, as an insult.

The man credited with being the prototypical social Darwinist was Herbert Spencer, Charles Darwin's contemporary and friend. In fact, Spencer was the prototypical libertarian – his chief concern was to keep government and the state out of human affairs to the greatest extent possible. He would certainly have opposed any coercive measures by the state, such as the programme of compulsory sterilization of defectives, which was an attempt to apply Darwinian science to the social field, later carried out by the eugenicists. Spencer was an anti-imperialist and a very early champion of women's rights, and in person was said to be a kinder, gentler figure than the representation handed down to us by intervening generations.

While working as a sub-editor on *The Economist*, the Derbyshire-born Spencer was taken up by a circle of intellectuals including John Stuart Mill, Harriet Martineau and Mary Ann Evans (the novelist George Eliot). Spencer is said to have come close to marrying Evans, but in the end remained a bachelor, spending what little leisure time his studies left him playing billiards with Charles Darwin's cousin Francis Galton at the Athenaeum. An autodidact who became a polymath, Spencer had from his early years a boundless ambition to develop a grand unifying theory of more or less everything. He studied and wrote about psychology, biology, politics, economics, sociology, and ethics in search of his all-embracing synthetic philosophy. The big idea he found to provide a naturalistic explanation of culture, society, the mind, economics and the natural sciences, was evolution. At least, evolution of a sort.

It was Spencer who coined the fateful term 'survival of the fittest', after reading Darwin's *Origin*. 'This survival of the fittest, which I have here sought to express in mechanical terms,' Spencer wrote in his *Principles of Biology*, 'is that which Mr. Darwin has called "natural selection", or the preservation of favoured races in the struggle for life.'[12] Spencer had not, however, cribbed the underlying idea from Darwin. He had been thinking along these lines for some time.

The poverty of the incapable, the distresses that come upon the imprudent, the starvation of the idle, and those shoulderings aside of the weak by the strong, which leave so many 'in shallows and in miseries,' are the decrees of a large, far-seeing benevolence ... It seems hard that an unskilfulness which with all his efforts he cannot overcome, should entail hunger upon the artisan. It seems hard that a labourer incapacitated by sickness from competing with his stronger fellows, should have to bear the resulting privations. It seems hard that widows and orphans should be left to struggle for life or death. Nevertheless, when regarded not separately, but in connection with the interests of universal humanity, these harsh fatalities are seen to be full of the highest beneficence – the same beneficence which brings to early graves the children of diseased parents, and singles out the low-spirited, the intemperate, and the debilitated as the victims of an epidemic.

That passage might strike a reader today as very 'social Darwinist' indeed; yet it was published in 1851, eight years before the *Origin*. Spencer's 'far-seeing benevolence' was not natural selection as Darwin would define it, but a curious idea of social evolution that was Spencer's own, a process that moved societies through stages of social progress, and shaped human character into ever more gentle and civilized states of being. Nevertheless, it was, Spencer believed, intimately bound up with the same fundamental laws of nature that governed the physical sciences.

Writing against the idea of poor laws, Spencer was even more brutally biological:

> There is . . . a normal amount of suffering, which cannot be lessened without altering the very laws of life. Every attempt at mitigation of this eventuates in exacerbation of it. All that a poor-law . . . can do, is to partially suspend the transition – to take off for awhile, from certain members of society, the painful pressure which is effecting their transformation. At best this is merely to postpone what must ultimately be borne. But it is more than this: it is to undo what has already been done. For the circumstances to which adaptation is taking place cannot be superseded without causing a retrogression – a partial loss of the adaptation previously effected; and as the whole process must some time or other be passed through, the lost ground must be gone over again, and the attendant pain borne afresh. Thus, besides retarding adaptation, a poor-law adds to the distresses inevitably attending it.[13]

This seemingly devil-take-the-hindmost insistence that aid should be denied to the poor, that, indeed, it might well be best for all of us if the weakest were allowed to perish, represented the essence of social Darwinism in the public mind. For many readers, Darwin's work appeared to validate it. Even before Darwin's *Descent*, people began to talk about natural selection as a general law that applied to human individuals and social classes as well as to animals: Those in society who fell behind economically deserved to be left to starve; giving them a helping hand was not only to act against nature, but to put at risk the development of the social organism as a whole. Moreover, what is natural came ever more to be regarded as what is proper. Unlike Malthus, who was the bleakest pessimist, Spencer, beneath the gritty hardheadedness, was a sunny optimist. He thought that as the poor died out, so too would laziness, stupidity and immorality. In parallel, there would be a corresponding growth in the industriousness, thrift and imagination that he believed had allowed the fittest to survive and prosper. Unlike Darwin's evolution, which had no purpose or direction, Spencer's evolution – until late in life, when he lost faith in it – meant things could only get better.

Probably the most commonly cited of Spencer's statements is one that spells out with chilling clarity the flip side of the survival of the fittest – the elimination of the unfit. 'If they are sufficiently complete to live, they do live,' Spencer said, 'and it is well they should live. If they are not sufficiently complete to live, they die, and it is best they should die.'

It has suited many of Spencer's critics to leave that passage there, without alerting their readers to the exculpatory evidence of the very next paragraph. 'Of course, in so far as the severity of this process is mitigated by the spontaneous sympathy of men for each other,' Spencer continued, 'it is proper that it should be mitigated.'[14] Spencer's hard-headedness went with a soft heart, it seemed. Though he resolutely opposed the state helping the poor, Spencer was keen that private charity should do so.

Later, Darwin himself would pronounce on the same subject in his *Descent*. Anyone seeking to establish whether or not Darwin really approved of eugenics should look here. Darwin wrote:

> With savages, the weak in body or mind are soon elimi-
> nated; and those that survive commonly exhibit a vigorous
> state of health. We civilized men, on the other hand, do
> our utmost to check the process of elimination; we build
> asylums for the imbecile, the maimed, and the sick; we
> institute poor-laws; and our medical men exert their
> utmost skill to save the life of every one to the last
> moment. There is reason to believe that vaccination has
> preserved thousands, who from a weak constitution would
> formerly have succumbed to smallpox. Thus the weak
> members of civilized societies propagate their kind. No
> one who has attended to the breeding of domestic animals
> will doubt that this must be highly injurious to the race of
> man. It is surprising how soon a want of care, or care
> wrongly directed, leads to the degeneration of a domestic
> race; but excepting in the case of man himself, hardly any
> one is so ignorant as to allow his worst animals to breed.[15]

Darwin too followed this brutal analysis with a 'neverthe-less', saying that though it may be injurious to the human race to look after the sick and needy, we should still do so, though we should perhaps discourage them from having children. Consequently, we are left with a puzzle. Both Spencer and Darwin set out essentially the same grisly universal law of nature. They said that it applied to human societies; but then both these amiable Victorian gentlemen recoiled from their own ideas, as if from a noxious smell. Did they mean it? Or were they just covering their reputations, uttering self-excusing pieties? It hardly matters, for their followers would not share their scruples, if scruples they were.[16]

Indeed, it was not long before Americans were being asked to check their sympathy by powerful figures in public life. In 1893, James Scrymser complained in the pages of the *New York Times* that there was too much charity in the city and that it was drawing in the indigent from the country towns of New York State and New Jersey. 'New York's fame has gone out far and wide as a place where a man will not be allowed to starve ... They come here and crowd everybody else a little closer, and make living a little harder all around ... They are intruders and aliens in New York, and they deserve much less sympathy than thoughtless and soft-hearted persons are apt to bestow upon them.'[17] It is not surprising that some people would think like that, but in this case, the writer was vice-chairman of the commission charged with improving the lives of New York's poor.

Even in what was known as the Gilded Age, not for the first time, and certainly not for the last, the presence in the streets of poor people gave rise to a nagging, existential fear. In 1879 William Graham Sumner, the father of American sociology, warned that 'if we do not like the survival of the fittest, we have only one possible alternative, and that is the survival of the unfittest. The former is the law of civilization; the latter is the law of anti-civilization.'[18]

This hobgoblin still haunts every consideration of welfare policy in our own times. Although perhaps political correctness nowadays moderates the language in which it is expressed, most politicians consider amongst themselves the long-term consequences of perpetuating circumstances in which the poorest and the least well educated breed faster and more plentifully than the professional middle class. Occasionally, the thought breaks out into the open, as it did in the notorious 'cycle of deprivation' speech given in 1972 by the Conservative government's Social Security Secretary, Sir Keith Joseph, whereupon the public reaction confirms that this anxiety is widely shared.

Genetic science, and the Darwinian synthesis, has given these still largely offstage ruminations a new vocabulary. Today's politician might fret about the effect on the quality of the 'gene pool' rather than the 'law of anti-civilization', but it amounts to much the same thing. During the coalminer's strike in Britain in 1984–5, there was debate not only about whether the pit villages were economically viable, but also whether they were really human communities at all, or merely genetic residue.

Once people start down the slope of Darwinist reference they find it hard to stop. Before long, a glancing allusion transmutes into a social theory and whole tracts of white working-class England are written off. In Westminster and Whitehall, any political journalist adept at drawing politicians out can hear this analysis all the time just so long as the tape-recorder and the television camera are switched off. It is a dismal analysis of how working-class communities have been stripped out during the course of the second half of the twentieth century. Grammar schools, and later good comprehensives, took those with academic talent and sent them away to the universities to become bourgeois; those who displayed a gift for boxing or football or musicianship skipped the middle class and went straight to join the celebrities, poolside; so that by the time Billy Elliot went off to the Royal School of Ballet, anyone who could read, write, kick a ball, pack a punch, sing, dance, or play the guitar had gone, leaving just the sludge at the bottom of the gene pool. So no wonder there is poverty, drugs and crime, and no – according to most of those who subscribe to this view of things – there is probably nothing anyone can do about it.

A similarly facile use of Darwinian metaphor can some-times be detected in American public rhetoric. Senator Daniel Patrick Moynihan once told the Senate Finance Committee, convened to discuss welfare reform, that the US could be witnessing the 'process of speciation' at work among the inner-city poor; that is, they were slowly turning, by the mechanisms of evolution, into a different species than the human one. As one disgusted observer recorded, 'Nod-ding their heads in agreement were the Secretary of Health and Human Services, Donna Shalala, and her two world-class poverty researcher undersecretaries, Mary Jo Bane and David Ellwood.'[19]

Social Darwinism most probably worked like this the first time around, though on a larger scale. Not so much a political programme or a social theory, but chiefly a matter of framing. It was a habit of reference and allusion; the making of easy analogies, with little thought for how apt they really were and without much moral awareness. 'Darwin used metaphors drawn from business, banking, industry and imperialism to depict animal behaviour,' the historian Paul Crook has pointed out. 'He spoke of profit and loss, increments, dili-gence, inheritance, saving, utility, success and progress through competition.'[20] No wonder then that they should be casually read back into economics.

Some historians have suggested that what has come to be known as social Darwinism really ought to be called 'social

Spencerism'. There is some truth in that idea, but so far as the wider public were concerned they were both part of the same new wave of thinkers, they were Box and Cox, the Castor and Pollux of the evolutionary firmament, interchangeable and simultaneously in vogue. Few troubled to note the technical distinctions between their interpretations of what evolution involved. Evolution itself was the thing. Of the two, Spencer's star shone more brightly. He was the first philosopher in history to sell more than a million copies of his books during his lifetime and was widely described as the greatest living philosopher. In America, the pair and their ideas featured in the leading current-affairs magazines from coast to coast. Both men were pointing to a modern, scientific way of understanding the world and doing so in the same language – using words like evolution, adaptation and selection. But Darwin was a great scientist and naturalist. So whose was the greater mind? Representatives of America's intellectual, scientific, commercial and political elite gathered at Delmonico's restaurant in New York in November 1882, almost seven months after Darwin's death, for a banquet to celebrate evolution as the greatest idea of all time and anoint Herbert Spencer as its originator and foremost champion. Posterity has not concurred.

Social Darwinism is frequently said to have had a significant role in justifying the worst excesses of laissez-faire capitalism. The evidence for this is flimsy. Businessmen did not generally go about giving ideological justifications for what they did, they were too busy making money. When they did feel they had to justify what they were doing, they tended to do so with references to what were seen as Protestant virtues: thrift, industriousness and so on.

There were, however, exceptions. Richard Hofstadter cites John D. Rockefeller Jr.'s 1903 American Beauty Rose speech as an important example of social Darwinist rhetoric. 'The growth of a large business is merely a survival of the fittest,' Rockefeller told his audience ... 'the American Beauty Rose can be produced in the splendour and fragrance that bring cheer to its beholder only by sacrificing the early buds which grow up around it. This is not an evil tendency in business. It is merely the working out of a law of nature.'[21] The allusions to Darwin and Spencer were certainly there, but the oil billion-aire's son's address to the YMCA at Brown University had no great impact on social thinking. It caused ripples at the time – ripples of mocking laughter in the main – because the news-papers liked to make fun of any Rockefeller.

There was certainly something risible about the sociologist William Graham Sumner's fulsome tribute to millionaires, whom he called the 'naturally selected agents of society' whose competence was assured 'by the intensest competition for their place and occupation'.[22] Sumner's aim was to reassure the American people that business was in safe hands, that a Darwinian process had guaranteed that the Masters of the Universe were selected for success.

This was a novel approach at the turn of the twentieth century, but probably not very convincing. Nowadays, evolu-tionary biology is on hand to make excuses for business leaders' failures. In the aftermath of the financial crash of 2008 John Chiao of Northwestern University published a study suggesting a link between genes governing the activity of the brain's signalling chemicals serotonin and dopamine with potentially catastrophic investment decisions. 'The monumental risks taken by Sir Fred Goodwin, who ran

DENNIS SEWELL

the Royal Bank of Scotland, and Andy Hornby, who ran HBOS, may have been partly ordained by their genes,' reported the *Times*. 'A pair of genes that influence financial risk-taking have been identified by scientists for the first time, in a study that could offer insights into the origins of the credit crunch.'[23]

The parallel between Darwin's struggle for survival among beasts in the wild and competition between businesses in the marketplace, which sees some enterprises fail and go under, while others succeed and grow, is an obvious one. But it was not Darwin's ideas that inspired capitalism; rather, it was the other way round.

The robber-baron capitalist who took most interest in the work of both Darwin and Spencer was the steel magnate Andrew Carnegie. He was a friend and patron of Herbert Spencer and an avid reader of Darwin, but far from refusing help to the poor or leaving them to perish, Carnegie gave away record sums of money. In his own lifetime he disbursed more than $4 billion in today's money to charitable causes, plus many millions more after his death through various endowments. Carnegie built more than three thousand public libraries for the intellectual betterment of the common man. For Carnegie, Darwin and Spencer's books were substitutes for the Bible. Carnegie recalled in his *Autobiography*:

When I, along with three or four of my boon companions, was in this stage of doubt about theology, including the supernatural element, and indeed the whole scheme of salvation through vicarious atonement and all the fabric built upon it, I came fortunately upon Darwin's and Spencer's works ... I remember that light came as in a flood and all was clear. Not only had I got rid of theology and the supernatural, but I had found the truth of evolution. 'All is well since all grows better' became my motto, my true source of comfort.[24]

Andrew Carnegie would not be the last of Darwin's readers to take away from Darwin's work the Spencerian notion of evolution-as-progress. Carnegie was a ruthless operator, who forced down the wages of his employees and made many of them work twelve-hour days. His company's major run-in with organized labour – the Homestead Mill strike of July 1892 – involved enormous loss of life, featuring a prolonged shoot-out between three hundred Pinkerton detectives and the striking steel workers, in which ten men were killed. The Pinkertons lost the battle and were forced to surrender, prompting the Governor to call out the Pennsylvania National Guard. Carnegie was on holiday in Scotland at the time, but remained in regular contact with his partner Henry Frick.

In a different intellectual climate, he might have been universally condemned for his brutal business methods. But though businessmen themselves may not have used evolutionary ideas to justify their behaviour, others would sometimes make excuses for them based on laws of nature elucidated by Darwin and Spencer. Though Darwin was clear that it was not the strongest or the most intelligent that survived, but those that had adapted best to a specific environment, those who wanted to curry favour with the rich would sometimes imply that the winners in the game of life were better in all respects than the losers. Those who prospered in the business world were portrayed as not only morally deserving of their riches, but as innately superior to the poor. However, this was a just a combination of sloppy reasoning and equally sloppy moral discernment. It was not by any stretch a vital ideological underpinning of laissez-faire. The free-market argument prospered on its own merits, before and after Darwin, and Adam Smith's 'invisible hand' certainly did not need an imaginary friend in the form of Herbert Spencer's theory of social evolution.

Besides, while Darwin and Spencer's ideas were being associated with American capitalism, in parts of Europe they were being promoted by Marxists. After the establishment of the Italian Socialist Party in 1893, one of its leading parliamentarians, Enrico Ferri, published his *Socialism and Positive Science – Darwin, Spencer, Marx*. Declaring himself a 'convinced follower of Darwin and Spencer', Ferri proposed that Marxian socialism was the logical outcome of the revolution in thought that 'has triumphed in our day thanks to the labours of Charles Darwin and Herbert Spencer.'[25] The fact that one could just as easily establish a Darwin–Spencer–Marx axis as Darwin–Spencer–Rockefeller one confirms that social Darwinism was, therefore, not a rigorous attempt to apply evolutionary ideas to economics, but chiefly a matter of the loose play of metaphor.

It was at Walt Disney World, in an address to Florida Democrats in December 2005, that Barack Obama first accused the then president, George W. Bush, of being a social Darwinist. It later became a recurrent theme of his campaign for the presidency. He said:

There are those who believe ... the best idea is to give everyone one big refund on their government – divvy it up by individual portions, in the form of tax breaks, hand it out, and encourage everyone to use their share to go buy their own health care, their own retirement plan, their own child care, their own education, and so on. In Washington, they call this the Ownership Society. But in our past there has been another term for it – Social Darwinism – every man or woman for him or herself. [26]

So universal is this lazy habit of using the term as a rhetorical brickbat to hurl at any right-wing politician (Margaret Thatcher and Ronald Reagan frequently got the same treatment) that it can surely only be a matter of time before some evolutionary psychologist steps forward to claim that it is something hard-wired into the brain, like the language instinct. Politicians generally have thick enough hides for it not to trouble them, but there are others in our society who are particularly vulnerable to simplistic representations or mis-representations of ideas about struggle, fitness and natural selection.

He was, he said, a social Darwinist. He wrote in his personal manifesto about his concern that natural selection appeared not to be working any more – had maybe even gone into reverse. He had noticed that 'stupid, weak-minded people reproduce faster than intelligent, strong-minded' ones. As an exception to the rule, as someone who felt he had evolved one step beyond the rest of a humanity that was otherwise in decline, he had thought long and hard what he should do about the problem. He understood that life was just a meaningless coincidence, the result of a long process of evolution, and that there might not, therefore, be much point in doing

# DENNIS SEWELL

anything at all. But he was not an out-and-out fatalist or determinist; rather, he believed that through bold choices a man might yet be the author of his own destiny. So he decided he would do his bit to put the survival of the fittest back on track. He would become a natural selector.

On 7 November 2007, in the municipality of Tuusula, Finland, Pekka-Eric Auvinen made Helena Kalmi, his head teacher, kneel down in front of him before he shot her with his SIG Mosquito pistol. He would kill a further seven people before turning the gun on himself. Some of the Jokela High School students would afterwards describe the way he prowled through the building pointing his gun at people's heads. Sometimes, he would squeeze the trigger and kill them; sometimes, after looking long and hard through the sights, he would suddenly turn away and let his terrified target go free. One witness said he seemed to be choosing his victims at random, but in fact he was making a very deliberate selection. He was trying to weed out the unfit.

'Death and killing is not a tragedy,' Auvinen wrote in the *apologia* he posted on the Internet, to be found when the shooting spree was over. 'It happens in nature all the time.'[27] Keen that he himself should not fall victim to the predictable condescension of posterity, he left a special plea, a dying boy's last wish, for his social Darwinist motivation to be taken seriously and for the world not merely to write him off as a madman or a psychopath, and *please, please* not to blame the movies, computer games, television or heavy metal music.

Fat chance. We always posthumously patronize our murderous misfits or use their stories to serve our own agendas. Michael Moore, for instance, turned the story of the Columbine Two into a film about the need for gun control.

For Eric Harris and Dylan Klebold, Columbine was not about guns so much as explosions. Their plan involved propane bombs designed to slaughter six hundred students in the school cafeteria, and car bombs to rip through the ambulance crews, police and rescue workers afterwards. They only carried guns to pick off the odd survivor fleeing from the wreckage. But something went wrong with the timing mechanisms of the bombs, so posterity will classify Columbine as a 'school shooting' just as Pekka-Eric Auvinen will always be remembered as the boy who went crazy after taking anti-depressants.

Eric Harris and Dylan Klebold also took their fatal cues from Darwin's theory of evolution. For just like Pekka-Eric Auvinen, the Columbine Two were amateur social Darwinists. After the killings, Darrell Scott, whose daughter had been one of the murdered, testified before the US Congress and made a moving appeal for better education about evolution:

> You should be aware that some students, surely not many, but some, will take the concept that we are 'nothing but animals' and the idea of 'the survival of the fittest' as justification for heinous behaviour. Eric Harris and Dylan Klebold who killed my daughter and twelve others at Columbine High School did just that. Harris wore a 'Natural Selection' T-shirt on the day of the killings and both had taken the evolutionary mindset to the conclusion that they had to help the process along. They made remarks on video about helping out the process of natural selection by eliminating the weak. They also professed that they had evolved to a higher level than their classmates. I was amazed at the frequent references to evolution and equally amazed that the press completely ignored that aspect of the tapes.[28]

What these and heaven knows how many other young men had in common was that the main, perhaps the only, lesson they took away from their classes in evolution at school was that inferior types were expendable, that only an elite deserved to live and that if pitiless Nature had no compassion for life's second-raters then there was no compelling reason why they themselves should either.

Sadly, it has not only been crazy teenagers who have taken up the idea of social Darwinism with eliminatory zeal. When state power was put behind such ideas, in Nazi Germany, the world witnessed human tragedy on a massive scale. The struggle for existence and the survival of the fittest may have been only overworked metaphors, but even clichés have consequences.

# CHAPTER THREE

Men and women of the present day are, to those
that we might hope to bring into existence, what the
pariah dogs of the streets of an Eastern town are to
our own highly bred varieties.

Francis Galton (1865)

Ever since men have bred horses, cattle, dogs or plants, they
have known of the possibility of improving a species through
selective breeding. Moreover, parents of children – and not just
those who fancy themselves as having some sort of important
pedigree to protect – have long been choosy about whom their
sons and daughters might marry. Yet although Plato debated
the idea more than two thousand years ago, it was not until
the late-nineteenth century when Francis Galton, Charles Darwin's cousin, floated his new scheme of eugenics, that people
took seriously the possibility of applying the principles of
animal breeding to human beings on a mass scale.

When Galton first began to consider the challenge, there
was not yet any consensus about which traits were actually
hereditary. Many held to an idea, derived from the Bible, that
all men and women had been made in the 'image and likeness'
of God: that they were born equal, in other words. Behavioural

differences between individuals were ascribed to their posses-
sion, or lack, of virtues such as industriousness, honesty and
kindness. A man was, it was widely held, whatever he made of
himself. Others, however, believed that even the moral aspects
of character ran in families; notions of 'bad blood' and being
'well bred' were widespread at the same time. Galton himself
had his eureka-moment as an undergraduate: 'I had been
immensely impressed', he would later recall, 'by many obvious
cases of heredity among the Cambridge men who were at the
University about my own time.'[1]

Galton set out to discover which talents were inherited,
painstakingly charting the incidence of various kinds of
'genius' down the generations. His researches led him to
believe that if the cleverest, healthiest and most gifted males
mated with the most talented females, and if they had large
numbers of children, then society would flourish and literature, music, art, science and politics would all be practised to a
higher standard in a golden age of eugenics. His great fear was
that if his ideas were not taken up, there would be an inevitable
reversion to mediocrity.

Though Galton himself liked to accentuate the positive,
others argued it was not simply enough to encourage the best
of the species to pair. By preventing, or at least limiting, breeding among those seen as degenerate or depraved, a bigger
boost might be given to the overall quality of mankind. Those
factors seen as contributing to the betterment of the species
were described as 'eugenic', while those that tended to make
the race less strong, less intelligent, less healthy were termed
'dysgenic', that is to say likely to cause the degeneration of the
breeding stock, or as we think of it nowadays, the gene pool.
To tackle the problem from both ends, it soon became clear,

would take not only 'positive eugenics' or exhortation, but 'negative eugenics' backed up by coercion.

'It is in the sterilization of failures, and not in the selection of successes for breeding, that the possibility of an improvement of the human stock lies,'[2] declared the novelist H. G. Wells, who had studied under 'Darwin's Bulldog', T. H. Huxley, at the Normal School of Science in South Kensington. But George Bernard Shaw, another very early proponent of Galton's idea, suggested that even sterilization itself might prove too soft an option when he addressed the Eugenics Society in 1910.[3] 'A part of eugenic politics would finally land us in an extensive use of the lethal chamber,' he argued. 'A great many people would have to be put out of existence simply because it wastes other people's time to look after them.'[4] Shaw was by nature a *provocateur* and not even his closest friends could be entirely certain when he was being serious and when he was merely trying to shock complacent or received opinion, or generate a headline in the press. Yet the reference to a 'lethal chamber' was readily understood by his audience; it was not one of Shaw's frequent coinings. Though more frequently employed by critics of eugenics than by its advocates, the currency of the phrase 'lethal chamber' in public debate attests to the fact that the possibility that eugenics might someday take an exterminatory turn was something understood almost from the very outset.

Yet for most of its advocates, eugenics was felt to be an upbeat project offering an optimistic hope of Utopia; its appeal was not confined to the misanthropic, but extended to the progressive and well meaning as well. Many of those whose professional or voluntary work took them among the poor embraced eugenics on the basis that it might help rid the world of the appalling misery they witnessed every day in the slums of industrial cities. But their sense of which traits might be construed as dysgenic was often coloured by underlying social assumptions. A good example of this tendency can be found in the writings of the socialist eugenicist Sidney Webb. 'In Great Britain at this moment, when half, or perhaps two-thirds of all the married people are regulating their families, children are being freely born to the Irish Roman Catholics and the Polish, Russian and German Jews,' Webb complained in a 1907 Fabian tract. These immigrant groups, he said, were 'thriftless and irresponsible', and their continued breeding, Webb warned, would lead to 'national deterioration'.[5]

The identification of Irish immigrants with degeneracy was common. In Scotland, newspapers published racist cartoons caricaturing the Irish as distinctly simian, suggesting they were a less highly evolved sub-species. But the eugenicists had more difficulty than the gutter press defining what made an individual or group 'unfit' from the start. Since they were not content to let natural selection take its course, intent instead on prescribing its outcome, they could not fall back on the common Darwinist tautology of proclaiming the survival of the fittest and then defining the fittest simply as those who survived and bred.

G. K. Chesterton, who campaigned against attempts to enshrine eugenic theories in English law, wrote:

The very word Unfit reveals the weakness of the whole of this pseudo-scientific position. We should say that a cow is fit to provide us with milk; or that a pig is unfit to provide us with pork. But nobody would call a cow fit without naturally adding what she was fit for. Nobody would call up the insanely isolated vision of the Unfit Pig in the abstract. But when we talk about human beings, we are bound to break off the sentence in the middle; we are bound to call them Unfit in the abstract. For we know how varied, how complex, and how controversial are the questions that arise about the functions for which they should be fitted.[6]

To begin with, the eugenicists concentrated on halting the transmission of hereditary diseases from one generation to the next – or at least those diseases they thought might be hereditary – proposing that men and women contemplating marriage should undergo rigorous medical examination. Should any weakness be discovered on either side, the couple would then be encouraged to sacrifice their personal love and happiness for the greater good of society. Naturally this required eugenicists to deny that there was any universal right to parenthood. Indeed Galton went further, disparaging the idea of the individual as being special or significant at all, insisting that each of us is merely a bud or outgrowth of a larger, organic system. Eugenics was essentially a collectivist project, and its practitioners would disparage their opponents as 'extreme individualists'.

Soon, however, the focus shifted from sharply defined diseases to a vaguer field of pathology – 'mental incapacity' and 'feeble-mindedness'. In the absence of diagnostic rigour, this category simply grew and grew. By 1914, the Eugenics Record Office in the United States had estimated that as many as *one in three* Americans were liable to pass to his or her heirs insanity, mental deficiency, epilepsy or some similar 'dysgenic' defect; and it is striking just how quickly the definition of feeble-mindedness was stretched beyond physiology to include moral or social shortcomings. Drunks, prostitutes, petty criminals, women who had babies outside marriage, even their bastard offspring, were soon classed as feeble-minded or as 'imbeciles'.

Chesterton was in no doubt about the lineage of eugenics itself. Its proponents, he said, were those whose 'creed is the great but disputed system of thought which began with evolution . . .'[7] Indeed, in the years leading up to the First World War, the eugenics movement looked like a Darwin family business. Charles Darwin's son Leonard replaced his cousin Galton as chairman of the national Eugenics Society in 1911. In the same year an offshoot of the society was formed in Cambridge. Among its leading members were three more of Charles Darwin's sons, Horace, Francis and George. The group's treasurer was a young economics lecturer at the university, John Maynard Keynes, whose younger brother Geoffrey would later marry Darwin's granddaughter Margaret. Meanwhile, Keynes's mother, Florence, and Horace Darwin's daughter Ruth, sat together on the committee of the Cambridge Association for the Care of the Feeble-Minded, which we might nowadays regard as nothing less than a front organization for eugenics.

The programme of the eugenics movement required an expansion of state agencies and an expansion of their scope for prying into – and ultimately directing – the lives of the poor. 'A system will also be established for the examination of the family history of all those placed on the register as being unquestionably mentally abnormal,' said Leonard Darwin, 'especially as regards the criminality, insanity, ill health and pauperism of their relatives . . . If all this were done, it can hardly be doubted that many strains would be discovered which no one could deny ought to be made to die out in the interests of the nation . . .'[8] Others actually called for the establishment of a dedicated health police who would have the authority to arrest without charge any member of the poorest third of the population and take the accused before flying squads of scientists for assessment.

Eugenics might have remained where it began, on the margins of British political life, something to be discussed in draughty temperance halls at meetings of the Rationalist Association (for the Darwinist/atheist axis had already become well established). However, unlike many other esoteric theories of the day, such as theosophy, the eugenics movement could count on the support not only of cranks, but of Cambridge academics, fellows of the Royal Society and large numbers of the medical profession itself. Together they were capable of launching what would prove to be an impressive political lobbying campaign. In a remarkably short space of time, the vocabulary and basic principles of eugenics spread through the middle class, becoming almost the rule rather than the exception. This rapid mainstreaming of what began as a quirky set of ideas was rather like the way that the environmental movement developed in our own times. In just a few decades the Green agenda has moved from being a minority concern associated with a tightly knit group of activists, to being something almost universally attended to and accepted. Just as it was an emerging consensus among scientists about the threat of global warming that led to an almost exponential growth of environmentalism, so it was scientists issuing dire warnings about the perils of genetic degeneration that gave eugenics a similar boost.

Ellen Pinsent of the National Association for the Care of

the Feeble-Minded wrote, under the combined letterhead of her own organization and the Eugenics Society, to every candidate in the 1910 General Election urging them to support measures to stop 'degenerates' from having any children.

At this time women did not yet have the franchise. But the women's suffrage movement was beginning to win more and more attention; in 1912 a number of suffragettes went on hunger strike; and in 1913 Emily Davison threw herself under the King's horse at the Epsom Derby. But though women could not vote, they could play a part in public life through committee work and campaigning. Throughout its history the Eugenics Society had broadly equal numbers of men and women among its membership. Committee women like Ellen Pinsent were the ones who really got things done. After the election, she was able to mobilize sufficient cross-party support to get a Private Member's Bill, the Feeble-Minded Persons (Control) Bill, introduced into the House of Commons in May 1912 by Gershom Stewart, the Conservative MP for the Wirral, and seconded by Willoughby Dickinson, the Liberal member for St Pancras North.

Stewart couched his proposals, in the jargon of eugenics, as a measure for 'the segregation of the unfit', prophesying 'the deterioration of the race' if nothing were done about 'a great army of people mentally defective, greater than the number of soldiers in the British Army'. He explicitly acknowledged that the bill's origins and objectives were drawn from the eugenics movement, talking of 'the scientific and benevolent people who have been trying to grapple with this problem' and through whose efforts the issue had been brought to the floor of the House. 'The object of this Bill is to regularise the lives, and, if possible, to prevent the increasing propagation of half-witted people,' Stewart explained. 'Have we a moral right to curtail the freedom of some of our weaker brethren?' Stewart asked rhetorically. 'I think we have.'

By a curious turn of the tide, opposition to the bill was actually led by another of Darwin's kinsmen. Colonel Josiah Wedgwood was the great-great-grandson of the potter Josiah Wedgwood, Darwin's maternal grandfather. They were related along other complex genealogical pathways too, owing to the Darwin–Wedgwood habit of marrying their cousins. The original patriarch, Josiah Wedgwood, married a cousin, and at least seven more of his extended family followed suit. Charles Darwin and his wife Emma (née Wedgwood) were cousins, and though Emma bore him ten children, of whom seven survived to adulthood, they were a notably sickly family. When Francis Galton raised the issue of the possible dysgenic effects of inbreeding, Darwin began to fret that he may have brought a curse upon his children, and began a series of experiments with hermaphrodite plants, the results of which gave him little solace on this score. During a holiday when half the family were simultaneously struck down by one illness or another, Darwin wrote to his friend Asa Gray: 'We are a wretched family & ought to be exterminated.'

Colonel Wedgwood would not have concurred. He did not approve of the fashion for sterilization and segregation, let alone extermination. In Parliament, he argued that the Feeble-Minded Persons (Control) Bill proposed the equivalent of life imprisonment for people who had committed no crime whatsoever, and exhorted his colleagues to put justice before brutal expediency.

Wedgwood described the science behind the bill as based upon 'experience of breeding cattle not of breeding men' and warned that a minimum of three hundred people in each parliamentary constituency would be incarcerated if the bill became law. He also warned against abandoning the fate of ordinary men and women to the mercy of scientists:

> Here you are alienating these powers . . . and you are going to entrust them to a body of specialists whose absolute remedies for disease change every year, and who invent year after year new fungoid growths, or something of the kind which may be stamped out by science if only you give them a free hand . . . Let any hon. Member who has got a daughter imagine for the moment whether he would allow the police to take that daughter away under these circumstances, and does he not think that the working classes may possibly have similar feelings as himself in this matter?

Wedgwood told the Commons that they had miscalculated the political mood in the nation. 'I do think it shows an absolute want of understanding of the feelings of the ordinary poor people of this country to imagine that they will tolerate such a Bill as this, or such a monstrous injustice as that people are to be sent to prison for life for merely being abnormal.'[9]

Wedgwood's speech, which languishes all but forgotten in the archives of *Hansard*, deserves to be remembered as one of the great eloquent defences of civil liberties in twentieth-century Britain. But Wedgwood was up against a House of Commons that had become seriously afraid of the most wretched and desperate members of the society it represented. In the autumn of 1910 a lockout of boilermakers and ship-builders had precipitated a wave of industrial and social unrest that lasted until March 1912. 'Real terror crept into the hearts of large sections of the public and loud clamour for displays of police and military force was made,' wrote the future Labour prime minister, Ramsay MacDonald in an analysis of the unrest. 'On several occasions, particularly during the short railway strike [of August 1911], we were on the brink of civil war.'[10]

One MP reported how only a few days before the debate a 'mental defective' had arrived in the Commons lobby demanding to see him, and when told his MP was not available had taken out a revolver and fired it into the roof. The same member told the Commons that he had been visited on the eve of the debate by a woman who told him she had a plan to blow up the Houses of Parliament.

Like so may others who had come under the influence of eugenics, this MP's fear of the 'feeble-minded' was laced with contempt. 'There is only one fitting description,' he said, 'they are almost like human vermin. They crawl about, doing absolutely nothing, except polluting and corrupting everything they touch. We talk about the liberty of the subject. What nonsense! What a waste of words!'

This politician's frankly expressed disdain for the historic liberties of the people was matched by a scornful and dismissive attitude to the constituents he was supposed to serve. 'A mother came to my door and cried for an hour, asking me to sign a paper to the effect that she was a fit and proper person to have her daughter home,' he told the House. 'She threatened suicide if I did not sign it. I made up my mind that that would not be at all a bad job, so I would not sign the paper.'[11] That MP was not some port-sodden, reactionary knight of the shires, but Will Crooks, a trade unionist, prominent Fabian, and the fourth Member to be elected to Parliament (after Keir Hardie, Richard Bell and David Shackleton) of the new Labour Party.

No matter how knowledgeable we all are now in the ways of politics, political cynicism and the abuse of power, it is still shocking to encounter attitudes like these from a politician from the party of the working class. But perhaps it should not be so surprising. Eugenics fitted in very neatly with the Fabian programme for social planning, with Sidney Webb's injunction to 'Interfere! Interfere! Interfere!' and was designed to solve the problems thrown up by what the Fabians liked to call the 'social residuum'.

'Negative eugenics,' the geneticist Lancelot Hogben argued '... is essentially en rapport with the social theory of the collectivist movement.'[12] And so it was – it represented a top-down, scientific solution to a social problem. H. G. Wells, imagining a new world order, voiced all the pent-up frustrations of the Fabians in his uncompromising message to the old order: 'We cannot go on giving you health, freedom, enlargement, limitless wealth, if all our gifts to you are to be swamped by an indiscriminate torrent of progeny. We want fewer and better children who can be reared up to their full possibilities in unencumbered homes, and we cannot make the social life and the world-peace we are determined to make, with the ill-bred, ill-trained swarms of inferior citizens that you inflict upon us.'[13] It was as if, as in the Brechtian joke, the Fabian Left had lost confidence in the people, and so had determined to dissolve the people and appoint a new one.

Had eugenics been taken up only by the Fabians, though, it would not have established itself to the extent it did – or would have done so only very slowly, Fabian gradualism being rather like the evolutionary process in this respect. But if a broader coalition of political groups and interests were required for eugenics to take off, social and economic progress had already prepared the ground, segmenting the old working class. A new breed of lower-middle-class, white-collar clerks had emerged. Lacking any serious capital, their position of superiority above the general mass was at best precarious. Eugenics offered a way for Mr Pooter to feel his social and professional status was not just down to luck, it was validated by biology.

A few rungs up the social ladder came the professional middle class. It was this class that provided the activists for the eugenics movement: academics, scientists, doctors, public health professionals, and the men and women who sat on committees of charitable and benevolent societies. Unsurprisingly, intelligence became the chief criterion for determining between the fit and the unfit. Francis Galton wrote a novel, *Kantsaywhere*, in which he described the power structure and social relations of a eugenic utopia called Kantsaywhere. The island was ruled over by the Eugenic College, whose fellows set the fitness examinations and administered the republic along the lines Galton remembered from his Cambridge days.

The Trustees of this College are the sole proprietors of almost all the territory of Kantsaywhere, and they exercise a corresponding influence over the whole population. Their moral ascendancy is paramount. The families of the College and those of the Town are connected by numerous inter-marriages and common interests, so that the relation between them is more like that between the Fellows of a College and the students than the Gown and Town of an English University.[14]

It is harder to see what eugenics offered the real ruling classes – the Edwardian aristocracy and plutocrats. There was never any suggestion, for instance, that business skills or entrepreneurial spirit counted among the heritable virtues or could help sort the eugenic sheep from the degenerate goats. Nor was there any cult of blue blood; on the contrary, some eugenicists actually called for the replacement of the upper house with a chamber that was more eugenically distinguished than the inbred peerage.

Nevertheless, many members of the ruling caste were willing to give the eugenicists their head. Eugenic theory provided a spuriously scientific underpinning for racism and imperialism, and at a stretch could be depicted as patriotic. It also promised to protect against several spectres that haunted the Edwardian imagination. The cruel but efficacious process of natural selection may have been suspended at home – drains, medicine and charity, the eugenicists believed, had stopped it in its tracks; but among the lesser breeds abroad, it rolled remorselessly on. They might even catch up one day . Eugenics promised to give Britain an edge in the supposed struggle for racial supremacy. And in its domestic application, it might help ward off those perennial bogeys of the ruling elite – men with flaming torches coming up the drive, rioters in the streets, a seething and volatile underclass.

These social, economic and political factors represented, however, merely the context in which eugenics began to flourish. The impetus, as Galton conceded, had been provided by Darwin. 'The publication in 1859 of *The Origin of Species* by Charles Darwin made a marked epoch in my own mental development,' Galton wrote, 'as it did in that of human thought generally. Its effect was to demolish a multitude of dogmatic barriers by a single stroke, and to arouse a spirit of rebellion against all ancient authorities whose positive and unauthenticated statements were contradicted by modern science.' So, it was all change, after Darwin. The old things no longer held. Those ancient authorities – the Christian Church and the European civilization built upon its principles – had, for men like Galton, totally lost their power to command. Even though these were the foundations of culture, they must nevertheless be uprooted. It was time for a re-evaluation of all values.

'To Sir Francis Galton belongs the honour of founding the *Science* of eugenics. To Friedrich Nietzsche belongs the honour of founding the *Religion* of eugenics,' wrote Maximilian Mügge in *Eugenics Review* in 1909.[15] That some people believed that the 'eugenic babies' gracing the covers of popular magazines of the period would grow up to be Nietzschean Supermen was only natural. 'Society . . .' Nietzsche wrote in *The Will to Power*, 'should in many cases actually prevent the act of procreating and may without any regard for rank . . . hold in readiness the most rigorous forms of compulsion and restriction, and under certain circumstances have recourse to castration.'[16]

Thomas Common, one of the philosopher's champions in England, gave Nietzsche's denunciation of Christian morals an evolutionary twist. 'From the standpoint of all Darwinian philosophy of history', he asserted, 'we now regard Christianity as an artful device for enabling inferior human beings to maintain themselves in the struggle for existence, a device analogous to, and serving the same purpose as, the ink of the cuttlefish, the venom of the snake, the stench of the skunk, the various forms of mimicry &c.'[17] Nietzscheans who wanted to shrug off the ethical constraints of a Christian culture could thank Darwin for showing the way to be rid of them.

For some bizarre reason, Francis Galton hoped that eugenics itself would one day become a religion. In some ways it did. The movement acquired a priestly caste in genetic scientists; it had its zealots and its liberal trimmers and was from time to time riven by schism, with each side accusing the other of rank heresy. It stopped short of formal ritual, bells and incense, but there was more than a touch of superstition to the project and some downright irrationality. The adherents of eugenics were genuinely and passionately committed to the long-term development of the human race. But why should they care? No one ever explained what conceivable moral imperative a person might have, in the absence of anything more numinous in life or death than an indifferent Nature, to give two hoots what became of the rest of the human race once he or she was dead. Moreover, this 'metabiological heresy' always comes at a price as C. S. Lewis, a critic of eugenics both in his fiction and his non-fiction, noted when taking issue with 'the belief that the supreme moral end is the perpetuation of our own species and that this is to be pursued even if in the process of being fitted for survival, our species has to be stripped of all those things for which we value it.'[18]

Nevertheless, care the eugenicists did. The Feeble-Minded Persons (Control) Bill was quietly dropped when the government promised to bring in a measure of its own, the Mental Deficiency Bill. Campaigners for eugenics then focused on getting the new bill through. The Home Secretary, Winston Churchill, was broadly sympathetic. Indeed, two years previously Churchill had written to Asquith voicing his own concern about what appeared to be growing numbers of mental defectives. Having read a pamphlet proposing sterilization, Churchill said he was inclined to support it.

In July 1912, the first International Congress on Eugenics was held in London. Arthur Balfour, who had been prime minister between 1902 and 1905, gave the opening address. This prestigious endorsement of the eugenicists' programme confirmed that eugenic science had now found a place for itself within the respectable mainstream of political life. Other confirmations could be found in the widespread use of the terminology of eugenics by establishment figures; the president of the British Medical Association, for instance, opposed the introduction of National Insurance on the grounds that it would encourage degenerates to 'multiply their breed at the expense of the healthy and intellectual members of the community'. To coincide with the opening of the 1912 Congress, the *British Medical Journal* ran an editorial explicitly endorsing the eugenic point of view.

The Mental Deficiency Act 1913, despite the best efforts of Josiah Wedgwood, gave the eugenicists much, but not all of what they had been asking for. It established colonies for the segregation of the unfit, classifying them under four headings: *idiots, imbeciles, the feeble-minded* and *moral defectives*. Unmarried mothers and petty criminals were sometimes detained under the latter category, and persons 'given to homosexual practices' could be locked in asylums and even lobotomized. There was, however, no compulsory sterilization of defectives and the scale of the operation was far smaller than the more ambitious eugenicists had at first envisaged. The system, which remained in place until 1959, segregated at its peak some 60,000 people in institutions, with a further 43,000 subject to supervision and control orders in the community.

There were, of course, many instances of injustice. Edith Haithwaite, from Yorkshire, was a sixteen-year-old girl when she was convicted by Ripon magistrates of a petty theft. Categorized as a defective, she was detained for eighteen years before her sister was able to spring her by bringing a writ of habeas corpus in the High Court. Another youngster, who underwent a lobotomy during her incarceration, was held up by the author of an article in the *Journal of Mental Science* as a success story. 'From being a depraved and hopeless little animal she is now quite a sociable, clean child,' reported George Mackay.[19] The girl had been sent to the asylum when she was only nine and was lobotomized at the age of fourteen.

Kathleen Bradley was locked up when she was nineteen. She had no record of delinquency, criminal or moral, and had been in the top class at her school, but was misdiagnosed as congenitally defective while recovering from rheumatic fever. She was detained for twenty years and only released after the National Council for Civil Liberties took up her cause and had questions asked in Parliament. The NCCL estimated in the 1950s that there were some six thousand similar cases waiting to be resolved, eight hundred and fifty of which they were able to identify. The organization despatched teams of volunteers to help patients bring appeals before tribunals and by 1958 had secured the release of eighteen hundred inmates.

The passage of the 1913 Act was celebrated by eugenicists not only for the practical measures it set in motion, but because it seemed to them to inscribe the hereditarian principle into English law. A lapidary precedent, they felt, had been set. Next on their agenda would come sterilization and the use of fiscal measures to promote eugenic ends. But before they had time to draw breath, Europe was at war. On the enemy side, a form of social Darwinism had contributed to the initial drive to war but Darwinists in Britain varied in their attitudes to the conflict. For some, war was the struggle for survival in rawest form, Nature's way of selecting the fittest and disposing of the second rate. Darwin had predicted a war of extermination waged by the more highly developed races against savages. Instead, Britain was locked in combat with the civilization that had produced Mozart and Beethoven, Schiller and Goethe.

On Alfred Wintle's first night at the front, a shell exploded nearby, splattering over him the entrails of his sergeant, to whom he had only just been introduced. In such circumstances it was no doubt helpful to believe one was a member of the most highly evolved race of them all. 'I get down on my knees every night and thank God for making me English,' Wintle wrote. 'After all, he might have made me a chimpanzee, or a flea, a Frenchman or a German!'[20]

For others, whose moral sense showed disconcerting signs of having atrophied under the influence of Darwinist thought, the fighting was a chance to have unrestrained fun. 'When I got the opportunity of killing other people during the war', recalled the evolutionary biologist J. B. S. Haldane, 'I enjoyed it very much.' This taste for killing, Haldane said, was 'really a quite respectable relic of primitive man'.[21]

Many eugenicists, though, fretted about the possible dysgenic effects of a prolonged struggle: with the fittest away at the front, the babies born at home would often come from inferior, rejected stock. Leonard Darwin, perhaps more anxious about the threat to the future of the race than the one facing our boys in the trenches, proposed that older men should be called up first so the younger ones would have a chance to breed. The appalling death rate among infantry officers was another cause of acute concern. The eugenicist

Harold Laski, who would later become chairman of the Labour Party, saw the terrible toll the war was taking on his own university cohort. 'Half the men you met in my room at Oxford have been killed,' he told a friend, 'and I wonder where we shall get the intellect for the next generation.'[22]

The Eugenics Society, allowing its class bias to be even more than usually blatant, had already set up the Professional Classes War Relief Council, which opened a maternity unit, reserved for the wives of officers, in a pair of townhouses facing onto Hyde Park. The little eugenic poppets born there were the offspring of former doctors, lawyers and academics posted to the front, a type referred to in eugenic circles as 'race heroes'.

In the aftermath of the war, the eugenics movement failed to recover the political momentum it had built up during the antebellum years. The world had changed. With victory in Europe, revolution in Russia and the emergence of the Labour movement at home as a force to be reckoned with, the project of sterilizing large numbers of the working class struggled to gain much traction. Besides, hard science was catching up with pseudoscience and threatening to pop its balloon.

The standard assumption among eugenicists at the time was one drawn from Mendelian theory: that traits such as criminality, idleness, and drunkenness were not only inherited, but their inheritance each depended on a single unit of hereditary transmission – a single 'gene' as we might say today. This made it possible to calculate the odds of anyone inheriting a particular trait if you knew whether it was present in parents and grandparents. Thus, the offspring of poor, feckless and degenerate couples were thought likely to be poor, feckless and degenerate themselves; the children of two middle-class intellectuals, by the same logic, were likely to be academically gifted. Science was challenging this assumption from two directions. First, it was becoming clear that the influence of environmental and cultural factors explained a great deal more than the eugenicists allowed. Second, that where traits were inherited, the mechanism of inheritance was much more complex, often requiring a combination of different units of transmission – they were, as we would understand it today, 'polygenic', requiring the combination of a set of different genes to bring them about.

It says a lot for the sheer power of scientific reputation that the eugenicists had won such enormous influence on the basis of next to nothing in terms of scientific experiment, discovery or knowledge. The early eugenicists, for instance, knew nothing of the gene as the basic unit of heredity; the Danish scientist Wilhelm Johannsen coined the word only in 1909. Before that they talked of 'gemmules', 'plastitudes' and 'pangens'.

Charles Darwin believed that the body shed 'gemmules' into the blood, which were then stored in the reproductive organs before fertilization. Although his cousin, Francis Galton, did not possess the great naturalist's encyclopaedic knowledge of flora and fauna – indeed, he once mistook a cow for a hippopotamus and shot it – it was Galton, to Darwin's evident pique, who proved the theory was wrong by exchanging the blood by transfusion between various kinds of rabbit and then studying their offspring.

The work of Gregor Mendel, which provided the underpinning of early genetic science, had lain dormant and undiscovered until almost the turn of the twentieth century.

The chromosome, though it had been spotted under the microscope much earlier, was something whose significance really was not properly understood before 1902 and it would take until 1956 for scientists to be agreed on how many chromosomes there were in human cells. DNA was again something that had been noticed and isolated, but its role would not be clarified until well after the Second World War. And on the theoretical side, the 'neo-Darwinian synthesis' that provides the current paradigm of evolutionary biology was still some decades off. Yet even though the science of heredity was in its infancy, the eugenicists were able to persuade large parts of the political class (and much of the general public too) that they knew and understood both the biological and the social implications of evolution.

Such presentational legerdemain would not have been possible if, as is sometimes claimed, eugenics did not represent what the mainstream of scientists believed but was rather the particular fixation of a small, though influential, group, who were interested in the social and economic applications of heredity. There is plenty of evidence that eugenics could claim very wide support and that the editors and editorial boards of a broad range of scientific journals came to be dominated by eugenicists.

'It is a consequence of the movement's popularity within the scientific community that eugenics was *science*, not *pseudoscience*,' wrote Jonathan Marks in his 1995 work *Human Biodiversity*. 'If all the relevant scientists believed it, how could eugenics possibly be pseudoscience? If eugenics represented a corruption of certain scientific principles, it is hard to escape the conclusion that it was the scientists themselves who were the corruptors.'[23] Though Marks was writing chiefly about the position of eugenics in the United States, his point holds good for the British eugenics scene too.

Moreover, the eugenicists kept up with scientific developments. Once they realized their mistake over the single Mendelian factors, they realigned their ideas with the new genetic science. Eugenics after this adjustment cannot today be dismissed as being based on mistaken science. Its practitioners could claim that they were at the leading edge of knowledge in the field. In the mid-1930s, the movement revived its campaigning for the sterilization of the unfit. Their message was taken up with enthusiasm by a number of women's sections of the Labour Party who put forward a draft sterilization bill.

The eugenicists mounted a grass-roots propaganda effort, despatching activists to address branches of the Women's Institute, meetings at the Ideal Home Exhibition, and a series of talks to Labour Party branches given by Dr Caroline Maule, an American physician who had moved to London, and who sat on the executive committee of the Socialist Medical Association. In 1936, Dr Maule persuaded the National Conference of Labour Women in Swansea to pass a motion calling for the sterilization of the blind.

During the 1920s and 1930s, some scientists on the Left turned against the 'mainline eugenics' preached by the society, if not wholly against eugenics as such. They were uncomfortable with the way eugenics was often a front for snobbish and racist attitudes, and advocated a 'reform eugenics' that recognized that there were valuable traits to be found in all classes and ethnic groups. Among those frequently cited as reformers was Julian Huxley (the grandson of Darwin's friend T. H. Huxley, and brother of Aldous, the novelist). His disagreement appears chiefly to have been more about tone rather than substance since Huxley continued to believe that the poorest were breeding too fast and that their access to welfare or medical treatment should be restricted. He also argued at various times that the long-term unemployed should be sterilized and that voluntary sterilization should be a condition of obtaining unemployment benefit. After the Second World War, Huxley was appointed the first Director General of UNESCO.

The eugenicists had enough friends in high places not to need to worry about being sniped at by the odd left-wing or Marxist critic. Neville Chamberlain, for example, a keen eugenicist and a former chairman of the Eugenics Society's Birmingham branch, was Minister of Health between 1924 and 1929 and Chancellor of the Exchequer from 1931 until he succeeded Stanley Baldwin as prime minister in 1937.

But during the troubled economic period of 1930s, the public tired of the constant badmouthing of the poor that formed the staple rhetoric of eugenics. Hard times proved that there were other causes of penury than inherited fecklessness – tens of thousands of previously hardworking, sober and thrifty people found themselves unemployed and flat broke. Eugenicists, now unable to win wide public appeal, devoted less time to public campaigning and began a long march through the institutions.

One institution in particular became positively riddled with eugenicists from top to bottom: the London School of Economics, founded by the Fabians Beatrice and Sidney Webb, and one of the world's leading centres in the study of the social sciences. The economist William Beveridge, best known for his 1942 report establishing the lineaments of Britain's Welfare State, was the director of the LSE between

1919 and 1937. Because of his association with the post-Second World War welfare state, Beveridge is generally thought of as having a benevolent, avuncular view of the worst off in society. In fact for nearly all his adult life Beveridge was an active eugenicist, who had a reputation for taking a particularly hard line in his earlier years. In a paper entitled 'The Problem of the Unemployed', written in 1909, Beveridge, accepting that though the 'unemployable' must be supported by the state, insisted they should be made to pay a price for society's indulgence, one that should involve '. . . complete and permanent loss of all citizen rights – including not only the franchise but civil freedom and fatherhood.'[24]

On the day the House of Commons met to debate the Beveridge Report in 1943, its author slipped out of the gallery early in the evening to address a meeting of the Eugenics Society at the Mansion House. Beveridge thanked his audience for the part they had played in developing the idea of child allowance – a key element of his proposals. His report, he was keen to reassure them, was eugenic in intent and would prove so in effect. Some of those present, though, were sceptical. The idea of child allowances had been developed within the society with the twin aims of encouraging the educated professional classes to have more children than they currently did and, at the same time, to limit the number of children born to poor households. For both effects to be properly stimulated, the allowance needed to be graded: middle-class parents receiving more generous payments than working-class parents. Many eugenicists believed that the reason the middle class had so few children was that they were being taxed so highly to support a vast number of feckless degenerates they limited the size of their own families as a necessary economy. The

Home Secretary had that very day signalled that the government planned a flat rate of child allowance. But Beveridge, alluding to the problem of an overall declining birth rate, argued that even the flat rate would be eugenic. Nevertheless, he held out hope for the purists. 'Sir William made it clear that it was in his view not only possible but desirable that graded family allowance schemes, applicable to families in the higher income brackets, be administered concurrently with his flat rate scheme,' reported the *Eugenics Review*.[25]

When he had first become the LSE's director, Beveridge had set up a department of Social Biology funded by the Rockefeller Foundation. The department's syllabus was laid out for internal consumption as 'Instinct in Man, Inherited and Acquired Characteristics, Quantity and Quality of Populations and Racial and Economic Tests of Fitness'; while for the purposes of securing Rockefeller's money, this was euphemized as 'variation and heredity in man, selective immunity, relative importance of environmental factors in social structure and change, questions of race and class in relation to hereditary endowment, economic and biological tests of fitness'. Either variant 'could have been the synopsis for a Eugenics Society Symposium' observed Harry Armytage, a President of the Galton Institute (as the Eugenics Society later became).[26]

There is probably no duller and more sterile field of enquiry that the who's up, who's down internal politics of an English academic institution. Nevertheless, it is worth taking a brief detour round the rabbit warren of the London School of Economics to get a feel for the pervasiveness of eugenic influence there. Beveridge's successor at the LSE was Alexander Carr-Saunders. Unusually for a social scientist, Carr-Saunders had taken a first in zoology at Oxford. Afterwards he studied biometry under Galton's protégé Karl Pearson, Galton Professor of Eugenics at the University of London. Joining the Eugenics Society in 1912, he was editor of *Eugenics Review* between 1922 and 1927. By the time he retired in his turn, the LSE had been under the stewardship of a eugenicist for an uninterrupted stretch of thirty-seven years.

Nor would the director's departure mark the end of the society's influence at the LSE. Carr-Saunders had befriended a bright young man who had become interested in eugenics during the late 1930s. Although he had left school at the age of fourteen with no formal educational qualifications at all, by 1942 Richard Titmuss was editing *Eugenics Review* and after spells at the Ministry of Economic Warfare and the Cabinet Office, was recruited to be professor of social administration at the LSE in 1950. Titmuss's appointment was vigorously supported by another senior member of the LSE faculty, the sociologist T. H. Marshall, who, it almost seems unnecessary to add, was a fellow and vice-president of the Eugenics Society at the time.

However effective and useful the Eugenics Society may have been as a social and professional network, it would be unfair to leave hanging in the air the suggestion that Richard Titmuss owed his chair merely to some kind of eugenicists' freemasonry. Titmuss had published his first book on poverty and population while still working as an insurance clerk and in 1942 joined a group of historians in compiling an official history and analysis of wartime social policy, later published as *Problems of Social Policy*. His work on this project earned him professional respect that more than compensated for any lack of paper qualifications. Indeed, Titmuss proved to be an extraordinarily successful head of department and played an important role in developing public policy in the years ahead – so much so that the social anthropologist Sir Edmund Leach dubbed him 'the high priest of the welfare state'. Titmuss also played an important part in taming and civilizing the Eugenics Society, or at least persuading its members to allow greater room in their considerations for environmental factors.

John Maynard Keynes also remained involved with the Eugenics Society after serving as the treasurer of its Cambridge branch. In 1937 he delivered the annual Galton Lecture, choosing as his topic 'Some Economic Consequences of a Declining Population', and for the next six years served the society as a fellow and director. Keynes, Beveridge and Titmuss: if they were, as they are generally held to be, the three main architects of the welfare state, the men chiefly responsible for the theoretical basis of Britain's post-war economic and social settlement, then the Eugenics Society had the trifecta.

Compared with brutal interventions such as forcibly sterilizing people, or locking them up so they cannot breed, post-war reform eugenics was a relatively milquetoast affair. The reformers were broadly egalitarian in outlook, seeking general environmental improvement and hoping that contraception would steadily reduce the 'problem class' (what the Fabians had called the 'social residuum'). Perhaps the chief consequence of the fact that so many of those who would influence social policy in the years ahead were drawn from the ranks of eugenicists has been a deep-seated pessimism or fatalism about the poorest of the poor. If governments are led to think that people are genetically handicapped and have little prospect of making anything of their lives, then they see no point in providing a trampoline rather than a safety net. Little effort has been made to equip and challenge those perceived to have lost out in life's genetic lottery to take responsibility for their own lives; the welfare establishment has been content to leave them dependent upon the state, something that has proved literally de-moralizing for those involved. Despite Gordon Brown's promises to lift a generation out of child-poverty, the approach his own government took was to concentrate on nudging those just under the poverty line just over it, while the worst off became even poorer.

Perhaps the eugenicists have been simply marking time, waiting for technology to deliver the dream. In September 1999, the Galton Institute (as the Eugenics Society had renamed itself) hosted a conference on 'Man and Society in the New Millennium' at London Zoo. One of the speakers was a behavioural geneticist from Florida State University who delivered a decidedly upbeat paper. Professor Glayde Whitney predicted a golden age for eugenics in the twenty-first and twenty-second centuries, bringing a 'Galtonian Revolution' to fruition. 'This new revolution will be more momentous for the future of mankind than was the Copernican Revolution or the Darwinian Revolution,' he declared. 'For with the Galtonian Revolution, for the first time, the major changes will not be to ideas alone, but rather . . . to mankind itself.'[27]

The professor's message was clear. In the future, defective or unsatisfactory genes would be fixed or replaced. The problem class need be problematic no more. One can only wonder how much his audience of mild-mannered English eugenicists knew of Whitney's background, associations and reputation back home. The previous year, for instance, Glayde Whitney had written the introduction for the memoirs of David Duke, a former Grand Wizard of the Ku Klux Klan. But then, America is another country; they do eugenics differently there.

# CHAPTER FOUR

Three generations of imbeciles are enough.

Oliver Wendell Holmes Jr.

When Darlene Johnson, twenty-seven, was brought before Judge Howard Broadman in a California court for sentencing, she was in for a shock. Her attorney had already agreed a plea bargain and she was only expecting one year in jail, followed by three on probation. Johnson's crime was one that a conservative Republican like Broadman might have overlooked, even condoned, a generation or two earlier: Johnson had punished her children by thrashing them with a leather belt. But by 1991 public attitudes had changed and the action was classed as a serious offence.

Judge Broadman sprang a surprise on Johnson. He was going to attach a condition to her three years of probation, which was that Johnson, an African American woman living on welfare, must agree to have a newly licensed pharmaceutical product known as Norplant surgically inserted in her upper arm. The matchstick-sized silicon implant would produce a steady drip of a contraceptive hormone. Either that, or receive a sentence of not one but seven years.

The case soon became notorious. Indeed, the controversy had begun even before the event. In an article announcing the licensing of Norplant by the Food and Drug Administration, the *Washington Post* had warned that the product might be used coercively against 'women who are seen as a source of social problems', and predicted that 'ethical debate is sure to get started the minute some benighted judge orders a woman to use it or go to jail.'[1] A few weeks later, Judge Broadman followed this prediction to the letter.

The sentence raised crucial legal and constitutional issues, not the least of which was the novel one Broadman threw into the ring when he went on television to defend his action. The judge claimed to have weighed Darlene Johnson's rights in the balance against those of the children she might have if she were not using contraception. It was a consideration without precedent. If there have been bitter differences among Americans during the past half-century over the mortal question of whether *unborn* children possess rights, no judge had so far asserted the rights of those who were yet to be conceived. Boardman threatened to take old arguments into a no-man's-land of debate by implying that to prevent a person being conceived might be in their best interests.

The more down-to-earth question was whether it could ever be appropriate for the state itself to violate a woman's right to fertility. In Darlene Johnson's case, however, this question could not be considered in the abstract; at least not in the media or the cockpit of public opinion. Two salient facts about Johnson kept pressing in upon every consideration of her plight. First, that she was black. Second, that she was a member of the social group all too commonly described in the early 1990s as 'the underclass'.

Just over a fortnight before Judge Broadman set his extra-ordinary probation condition, the editorial department of the *Philadelphia Inquirer* (which was customarily calm and consensus-seeking to a fault) had erupted in uproar over an editorial that appeared under the headline 'Poverty and Norplant – Can Contraception Reduce the Underclass?' David R. Boldt, the newspaper's comment editor, found himself compared in his own pages – indeed by one of his own columnists – to the white supremacist David Duke, the Louisiana politician who had once held high office among the Grand Wizards of the Ku Klux Klan. Both in the *Inquirer*'s editorial and in the Johnson case, three factors had come together to reawaken a dormant political banshee: race, poverty and the belief that society would benefit from limiting the procreation of the unfit – the three obsessions of eugenics.

Inspired by Darwin, many American scientists determined in the early years of the twentieth century that the old political dispensation must be done away with and a new one put in its place. As one of them put it, 'The world is to be operated on scientific principles. The conduct of life and society are to be based, as they should be, on sound biological maxims.'[2] This remarkable scale of ambition characterized the US eugenics movement, along with the fierce urgency of *now*. If eugenics in Britain was mostly a matter of earnest talk, in America it was all about action. But, as in Britain, the new ideas were capable of forging coalitions that cut across conventional political boundaries. 'Socialist, progressive, liberal and conservative eugenicists may have disagreed about the kind of society they wished to achieve,' observed Daniel Kevles, the author of the most comprehensive history of eugenics, 'but they were united in a belief that the biological expertise they commanded should determine the essential human issues of the new urban industrial order.'[3]

One of the most energetic popularizers of eugenics in the United States during its heyday in the 1920s was the science writer Alfred Wiggam, a man who didn't trouble himself with euphemism. 'Evolution is a bloody business, but civilization tries to make it a pink tea,' Wiggam said, calling for scientists to be given a free hand in the elimination of the unfit. 'Civilization is the most dangerous enterprise upon which man ever set out. For when you take man out of the bloody, brutal, but beneficent hand of natural selection, you place him in the soft, perfumed, daintily gloved, but far more dangerous, hand of artificial selection. Unless you call science to your aid and make this artificial selection that we call civilization as efficient as the rude methods of nature, you bungle the whole colossal task.'[4]

Wiggam, like many other eugenicists, believed there was not a moment to lose. The findings of the new science of statistics were raising the alarm. A rising tide of undesirables threatened to swamp America's pure and pioneering *Mayflower* stock and the evidence was there for all to see in the differential birthrate, the fact that the poor tended to have more children per family than the rich or middle classes.

One of the first to be driven to act by the supposed threat had been the eminent Harvard zoologist Charles Davenport. He had been the organizing secretary of the celebrations to mark the fiftieth anniversary of Darwin's *Origin* held in New York in 1909, and had contributed an essay to the book *Fifty Years of Darwinism*, published by the American Association for the Advancement of Science in the same year. At the time of the anniversary, Davenport had felt the need was urgent to do something about 'the delinquent, defective and dependent classes' and 'take the steps that scientific study dictates as necessary to dry up the springs that feed the torrent of defective and degenerate protoplasm.'[5] Having secured enough funding from the Carnegie Institution to establish in 1910 a well-appointed research facility for the study of evolution at Cold Spring Harbor on Long Island, Davenport also managed to acquire an adjacent site for his new Eugenics Records Office (ERO), with money given by Mary Harriman, the widow of the railroad baron E. H. Harriman and mother of the future politician Averell. The ERO would be separate from the Carnegie Institution laboratory, though Davenport would be in charge of both.

The ERO was formally an offshoot of the American Breeders Association (ABA), an organization set up by agricultural scientists in 1903 for the promotion of better livestock and pastures. As cattle, now people. Davenport had successfully lobbied for the ABA to set up a eugenics committee to draw up the strategy, and the ERO would carry out the practical work. This broad approach combining Mendelian, biometric and cytological studies, references to animal and plant breeding methods, and the latest genetic science, explains the extraordinary rapidity with which eugenic ideology became accepted. Davenport appointed a thirty-year-old former teacher and enthusiastic eugenicist, Harry Laughlin, as superintendent of the ERO. Cold Spring Harbor soon became the campaign headquarters for the movement.

Laughlin recruited eugenics field-workers (most of them young women), and sent them out to interview people in their homes, to compile family trees and to flag up all suspected inherited defects. Under pressure from the eugenics lobby, many states were soon passing laws authorizing the compulsory sterilization of anyone deemed 'unfit' and Laughlin himself drafted the 'Model Eugenical Sterilization Law' which became the basis of the statute adopted in Virginia. The eugenicist cast his net so wide it included almost every American with a problem. Any person should be sterilized, Laughlin argued, if they were 'potentially the parent of socially inadequate offspring'.

Laughlin's definition of 'socially inadequate' was set out in Section 2 (b) of his model law. It included the feeble-minded; the insane; persistent criminal offenders (including the 'delinquent and wayward'); epileptics; alcoholics and drug-users; the diseased; the blind; the deaf; the crippled or deformed; and a class designated the 'dependant', which comprised 'orphans, ne'er-do-wells, the homeless, tramps and paupers'.[6] And one did not even have to be any of the above to be selected for sterilization, merely the potential parent of such a social inadequate.

Since anyone without capital or savings could become the parent of a pauper, his model law brought all of the poorest section of society within target range of the statute. And the practical implementation of the sterilization laws in different states was variously obtuse and malicious. Categories such as 'blind' and 'deaf' were interpreted very loosely to encompass the visually impaired and the hard of hearing. In California, one woman was actually sterilized for suffering from post-natal depression.

On Harry Laughlin's part, this broadly drawn, almost catch-all set of taxonomic categories for the 'cacogenic' was very deliberately contrived. During the course of 1911, at a series of meetings, the eugenicists within the ABA developed a master plan to cleanse the blood of the American people. Compulsory birth control, restrictive marriage laws, segregation of the unfit in secure institutions, enforced sterilization and selective euthanasia: all these measures were not just considered but approved. Around this time, Laughlin estimated that some action would need to be taken against at least 10 per cent of the American population and even this vast number might not be enough. He was particularly concerned with identifying those people who appeared perfectly normal and lived perfectly blameless lives, but who carried in their genetic make-up the seeds of vice, degeneracy and feeble-mindedness that might yet find expression in future generations.

Advances in evolutionary science were frequently invoked in calls for eugenic sterilization. Until the early years of the twentieth century, many scientists had speculated that traits acquired during an organism's lifetime could be passed on to subsequent generations. The idea is frequently associated with the French naturalist Jean-Baptiste Lamarck – hence the shorthand *Lamarckism* – though it was widely held by most of Lamarck's generation of evolutionary theorists, and in an adapted way by Darwin himself in his theory of pangenesis. Galton questioned the idea, and it was finally rejected by the scientific mainstream. Giraffes did not get their long necks by constantly stretching to reach leaves on a high branch, they got them through natural selection. For as long as belief in the inheritance of acquired characteristics persisted, scientifically minded social reformers saw a point in taking action to improve the environment. Cure a man's alcoholism, and his descendants might not turn out to be drunkards. Give a family decent housing, and their children might become decent and responsible members of society. However, once scientists took the view that the heirs of the improved of today might revert to type tomorrow, the eugenicists could argue without much fear of contradiction from the scientific community, that there was no point in improving the living conditions of the poor; indeed, it would be dysgenic to do so.

The growing use of intelligence tests gave the eugenicists a further tool to help them sort the fit from the unfit. One of the pioneers in this field was the psychologist Robert Yerkes, working first at Harvard and later at Yale. Heavily influenced by Darwinism, Yerkes (pronounced Yerk-eez) was particularly interested in the cognitive similarities between humans and apes. A convinced eugenicist, Yerkes nevertheless realized that eugenic proposals would need some selling to politicians and the public. To this end, he contemplated the idea of developing a 'perfect chimpanzee' notable for being dependable, trustworthy, self-controlled and considerate.[7] Having once set eyes upon this paragon of an animal, Yerkes speculated, people would be all the more keen to breed better Vermonters and Oregonians. For a while it looked as if Yerkes might succeed. In the 1920s he adopted a bonobo, Prince Chim, which moved in with him, slept in its own bedroom and sat up at the table to eat with a knife and fork. Yerkes described Chim as an intellectual genius in his memoir *Almost Human*, published not long after the creature caught pneumonia and died.[8]

During the First World War, Yerkes was made chairman of the Committee on the Psychological Examination of Recruits, with a brief to set up a system of assessing all soldiers joining the US Army, so that they could be allocated the most appropriate roles. Yerkes developed a set of intelligence tests that were applied to nearly 1.75 million soldiers. This was the largest survey of its kind ever conducted and provided the data for authoritative scientific pronouncements on intelligence for many years to come. It also provided an enormous propaganda opportunity for the eugenics movement.

Alfred Wiggam, who became chairman of the American Eugenics Society, interpreted the army mental-test results as showing that close to forty-five million Americans were mentally defective. Wiggam reported estimates that the mental powers of this vast body of near-imbeciles would never be greater than those of twelve-year-old children. In addition, he estimated there were a further twenty-five million whose capacity for mental development was only that of thirteen- or fourteen-year-old children, and Wiggam was adamant that education could add nothing to their intelligence. Yerkes's army researches, it seemed, had placed no fewer that sixty-five million Americans in the eugenicists' free-fire zone.

The supposed new ability to quantify aspects of feeble-mindedness did not always operate in the eugenicists' favour. The Mayor of Chicago scored in the 'moron' range when he took a sample test and Virginia legislators were only half joking when they attributed their tardiness in implementing Harry Laughlin's model sterilization statute to a pervasive fear among their colleagues that they too might come under the knife. However, quantitative methods indubitably added what passed for evidential substance to the theoretical claims being made by the zoologists, psychologists and public health physicians who constituted the core of the eugenics movement.

Not that their authority was in any serious doubt. Though both the methodology and the conclusions of the army tests were subjected to a rigorously critical analysis by the journalist Walter Lippman in a series of four articles in the *New Republic* in 1922, who was Lippman, a mere scribbler, to contradict men such as Yerkes, president of the American Psychological Association and an officer of the National Research Council, or Charles Davenport, elected to the National Academy of Sciences? American eugenics was rooted in the technocratic and scientific establishment to an even greater extent than the British variety. Davenport himself had taught genetics at Harvard. By 1929, he had recruited to the advisory board of the American Eugenics Society eminent geneticists from the universities of Princeton, Stanford, Brown, MIT, and Chicago. In a society that set great store by academic credentials, eugenics could offer the best.

Their professional eminence and close connections with the most powerful figures in political and public life gave the eugenicists unbounded arrogance. 'It would not be a matter of great difficulty to secure a general consensus of public opinion as to the least desirable, let us say, ten per cent of the community,' wrote one leading member of the movement. 'When this unemployed and unemployable human residuum has been eliminated, together with the great mass of crime, poverty, alcoholism, and feeblemindedness associated therewith, it would be easy to consider the advisability of further restricting the perpetuation of the then remaining least valuable types.'[9]

Eugenics was also riding the slipstream of progressivism, a movement that crossed party political lines, which saw social problems as things to be solved by experts. Organization, planning, efficiency and intervention were not yet regarded as the buzzwords of bloated and sclerotic state bureaucracies, but as the virtuous and benign hallmarks of modernity. The biologists *were* experts, and if they diagnosed poverty, crime and unemployment as biological problems, and said they had a biological solution to hand, many American politicians were happy to let them get on with it. Indeed, it would take a very brave or foolhardy man to stand out against the zeitgeist and criticize them.

Besides, the eugenicists were taking their message directly to the people. It is remarkable how similar to a political campaign the eugenics project was. Its leaders were adept at advertising, spin and PR. They came up with the idea of better baby contests and held fitter family competitions at agricultural fairs across America. While the Holstein bulls and Jersey cows waited for the judges in one tent to decide which beast would get the coveted rosette, in the next tent families would queue to be physically and psychologically assessed according to eugenic criteria. Those who passed muster would leave proudly clutching a medal with the inscription 'Yea I have a Goodly Heritage', though not before being exposed to a flashing light display that demonstrated just how small a time interval there was between one and another 'unfit' person being born, or how frequently one of the unfit is sent to jail. 'Very few normal people go to jail' the sign proclaimed.

Despite being supposedly an expression of leading edge science, eugenic propaganda was often of this crude, almost brutal kind. Charles Darwin had enjoined that 'all ought to refrain from marriage who cannot avoid abject poverty for their children; for poverty is not only a great evil, but tends to its own increase by leading to recklessness in marriage.'[10] With this in mind, the eugenics movement paid vagrants to walk the streets of the cities carrying placards bearing a humiliating message:

I am a burden to myself and the state.
Should I be allowed to propagate?
I have no opportunity to educate or feed my children.
They may become criminals.
Would the prisons and asylums be filled if my kind
had no children?
I cannot read this sign.
By what right have I children?[11]

Were these poor men and women ever told the true burden of the message they carried? Almost certainly not. The breathtaking heartlessness and cynicism of this exercise is surely enough to make one wonder whether perhaps too much exposure to evolutionary science might itself lead to a degeneration of the faculty of moral discernment. A wildly speculative notion, of course; but arguably no wilder than the message the eugenicists were peddling as hard, scientific fact.

As the campaign developed, eugenics became popularized in newspapers such as the *Saturday Evening Post* and the *Los Angeles Times* and penetrated many aspects of popular culture. The jargon of eugenics – *moron, imbecile, feeble-minded* – became part of the currency of general conversation. Between 1915 and 1919, a leading Chicago surgeon, Harry Haiselden, became the protagonist of a true-life drama by publicly allowing six infants he diagnosed as hereditarily unfit to die by the peculiarly cruel act of withholding treatment. There was even some suspicion that in at least one case he actively brought about the child's death. Amazingly, Haiselden did not pursue his euthanasia in secret. Wanting to start a public debate over eugenic euthanasia, he decided to make his own refusal to treat sick children into a cause célèbre. Haiselden lambasted a society in which 'horrid semi-humans drag themselves along all of our streets' and put the dying babies and their mothers on show to journalists as he explained why he thought these babies should not be allowed to live.[12]

Not only was Haiselden never prosecuted – indeed he seems to have used the press as a cover, hiding as it were in full view – he went on to make an enormously popular, if controversial, film called *The Black Stork*. In this cautionary melodrama a young man afflicted with an unnamed but inherited disease fails to listen to his doctor's warnings against marriage and weds his childhood sweetheart. In due course their baby is born 'defective' and requiring immediate surgery to survive. However the doctor (played by none other than Haiselden himself) refuses to treat the infant despite the imprecations of the desperate parents. Fortunately, God grants the mother a vision of the bleak future of poverty, misery and crime that would be her baby's lot if it were to go on living, and she concedes that the doctor is right. In a happy eugenic ending, the dying baby's soul is received into the arms of Jesus. The film was shown around America from 1916 right up to 1928 and in some venues as late as the 1940s.

If eugenic cinema defied conventional ideas about the sacredness of all human life, eugenic literature set out to scotch the illusion of rural America as some kind of Arcadia. What emerges from the volumes of 'cacogenic' findings published by the eugenics movement between 1912 and the mid-1930s, is a sinister land seething with degenerates practising every imaginable depravity. The original inspiration for this genre was a famous 1877 study by the sociologist Richard Dugdale of a New York hill family he called the Jukes. This focused on a seven-hundred-strong cohort of prostitutes, indigents and criminals whose ancestry could be traced back to one man, Max, a descendant of early Dutch settlers and one woman, 'Margaret the Mother of Criminals'. Dugdale had come upon six of the Juke men while visiting jails as a member of the Prison Association and on investigation discovered that seventeen more of their immediate relatives were also convicted felons. He set out to examine their entire history in the United States, concluding that poverty, disease and criminality had plagued each generation.

Dugdale was no eugenicist, indeed he believed that environmental factors mostly accounted for the wretched condition of the extended Juke family. 'Public health and infant education', he wrote, '. . . are the two legs on which the general morality of the future must travel.'[13] But his research was given a eugenic spin by Arthur Estabrook of the ERO at Cold Spring Harbor in *The Jukes in 1915*, which re-analysed and updated Dugdale's data to include almost three thousand more of the Jukes declared to be suffering from 'feeblemindedness, indolence, licentiousness and dishonesty' and to have cost the public at least $2 million. Calculating the cost to the taxpayer of supporting the unfit would become a standard propaganda technique in eugenics. Photographs of the Jukes were even displayed as evidence – they were perceived to have 'a look' about them – at the Second International Congress of Eugenics, held at the American Natural History Museum in 1921. Naturally, Estabrook's study called for the Jukes to be prevented from reproducing.[14]

Meanwhile, the psychologist Henry Goddard had discovered another family. He called them the Kallikaks – *kalos* being Greek for good, *kakos* for bad – who neatly demonstrated, at least to the satisfaction of eugenicists, the hereditary nature of both vice and virtue. The original Martin Kallikak, a hero of the Revolutionary War, had planted two distinct family trees: one stemming from a casual relationship with a woman of ill repute; the other from a respectable marital union with a Quaker. Down the generations, the products of his drunken, casual coupling at an inn proved to be – what else? – 'feeble-minded, criminal and poor', while those of the marriage bed were of course intelligent, mannerly, law-abiding and went on to pursue successful careers in medicine, law and the Church.

Even at the time there was good reason to doubt Goddard's account. Deborah Kallikak, the contemporary representative of the supposedly degenerate line, did not in fact display the characteristics that led Goddard to regard her as a public menace. Her teachers noted that she was accomplished with an electric sewing machine, could cook and performed exemplary housework and had 'no noticeable defect'. Goddard, who coined the term 'moron' in his proposed system for classifying mental retardation on the basis of IQ (morons were 51–70, anyone below this an imbecile), was frustrated by their refusal to acknowledge that Deborah was feeble-minded. Alas, his eugenicist claims prevailed. Although he may not have recommended sterilization, Goddard did propose the segregation of those he regarded as morons in institutions exactly like the one he ran himself, known as Vineland, in New Jersey. It was here that Deborah Kallikak spent most of her life, locked away until she died in the 1970s.

*The Kallikak Family* became a raging best-seller and there was even talk of adapting it for Broadway, pseudo-science once again construed as potential entertainment. Like Haiselden, Goddard understood the commercial value of edifying the public, not just to himself, but to the popular newspapers who knew that there was no better way to add circulation than by frightening the readers. 'There are Kallikak families all about us,' Goddard warned, and worse 'they are multiplying at twice the rate of the general population'.[15] And sure enough, with very little effort other eugenicists were able to summon demons that made the Kallikaks look relatively harmless.

In Indiana during the 1880s, Oscar McCulloch, the minister of Indianapolis's Plymouth Congregational Church, began investigating a clan of local paupers. He reported his findings to the National Conference of Charities and Corrections in Buffalo:

> Since 1840, this family has had a pauper record. They have been in the almshouse, the House of Refuge, the Woman's Reformatory, the penitentiaries and have received continuous aid from the township. They are intermarried with the other members of this group and with two hundred and fifty other families. In this family history are murders, a large number of illegitimacies and of prostitutes. They are generally diseased. The children die young. They live by petty stealing, begging, ash-gathering. In summer they 'gypsy' or travel in wagons east or west. In the fall they return. They have been known to live in hollow trees or the river bottoms or in empty houses.[16]

McCulloch died shortly after providing this account, but his papers found their way to Estabrook who continued the investigation and presented the results at the Second International Eugenics Conference. A relatively recent common ancestor of this clan, or 'tribe' in Estabrook's demeaning term, had been discovered. Call him Ishmael. The Tribe of Ishmael, according to Estabrook, most likely originated among the off-spring of petty criminals transported to the Virginia colony from England. 'It is estimated that the Tribe numbered six thousand people in 1885, coming from about four hundred different family heads. Today . . . the number would not be less than ten thousand. They are now found in Indiana, Kentucky, Illinois, Ohio, Michigan, Iowa and Kansas,' ran Estabrook's sensational claim, implying that any day now they would be coming to a state near you.[17]

Indiana had been the first state to pass a forced sterilization law in 1907. The eugenicists were determined to encourage more states to follow suit. Accordingly they emphasized the practical social benefits that sterilization could bring, stressing the potential savings to legislators – and thus, of course, the public – in terms of welfare costs but also in terms of resources expended on the police and the criminal justice system. 'At one time the greater proportion of the women keeping houses of prostitution in Indianapolis belonged to the Tribe,' Estabrook asserted, establishing a link between the Ishmaelites and semi-organized crime.[18]

'The other marked characteristic of the Tribe has been the wandering or "gypsying" as it is called by the Ishmaelites,' Estabrook went on, hitting another perennially hot button among both big-city and small-town mayors. 'They would go often with several "wagons" in a party, sometimes alone. They camped in creek bottoms, near a settlement if possible, and lived off the country, begging and stealing. When they became tired of the place or, as often, were told to move on by the people who could no longer stand their depredations, they travelled on to the next place to do the same.' Worried he might actually have understated his case, Estabrook wound up with a warning of nothing less than genetic contagion: 'These germ plasms have now spread through the whole middle west and are continuing to spread the anti-social traits of their germ plasm with no check by society.'[19]

The Ishmaelites were only one of a series of similarly extended families traced and charted by the eugenic sleuths of Cold Spring Harbor in their campaign to spread fear and loathing of America's rural poor. In upper New York State, they discovered the Nams: two thousand related individuals who were often illegitimate, frequently engaged in prostitution and allegedly feeble-minded. In Vermont, Henry Perkins, yet another zoology professor with a mission, came across the Doolittles – four generations of 'degenerates'.[20] In Ohio, there were the Happy Hickories; in Amherst County, the Mongrel Virginians, and in Massachusetts, the Hill Folk.

Davenport had warned against too great a reliance on intelligence testing in identifying the cacogenic, warning that there were moral imbeciles who could answer all the questions except the moral one. This advice, impressed upon the prim young women with notebooks who were sent out as eugenics field workers, led to a creepy prurience in their investigations. Sexual attitudes, sexual behaviour: both became false criteria in judging imbecility. Persistent masturbation was a factor in assessing feeble-mindedness, even – absurdly – among teenage boys. The slightest sexual peccadillo could lead to a young woman being branded a moral imbecile. This linkage between moral traits and mental defects, so important to Davenport and the eugenicists, was something that had struck Charles Darwin too. 'That the state of the body by affecting the brain, has great influence on the moral tendencies is known to most of those who have suffered from chronic derangements of the digestion or liver,' Darwin wrote in the *Descent*. 'The same fact is likewise shewn by the "perversion or destruction of the moral sense being often one of the earliest symptoms of mental derangement"; and insanity is notoriously often inherited. Except through the principle of the transmission of moral tendencies, we cannot understand the differences believed to exist in this respect between the various races of mankind.'[21] As the eugenicists cast their net wider, a boy who smiled too readily when brought for inquisition before public health officials would be written down as an idiot, particularly if he were related to one of the demonized 'tribes'; while a girl who smiled in too flirtatious a manner was branded a moral defective. The Darwinists had truly taken over the asylum.

The Hill Folk of Massachusetts became the subject of a study by the field worker Florence Danielson and Charles Davenport himself. Their report examined two interconnected family trees, being respectively the progeny of one Old Neil Rasp and another man known only as Nuke. 'From the biological standpoint, it is interesting to note that mental defect manifests itself in one branch of the pedigree by one defect and in another branch by a quite different one,' Davenport and Danielson observed. 'In one line alcoholism is universal among the men; their male cousins in another line are fairly temperate, plodding workers, but the women are immoral.' Getting into the detail, we learn that 'the descendants from the most feebleminded daughter of the second generation' display 'abnormal sex instincts'. The daughter of another 'has a mulatto child', while several of her cousins display 'uncontrolled sexual instincts' and another is simply 'immoral'.[22]

Given this preoccupation with sex on the part of the field workers, it is hardly surprising that when sterilization began in earnest, no fewer than two out of every three of the women subjected to the procedure in California were categorized as sexually delinquent.

Carrie Buck was three years old when her mother, Emma, unable to cope, gave her up for fostering. Emma's marriage to Frank Buck had broken down, possibly as a result of her infidelity. Whether Carrie was Frank's child, or the result of one of her mother's affairs, nobody knows for sure. Carrie was placed with the family of a local policeman in Charlottesville, Virginia, where she performed adequately in school and was generally considered to be well adjusted and hard working. However, in 1923 she became pregnant after being raped by her foster parents' nephew. The family closed ranks. Carrie, the outsider, was thrown to the wolves.

Neither her previous good behaviour nor her evident intelligence would carry any weight with the Commission on Feeblemindedness, when she was examined the following year. Even if she had been given a chance to state her case before a disinterested tribunal, it would not have made any difference. Carrie came from tainted stock. For on All Fools' Day 1920, almost four years before, Emma Buck had herself been brought before the Commission. Infected with syphilis, and with a previous conviction for prostitution, her hearing before the panel was brief and conclusive. She was committed to the Colony for the Feebleminded immediately. It was effectively a life sentence – she would remain incarcerated for twenty-four years until her death.

As the offspring of a feeble-minded mother and with an illegitimate child of her own on the way, Carrie stood no chance of avoiding the Colony herself. Her foster parents need hardly have gone to the bother of inventing tales about her wild hallucinations and weird behaviour.

The teenager was allowed to have her baby in freedom. At the end of March she gave birth to a daughter whom she named Vivian. The child was soon taken away from her and handed over to the very same foster family in whose home she had grown up. Carrie herself was sent to the Colony. Meanwhile, the Commonwealth of Virginia had finally got round to passing the Eugenical Sterilization Act, based on Harry Laughlin's proposed law.

The details of what happened next have only come to light relatively recently thanks to the research of Paul Lombardo, a legal and bioethics scholar at the University of Virginia. Carrie Buck was examined and selected for sterilization. However, she was also chosen to test the constitutionality of Virginia's new law. For the eugenicists had encountered considerable difficulty getting the measure through the state legislature, where it had been held up for a long period. They knew their opponents had not given up and, anticipating a legal challenge once the sterilizations began, decided to fight the battle on their own terms with a test case of their own devising, which they felt certain would survive judicial scrutiny. A bewildered Carrie Buck suddenly found she had been granted a lawyer.

It was all a squalid fix. Carrie was represented by an active eugenicist, Irving Whitehead, who had personally campaigned for sterilization. Whitehead, what is more, was one of the original trustees of the Colony and had been a member of the panel that appointed the superintendent, Albert Priddy, against whom the case would nominally be brought. The two were hand in glove, and not only was Carrie's lawyer colluding with Priddy, but so were most of the witnesses who would testify in court. A social worker, Miss Wilhelm, was sent to examine baby Vivian, and conveniently concluded the little girl, who was still only about seven months old, was defective. 'There is a look about it that is not quite normal,' she told the judge.[23] *A look about it . . .*

Expert testimony was provided at various stages in the legal process by a doctor, Joseph DeJarnette, of the Western Lunatic Asylum in Staunton, Virginia; Arthur Estabrook from Cold Spring Harbor and Harry Laughlin himself. Estabrook claimed that a standard intelligence test administered to tiny Vivian had established that she was feeble-minded; although he had never actually met or examined her. Laughlin's evidence confirmed that Carrie Buck fitted the description of 'a low grade moron' and opined that the chances of her being feeble-minded through environmental or non-hereditary causes were exceptionally remote. Laughlin's testimony also placed before the court the details of Emma Buck's genetic and clinical history. It was all deceitfully contrived to demonstrate three generations of hereditary defect.

Whitehead did not challenge the diagnosis of Carrie as a moron at the circuit court hearing, allowed false testimony vilifying her as sexually promiscuous to pass undisputed, and called no witnesses on her behalf. However, when the court, unsurprisingly, found in Superintendent Priddy's favour, Whitehead lodged an appeal and the case went forward for consideration by the Virginia appellate bench. This was all part of the plan. From the outset, the conspirators' aim had been to take the case all the way to the Supreme Court of the United States. Priddy had died while the circuit court was considering its decision and had been replaced by his assistant, J. H. Bell, so when the suit was finally decided in Washington DC in May 1927, it entered American legal history as the landmark case of *Buck vs. Bell*.

The eugenics movement had plenty of friends in the United States Congress and had received words of encouragement from three Presidents – Teddy Roosevelt, Woodrow Wilson and the incumbent, Calvin Coolidge. Now they would obtain the explicit endorsement of the third branch of government. Writing for the majority in finding against the plaintiff, Carrie Buck, Supreme Court Justice Oliver Wendell Holmes Jr. said: 'It is better for all the world, if instead of waiting to execute degenerate offspring for crime or to let them starve for their imbecility, society can prevent those who are manifestly unfit from continuing their kind. The principle that sustains compulsory vaccination is broad enough to cover cutting the Fallopian tubes. Three generations of imbeciles are enough.'

One might be forgiven for assuming that Supreme Court Justices, whose job is to interpret the constitution of the United States, would believe in the rights and values enshrined in that founding document. But that would be a mistake. Like many of his contemporaries in the immediate post-Darwin period, in 'the midst of doubt, the collapse of creeds', Holmes had abandoned any kind of faith and turned instead to philosophical scepticism and pragmatism, eventually arriving at a pessimistic moral relativism.[24] He recognized no law from Heaven to inform our laws on Earth. He viewed natural rights as nonsense, and regarded moral choices as arbitrary. He was a keen reader of the work of Herbert Spencer, respected force and believed that it was what decided most things in the end. Grant Gilmore, in his 1974 Storrs Lecture at Yale, challenged the then prevailing view of Holmes as the 'Yankee from Olympus'. Instead, Gilmore portrayed him as 'harsh and cruel . . . who saw in the course of human life nothing but a continuing struggle in which the rich and powerful impose their will on the poor and the weak.'[25]

Human beings, Holmes came to believe, had far too big an idea of their own significance – a train of thought he expanded upon in a letter to his friend, Lewis Einstein, concerning the novels of Henry James. 'My general attitude is relatively coarse: let the man take the girl or leave her I don't care a damn which,' Holmes wrote in his brusque way. 'Really, I suppose, he [James], like his brother and the parsons, attaches a kind of transcendental value to personality; whereas my bet is that we have not the kind of cosmic importance that the parsons and philosophers teach. I doubt if a shudder would go through the spheres if the whole ant heap were kerosened.'[26]

Such sudden turns of phrase – and ideas – were part of Holmes's theatre when delivering Supreme Court opinions. At the time when *Buck vs. Bell* was proceeding before the court, the judge was in almost daily exchange by letter with the British Fabian socialist Harold Laski, with whom he maintained an unusually close friendship despite a difference in age of more than fifty years. 'I wrote and delivered a decision upholding the constitutionality of a state law for sterilizing imbeciles the other day and felt that I was getting near to the first principle of real reform,' he wrote to Laski. He goes on to complain, however, that his fellow justices had tried to bowdlerize his text. 'I am amused (between ourselves) at some of the rhetorical changes suggested, when I purposely used short and rather brutal words for an antithesis . . . I am pretty accommodating in cutting out even thoughts that I think important, but a man must be allowed his own style.' *Three generations of imbeciles are enough.* 'Sterilize all the unfit, among whom I include all fundamentalists,' Laski wrote back to Holmes. The exhortation was perhaps genuine. The younger man had worked for a brief period at the Galton Laboratory for National Eugenics, and in the year following the Buck case Laski was appointed professor of political science at the LSE.[27]

Carrie Buck was sterilized on the morning of 19 October 1927. She was just twenty-one. In the months and years ahead, suspected imbeciles would be hunted down all over the state and put beneath the blade. In some rural areas, such as the mountain country of Virginia, vast sweeps were made, roadblocks set up, doors broken down and teams of sheriffs' deputies seen dragging whole families away. Some people have found it hard to summon much sympathy for the hill folk of the Appalachians, their prejudices no doubt abetted by the scene in John Boorman's 1972 film *Deliverance* in which two inbred mountain men rape Ned Beatty and Jon Voight at gunpoint; but that was just a movie, while the brutality visited upon the people of America's rural heartlands was real, and has left a long trail of agony leading to the present day.

Carrie Buck had a sister. For years Doris Buck Figgins and her husband tried unsuccessfully to have a child. It was not until 1979 that she found out that the operation she had undergone under the supervision of the Virginia authorities at Lynchburg was not, after all, an appendectomy, as she had been told at the time. 'I'm not mad about it,' she said after she discovered the appalling truth, 'just broken hearted.'[28]

Carrie herself was released from the Colony in due course, married, and lived a life that showed no trace of imbecility, feeble-mindedness or hereditary vice whatsoever. She died in 1983. Back in 1925, while her case was going through the courts, the then Governor of Virginia, E. Lee Trinkle, who signed the state's eugenical sterilization measure into law, had written to the superintendents of the Virginia State Hospital urging them on to make as vigorous use of it as they could, once it was confirmed as being constitutional. In May 2002, timed to coincide with the seventy-fifth anniversary of the Supreme Court's decision in *Buck vs. Bell*, Governor Mark Warner made a public statement formally apologizing on behalf of the Commonwealth of Virginia for the forced sterilizations. 'The eugenics movement was a shameful effort in which state government never should have been involved. We must remember the Commonwealth's past mistakes in order to prevent them from recurring.'[29]

There can be no certainty about how many people were sterilized as a result of the programme that the eugenics movement set in train. Thirty-three states passed sterilization laws, and an estimate of sixty to sixty-five thousand is commonly cited for those subjected to the procedure. However, many centres that were performing mandatory operations also tried, as a matter of policy, to obtain the patient's consent to sterilization. Where consent was obtained, the very fact of the operation having taken place could be concealed under rules governing patient confidentiality. In many cases there would be good grounds for scepticism about how well informed this consent was likely to be. There are a number of documented cases where men and women consented to a procedure they did not understand only because they had been assured by a medical professional that it would be good for their health. Compulsory sterilization laws remained in force in some states well into the 1970s, and in Oregon as late as 1983. The decision in *Buck vs. Bell* has never been overturned.

In 1973, the Southern Poverty Law Centre filed suit on behalf of two young girls, Alice and Minnie Relf, in the US District Court in Washington DC, against Caspar Weinberger, then the Secretary of the US Department of Health.[30] The Relf sisters were fourteen and twelve years old respectively when their mother, an illiterate African American woman, made a mark on a form, believing that she was authorizing doctors to provide contraceptives to her daughters. Instead, both of her daughters were surgically sterilized.

Others joined the suit, making it effectively a class action. When the case came to decision, Federal District Judge Gerhard Gesell estimated that during the previous few years somewhere close to a hundred and fifty thousand poor people had probably been sterilized under federal programmes. An unknown number of these, he said, had been coerced into accepting the procedure. A common method of coercion, it appeared, had been the threat to withdraw welfare payments if the victims did not agree.

The sheer scale of the assault launched against America's poor by eugenics is astonishing. For every Carrie Buck or Minnie Relf there are tens of thousands more whose names we do not know. As we shall see in the next chapter, eugenics had a strong racialist dimension. In the early stages, those selected for sterilization tended to be the sort of people often dismissed as 'white trash', and the whole project sometimes seemed to be aimed at purifying the Caucasian bloodline. In Vermont, Native Americans were targeted, and after the Second World War, particularly in the southern states, African Americans became the most frequently victimized group. In medical slang, the sterilization operation was even known as a 'Mississippi appendectomy'. In California, another class action,

*Madrigal vs. Quilligan*, mounted in 1975, exposed the increasing use of sterilization against Latina women.

And it was against this historical background that Judge Broadman would issue his order seeking to control the fertility of Darlene Johnson with Norplant – sterilization-lite. It was not, as some said, that the sentence raised a long-buried spectre from the darkness of the American past. After all, plenty of men and women are still living with daily pain and anguish, having been forcibly sterilized or tricked into volunteering.

But almost immediately politicians at state level began considering the advantages of Norplant as what can only be described as eugenics by the back door. In 1991, 1992 and 1993, legislators in more than a dozen states introduced measures that, had they passed, would have coerced women into submitting to Norplant. The American Civil Liberties Union has produced evidence that some of these bills would have bribed women on welfare with financial incentives. Others would have blackmailed them into using Norplant by threatening them with the loss of benefits.

The ACLU argues that the enthusiasm for using Norplant as a social tool arose from 'erroneous notions that women on welfare have children indiscriminately and remain on welfare indefinitely'. In fact, the ACLU says, 'the average number of children in a family on welfare is 1.9 (a figure no larger than that for the general population), and in 1990 the median period for receipt of Aid to Families with Dependent Children was 23 months.'[31]

The Norplant controversy shows how the ideas propagated by the eugenics movement continue to colour many people's perceptions of the poor, as well as continuing to influence political approaches to poverty and welfare reform.

The history of eugenic sterilization in the United States reveals how imperilled freedom can be – even in the freest and most decent of societies. The generation of biologists that came after Darwin, determined to remake the world along rational and scientific lines, created a demon. Their Darwinism was not a science that dealt purely in facts and left values aside; it took on many of the characteristics of an ideology. It was a supposedly utopian political project, and an affirmation of a philosophical system that threatens to subvert the ethical foundations of a free society even now.

# CHAPTER FIVE

Give me your tired, your poor,
Your huddled masses yearning to breathe free,
The wretched refuse of your teaming shore,
Send these, the homeless, tempest-tossed to me,
I lift my lamp beside the golden door!

Emma Lazarus

'I think we now have sufficient population in our country for us to shut the door and to breed up a pure, unadulterated American citizenship,' Ellison DuRant Smith told the United States Senate in April 1924. 'I would like for the Members of the Senate to read that book just recently published by Madison Grant, *The Passing of a Great Race*. Thank God we have in America perhaps the largest percentage of any country in the world of the pure, unadulterated Anglo-Saxon stock; certainly the greatest of any nation in the Nordic breed,' he went on. 'It is for the preservation of that splendid stock that has characterized us that I would make this not an asylum for the oppressed of all countries, but a country to assimilate and perfect that splendid type of manhood that has made America the foremost Nation in her progress and in her power.'[1]

'Cotton Ed' Smith was a Southern Democrat of the old

sort. He was born and died in the same bed in his slave-owning family's antebellum mansion on Tanglewood Plantation in Lee County, South Carolina. During more than thirty years in the Senate, Smith opposed just about every enlightened or progressive cause that presented itself, including women's suffrage, the New Deal and civil rights. 'To Cotton Ed, White Supremacy is real,' reported *Time* magazine, 'as real as the population of his beloved Lee County: White, 7,850, Negro, 16,246.'[2]

The author whose book the senator was puffing, Madison Grant, was one of those responsible for putting Ota Benga on display in the Bronx Zoo. A close friend of Presidents Theodore Roosevelt and Herbert Hoover, Grant embodied the twin spirits of the Progressive Era and the Efficiency Movement in seeing social problems as susceptible to technocratic or scientific remedy. He divided his time between political activities and scientific work and brought the two together in *The Passing of the Great Race,* a book that would have disastrous consequences as one of the seminal works of scientific racialism. Adolf Hitler wrote to Grant, praising the book as 'my Bible'.[3]

Scientific racism is distinguished from the common or garden variety by its use of Darwinian evolutionary ideas, genetic science and physical anthropology to establish a supposed hierarchy of races, designating some superior, others inferior, according to supposedly objective, scientific criteria. It did not establish the racist mindset, which had been manifest for all human history, but it sought to elevate racism by putting it on a biological footing. Its initial reference point in Darwinian evolutionary science was Charles Darwin's observation that man 'has diverged into distinct races, or as they may be more appropriately called, sub-species. Some of these, such as the Negro and European, are so distinct that, if specimens had been brought to a naturalist without any further information, they would undoubtedly have been considered by him as good and true species.'[4]

Had Darwin limited his theorizing about the distinctness of the races to a discussion of their physiological differences alone, then scientific racialism would have had a very short life. Scientists soon found that the 'Negro and the European' had an enormous amount in common beneath the skin, and that the differences between them were mostly superficial. Thanks to progress in genetic science, we now know there would be as much variation between any randomly chosen group of Africans or Europeans as would be found in a comparison of the racial groups themselves, and that though it is possible to determine ethnic origin from DNA, the commonality is more striking than the differences. Even in Madison Grant's time, it would not have been plausible to base a claim that the European was more 'highly evolved' than Africans merely on the basis of physiological make-up.

Those who seek to absolve Charles Darwin of any responsibility for the consequences of scientific racialism like to point out that he was himself no more of a racist than any other English gentleman of his times; that he passionately opposed slavery; and that he sometimes spoke and wrote warmly and in complimentary terms about people of African descent. More recently, his biographers Adrian Desmond and James Moore have argued that Darwin's abolitionism was an important factor driving him in his work to develop a theory of common ancestry and racial unity.[5] All this may be true, but it is beside the point. For what gave the scientific racists their impetus were not Charles Darwin's personal feelings or opinions, but his speculations on the origins of social behaviour and moral qualities in man. If the qualities that characterize civilization are rooted in culture, then societies may vary immensely in terms of the level of civilization they achieve, while remaining biologically equal in terms of evolutionary development. But if social behaviour and moral faculties are to any significant extent biologically determined, then inevitably any disparities in the way different groups behave will prompt the drawing up of biological hierarchies.

Darwin addressed himself to the ways in which social co-operation might have developed in primitive man. 'A tribe including many members who, from possessing in a high degree the spirit of patriotism, fidelity, obedience, courage, and sympathy, were always ready to aid one another, and to sacrifice themselves for the common good, would be victorious over most other tribes; and this would be natural selection,' he wrote. 'At all times throughout the world tribes have supplanted other tribes; and as morality is one important element in their success, the standard of morality and the number of well-endowed men will thus everywhere tend to rise and increase.'[6]

Once man had crossed the threshold of moral reasoning, Darwin argued, civilization became self-developing. 'The moral nature of man has reached its present standard, partly through the advancement of his reasoning powers and consequently of a just public opinion, but especially from his sympathies having been rendered more tender and widely diffused through the effects of habit, example, instruction, and reflection. It is not improbable that after long practice virtuous tendencies may be inherited.'[7]

Darwin had little to say, however, about those peoples who had not followed this pattern of development. He noted that 'savages' persisted, and showed little sign of change over recent centuries. He had himself encountered savages – Fuegians, who had so revolted him by their feral behaviour that he said he felt more comfortable thinking of himself as the descendant of a baboon than of men like them. 'The astonishment which I felt on first seeing a party of Fuegians on a wild and broken shore will never be forgotten by me,' Darwin wrote in the *Descent*, 'for the reflection at once rushed into my mind – such were our ancestors.'[8] Here, at least, Darwin acknowledged a common humanity with the savage. In an earlier account of contact with Fuegians, he found it hard even to admit them to the animal kingdom. 'These poor wretches were stunted in their growth, their hideous faces bedaubed with white paint, their skins filthy and greasy, their hair entangled, their voices discordant, their gestures violent and without dignity,' Darwin recorded in his memoir of the voyage of the *Beagle*. 'Viewing such men, one can hardly make oneself believe they are fellow-creatures, and inhabitants of the same world.'[9] In the *Descent*, Darwin predicted that the more advanced races would supplant – or even exterminate – the savage races wherever they were, and certainly gave little sign of regarding them as his own biological equals.

Behind the seeming ambiguity of his attitude – stressing the unity of common descent, and at the same time seeming to suggest a hierarchy of evolutionary gradation among the various races – perhaps lay a genuine uncertainty. Certainly there appears to be an inconsistency between the public and private Darwin on the question of the possibility of civilizing these savages. In the *Descent*, published in 1871, Darwin emphasizes the stasis in their development. 'Many savages are in the same condition as when first discovered several centuries ago,' he laments. 'As Mr. Bagehot has remarked, we are apt to look at the progress as normal in human society; but history refutes this.'[10]

For many years Darwin had taken the view that it was useless to send missionaries among the Fuegians, whom he considered the very lowest of the human race. However, since 1867 he had been quietly sending money to support missionaries in Tierra del Fuego. They had established farms, built a school and converted a number of the Fuegians to Christianity. A year before the publication of the *Descent*, Darwin wrote to his friend James Sulivan, who had served as an officer aboard the *Beagle*: 'The success of the Tierra del Fuego Mission is most wonderful, and shames me, as I had always prophesied utter failure.'[11] It clearly did not shame him enough to modify his general scepticism about the prospect of bringing savages to civilization in his book published the following year, and this scepticism created a gap in evolutionary theory that the scientific racialists like Madison Grant would be only too pleased to fill.

Madison Grant was scornful of an approach to anthropology that concerned itself with linguistics, religion, marriage customs, designs of pottery or blanket weaving. 'Man is an animal differing from his fellow inhabitants of the globe, not in kind but only in degree of development,' he insisted in true Darwinist style, 'and an intelligent study of the human species must be preceded by an extended knowledge of other mammals, especially the primates.'[12] His own studies of animals led him to seek a revival of racial consciousness and promote an anti-democratic politics based on concentrating power in the hands of a technocratic elite.

'A majority must of necessity be inferior to a picked minority, and it always resents specializations in which it cannot share,' Grant argued. His own back-to-basics programme called for a return to the forms of social organization that first made civilization possible. 'Mankind emerged from savagery and barbarism under the leadership of selected individuals whose personal prowess, capacity, or wisdom gave them the right to lead and the power to compel obedience . . . In a democratic system this concentrated force at the top is dispersed throughout the mass, supplying, to be sure, a certain amount of leaven, but in the long run the force and genius of the small minority is dissipated.'[13]

In the context of the United States, Grant identified the gifted and valuable minority with a particular racial type. Looks, once again, become a mortal question. Grant's model of perfection was his own type. The native New Englander with his clean-cut face, high stature, grey or blue eyes and light brown hair, he asserted, represented a particularly pure strain of the Nordic race. The pioneer stock of the American colonies and the early wave of immigrants, Grant argued, had been very largely Nordic. A wide swathe of Northern Europeans – Scandinavians, Germans, Balts, Dutch, the English (but not the Welsh), the Scots, and the fairer and red-headed among the Irish, qualified as Nordic.

Dr Lothrop Stoddard, one of the founding directors of the American Birth Control League, agreed with Grant that of all the Nordic groups in the United States, the original settlers possessed the finest pedigree. 'The immigrants of colonial times were largely exiles for conscience's sake,' he pointed out, 'while the very process of migration was so difficult and hazardous that only persons of courage, initiative, and strong will-power would voluntarily face the long voyage overseas to a life of struggle in an untamed wilderness.' America's best bloodlines, Stoddard claimed, had been established by nothing less than Darwinian natural selection: 'Only the racially fit ordinarily came, while the few unfit who did come were mostly weeded out by the exacting requirements of early American life.'[14] Stoddard was not venturing a dubious scientific speculation here; Charles Darwin had said something similar himself. 'There is apparently much truth in the belief that the wonderful progress of the United States, as well as the character of the people, are the results of natural selection,' Darwin wrote in the *Descent*.[15]

Darwin had not distinguished between north and south Europeans in his assessment; but for the scientific racialists, the distinction was an important one. The new wave of immigration from around 1890 brought an influx of people from Southern and Eastern Europe. These Italians, Greeks, Southern Slavs and Jews were classed by Madison Grant as being from two races – the Alpine and the Mediterranean – both of which, he maintained, were genetically inferior to the Nordics.

Lothrop Stoddard thought the new immigrants should be subject to the closest scientific attention. 'Since the various human stocks differ widely in genetic worth, nothing should be more carefully studied than the relative values of the different strains in a population, and nothing should be more rigidly scrutinized than new strains seeking to add themselves to a population,' he warned. 'The introduction of even a small group of prolific and adaptable but racially undesirable aliens may result in their subsequent prodigious multiplication, thereby either replacing better native stocks or degrading these by the injection of inferior blood.'[16]

Madison Grant, however, felt no need to be sensitive to the distinctions between each group of incomers. He had already smelled the future. 'New York is becoming a *cloaca gentium* which will produce many amazing racial hybrids and some ethnic horrors that will be beyond the powers of future anthropologists to unravel,' he railed, setting aside the language of science for some old-fashioned, tub-thumping populism. 'The man of the old stock is being crowded out of many country districts by these foreigners, just as he is to-day being literally driven off the streets of New York City by the swarms of Polish Jews. These immigrants adopt the language of the native American; they wear his clothes; they steal his name; and they are beginning to take his women.'[17]

There was really no need to lower the tone. The public and the politicians were already falling into step, and science appeared to be on his side. In 1917, Seth K. Humphrey, a Boston-based biologist and popular science writer, mounted a critique of the fashionable idea of America as a 'melting pot' on the basis of contemporary genetic thinking: 'What appears to the eye as a blend is an intimate mixture in new combination . . . our melting-pot would not give us in a thousand years what enthusiasts expect of it – a fusing of all our various racial elements into a new type which shall be the true American.' Instead, future generations would be bewildered by their own genetic endowment. 'They will inherit no stable blended character, because there is no such thing. They will inherit from a mixture of unlike characteristics contributed by unlike peoples, and in their inheritance they will have certain of these characteristics in full identity, while certain others they will not have at all.' After the First World War, Humphrey drew a causal connection between 'a degenerative change taking place in the quality of the race itself' and political and social unrest across the world. His meaning was clear: the roots of Bolshevism were biological.[18]

During the first two decades of the twentieth century, some 14.5 million immigrants entered the United States. Madison Grant blamed the 'suicidal ethics' of churchmen and those who insisted on upholding the traditional values of the United States constitution for bringing the American people to the brink of 'race suicide'. He warned:

> We Americans must realize that the altruistic ideals which have controlled our social development during the past century and the maudlin sentimentalism that has made America 'an asylum for the oppressed,' are sweeping the nation toward a racial abyss ... If the melting-pot is allowed to boil without control and we continue to follow our national motto and deliberately blind ourselves to 'all distinctions of race, creed, or colour,' the type of native American of colonial descent will become as extinct as the Athenian of the age of Pericles and the Viking of the days of Rollo.[19]

Grant's alarmist rhetoric might have gone done well on the stump except that, given his allies, he had no need to be a politician himself.

Albert Johnson had been a newspaper man. He worked for a while as news editor of the *Washington Post* before getting a paper of his own to edit in Washington State. In 1912, Johnson went into politics, running for a seat in the House of Representatives. He soon found that trading on popular prejudice against Japanese immigrants was an effective way to garner votes in this north-western state on the Pacific seaboard. Johnson was elected to the 63rd Congress of March 1913.

Some three years after he had returned to the District of Columbia, a friend gave him a copy of Madison Grant's *The Passing of the Great Race*. Johnson was so impressed he wrote Grant a congratulatory letter and soon the pair were regular correspondents. In Congress, Johnson decided to make immigration his special forte, and he looked to Grant to provide him with background briefings on the racial aspects.

Grant had become one of the leading members of the Immigration Restriction League and when the Republicans took control of the House of Representatives in 1919, the League lobbied to have Johnson picked as chairman of the Committee on Immigration and Naturalization. Grant invited the politician up to stay at his New York home, encouraged Johnson's interest in eugenics and eventually signed him up as a member of the Eugenics Research Association and of the Galton Society, of which Grant was a founding member. Scientific racialism and eugenics went hand in hand. The leading anti-immigration campaigners were active eugenicists, and the leading eugenicists campaigned for restricting immigration as well as the sterilization of the unfit.

Presumably at Grant's suggestion, Albert Johnson invited Harry Laughlin from the Eugenics Record Office to give evidence before his committee, laying out the eugenicists' arguments to a hearing convened to discuss biological aspects of immigration. Laughlin warned the congressmen that 'our failure to sort immigrants on the basis of *natural worth* is a very serious national menace'.[20] His initial presentation was so well received that Chairman Johnson decided to appoint him as the committee's 'Expert Eugenics Agent'.

Laughlin began writing, under the letterhead of the House committee, to mental-health institutions across America. His aim was to assemble evidence that would cast the immigrant groups of southern and eastern Europe as a genetic menace. Predictably, he found what he sought, though only by adopting a cavalier approach to statistical methodology; though Henry Goddard, the author of *The Kallikaks*, had already done some of Laughlin's spadework for him.

Charles Davenport had suggested to Goddard that he should use intelligence tests to discover hereditary defects among immigrants being processed at New York's Ellis Island. Goddard's first trawl concluded that more than 80 per cent of the Jewish, Hungarian, Italian, Polish and Russian immigrants he examined were hereditary defectives. Even to some hardened eugenicists this result seemed too good to be true. Goddard sent another team of researchers back, this time specifically to test a cohort of women. The results were even more astounding. They managed to write off 83 per cent of the Jews, 79 per cent of the Italians, 80 per cent of Hungarians and 87 per cent of Russians in their survey as feeble-minded.

Goddard cautioned those sceptical of his conclusions, and indeed his methods, that 'it is never wise to discard a scientific result because of apparent absurdity'.[21] In the course of 1913, several members of Goddard's staff from the Vineland Training School spent two and a half months on Ellis Island. Now they found that 40 per cent of the tested group were feeble-minded. But this time, they only tested immigrants who had been pre-screened by the Ellis Island medical staff. Any obvious mental defectives had thus already been excluded, and the Vineland researchers then de-selected anyone else of obviously high intelligence. The remaining sample they thought would represent a typical cohort of 'average immigrants'. Goddard first looked at the scores of the Russians in the group, finding that 83 per cent scored as feeble-minded. Perhaps fearing that his results would excite too much scepticism, he then ditched a number of the questions – those that more than 75 per cent of the immigrants had got wrong – and drew up a new scale. According to these figures, 40 per cent of the Jews were found to be feeble-minded, with the other groups achieving a similar result. The Ellis Island immigrants were the first people to be tested in America. The commonest criticism of intelligence testing all through the twentieth century – that the testers always seemed to find precisely what they wanted – began with Goddard and his teams.

Carl Brigham, a professor of psychology at Princeton, addressed himself to analysing the performance of various ethnic groups in Robert Yerkes's army tests, which Brigham had himself helped to administer. Adopting Madison Grant's racial taxonomy, he concluded that the Nordic type was by far the best performer, with Poles and Italians scoring very badly. With an eye on the current immigration debate, Brigham lamented that more than two million immigrants with intelligence 'below that of the average negro' had been allowed into the United States during the previous two decades.[22]

The army had classified its recruits only by country of origin, so Brigham found it difficult to produce any hard, quantitative evidence about the performance of Jews. Nevertheless, this was a subject upon which he felt compelled to pronounce. Accordingly, Brigham made some guesstimates as to the proportion of Jews in a number of national samples. 'Our figures, then, would rather tend to disprove the popular belief that the Jew is highly intelligent,' he reported. 'If we assume that the Jewish immigrants have a low average intelligence, but a higher variability than other nativity groups, this would reconcile our figures with popular belief, and, at the same time, with the fact that investigators searching for talent in New York City and California schools find a frequent occurrence of talent among Jewish children. The able Jew is popularly recognized not only because of his ability, but because he is able and a Jew.'[23]

It is not surprising that 'popular belief' held Jews to be intelligent. Today, Ashkenazi Jews are well known to be among the highest-scoring groups in IQ tests. What is remarkable is that the eugenicists had such confidence in their science as to assume that they could convince the American public to disbelieve the evidence of their own daily experience. In the end, the Jews who passed through Ellis Island and their descendants, though branded as hereditary defectives by Goddard's researchers, would contribute more Nobel laureates than any other immigrant community.

Brigham's speculations about the Jews, no matter how counter-intuitive they may have seemed to the man in the street, were of course precisely what Grant and Laughlin were looking for. Brigham also pointed to evidence that the country's Nordic genetic elite were already sleeping with the racial enemy. 'The 1920 census shows that we have 7,000,000 native born whites of mixed parentage, a fact which indicates clearly the number of crosses between the native born stock and the European importations', Brigham noted. 'According to all evidence available, then, American intelligence is declining, and will proceed with an accelerating rate as the racial admixture becomes more and more extensive.' The report concludes with the pious sentiment that: 'The steps that should be taken to preserve or increase our present intellectual capacity must of course be dictated by science and not by political expediency.' But it was his recommendation that 'immigration should not only be restrictive but highly selective.'[24]

The details of intelligence testing of immigrants were not much debated either in Albert Johnson's committee or on the floor of the House when the content of the Immigration Act of 1924 was being discussed. Yerkes had been in contact with the committee chairman, but by the time the committee was holding its hearings he had begun to have severe doubts about the whole area of ethnic differences. That he was never called to give oral evidence is surely significant, and neither were any of the other leading psychologists in the field. Johnson knew what he wanted and what he wanted was to give Harry Laughlin not just pre-eminence but a near monopoly as source and supply of scientific evidence to the committee.

However, a great deal of the decision-making for what would become known as the Johnson–Reed Act took place away from open session, behind closed doors. Madison Grant had put together a team of special advisers drawn entirely from the eugenics movement and the Immigration Restriction League, of which he was president, to keep the chairman on message. The IRL had worked obsessively since the 1890s to establish literacy as a criterion for entry into the United States, and despite the opposition of successive Presidents Cleveland, Taft and Wilson had managed to get Congress to include a literacy test in its Immigration Bill of 1917, another outrageous discrimination against the uneducated, the outcast and the poor, none of whom would be able to experience the irony of Emma Lazarus's sonnet lettered in bronze at the Statue of Liberty. Now another of its founder members, the Harvard climatologist Robert DeCourcy Ward, joined the panel of the wholly unofficial Committee on Selective Immigration alongside Johnson and Grant, with Harry Laughlin acting as secretary. The propriety of a congressional committee chairman sitting on the board of a pressure group involved in lobbying his own committee might be questioned, even in Washington. Yet Johnson was quite blatant in his extramural activities, actually taking on the presidency of the Eugenics Research Association himself in 1923.

The political manoeuvrings to limit immigration in the United States in the early 1920s were highly complex and involved several false starts. But Albert Johnson was always indefatigable, always the political point man to Madison Grant's fixer working away assiduously in the background. In 1920, Grant told Johnson that the time was right to introduce a bill to set quotas on immigration from various European countries: the proposal could be sold as an emergency measure to cope with the post-war surge in immigration that brought a million new arrivals in that calendar year. F. A. Wallis, the Commissioner of Ellis Island, warned that 'whole races of Europe are preparing to remove to the United States', presumably a coded way of announcing that there had been a particularly substantial increase in Jewish immigration, which was indeed the case.[25]

To mobilize support for emergency legislation, it was crucial to create an atmosphere of fear. Grant and his circle chose the Jews as their bogeymen. Johnson wangled copies of diplomatic cable traffic from the State Department alerting

Washington that a large number of Eastern European Jews were preparing to embark for the United States. These were, the consular officials said, 'filthy and ignorant and the majority are verminous'. Another set of diplomatic service documents described the Jews as 'evasive and dishonest' and concluded that they did not have 'the moral qualifications for American citizenship'.[26]

The influence of Madison Grant was everywhere apparent in the ensuing debates in the press and on Capitol Hill. A number of politicians even adopted his idiosyncratic system of racial classification, publicly extolling the virtues of the 'Nordic type'. Congressman Will Taylor of Tennessee distilled the question before the House in words that could have been written by Grant himself: 'The issue, stripped of its frills and furbelows and without any varnish or veneer, is simply this: Shall we preserve this country, handed down by a noble and illustrious ancestry, for Americans, and transmit it to our posterity as our forefathers intended; or shall we permit it to be overrun and submerged by a heterogenous, hodgepodge, polyglot aggregation of aliens, most of whom are the scum, the offal and the excrescence of the earth?'[27]

In case the upper chamber of the legislature remained in any doubt about the genetic peril that faced the nation, Charles Davenport provided evidence to the Senate Immigration Committee about the many and terrible defects he claimed the immigrants carried in their germ plasm, and which threatened to pollute the American heritage. Madison Grant then spent two days seeing members of the Senate in private and finally managed to persuade the sceptical LeBaron Colt, the Senate committee chairman, to endorse the measure.

The Emergency Quota Bill passed through Congress with

remarkable speed. It took just two months from the moment Albert Johnson proposed it to the arrival of the completed legislation in the Oval Office for the president's signature. But then there was a hiccup. President Woodrow Wilson refused to sign it. It was by now February 1921, and his term of office was due to expire on the 4th of March. He still retained his prerogative of veto, however, and he used it, just as he had used it previously to try to prevent the literacy requirement for immigrants being imposed by Congress. But Madison Grant had already squared president-elect Warren Harding, and the bill was brought back to Congress straight after his inauguration. This time the legislative process was even brisker: on the 19th of March, just a fortnight after its reintroduction, the new president signed the Emergency Quota Act into law. The measure had two chief effects: reducing the absolute number of immigrants who could enter the United States, and establishing quotas for each country of origin. These quotas had been carefully designed to favour the Nordic stocks so beloved of Grant, and powerfully discriminated against countries in eastern and southern Europe. The number of immigrants from Italy, for instance, was reduced from well over 200,000 to 40,000. Overall, immigration was more than halved.

The Emergency Quota Act had been sold to the American people as a short-term measure to cope with the sudden peak in post-war numbers. The challenge the eugenicists set themselves was to make it permanent. A terror of Bolshevism had helped fuel anti-immigrant, and especially anti-Semitic, feeling; but they could not count on this to last forever. Besides, the public's enthusiasm for Madison Grant's brand of Nordic supremacism was beginning to wane. The next round of legislative activity would depend upon more science and less populism. At which precise point, the eugenics movement received a considerable fillip from the Second International Eugenics Congress in the autumn of 1921. Leonard Darwin came from London, and funds were augmented with donations from billionaire philanthropists such as the Kelloggs and Harrimans. The issues of sterilization and immigration restriction remained linked and stayed in the news.

Harry Laughlin travelled to Europe to research the genealogy of would-be immigrants from various countries, returning to give further presentations to Albert Johnson's congressional committee and to erect an enormous eugenics exhibition display under the very dome of the Capitol. Laughlin reiterated all the usual warnings of genetic contamination and adduced figures, charts and tables purporting to show greater criminality and moral-imbecility among disfavoured immigrant groups. By unrelenting action and propagandizing, the eugenicists were able to sustain the political momentum they had built up during the quota campaign.

Charles Davenport and Harry Laughlin proposed a system whereby immigrants would be pre-screened in their countries of origin by trained eugenicists, who would make a close examination of the pedigree of the applicant. Davenport further argued that once in the United States, immigrants should have to register and make themselves available for eugenic assessment until naturalization. They took heart, therefore, when Calvin Coolidge, who had succeeded to the presidency on the death of Warren Harding, gave a supportive first address to Congress. 'America must be kept American,' he insisted, before promising to deliver the whole of Davenport's shopping-list. 'For this purpose, it is necessary to continue a policy of restricted immigration. It would be well to make such immigration of a selective nature with some inspection at the source . . . We should find additional safety in a law requiring the immediate registration of all aliens.'[28]

The following year, the Johnson-Reed Immigration Act was passed, further tightening the numbers and hardening the quota preferences in favour of the Nordic type. More lobbying by Grant and his team had facilitated the passage of the act, together with a well-planned media blitz. Newspapers and magazines ran a string of supportive articles and letters written by eugenics-friendly luminaries. Grant himself contributed an article to the *North American Review*, while both Lothrop Stoddard and the historical novelist Kenneth Roberts (a keen supporter of Grant) argued the case in no fewer than four articles in the *Saturday Evening Post*. One of Roberts's features was illustrated with a powerfully emotive photograph of a line of Jews queuing for visas in Poland. The *Post*'s leader writers joined in, endorsing the scientific case for restricting immigration. The most authoritative newspaper of the day was the *New York Times*, which ran a special feature on immigration giving prominence to Harry Laughlin's evidence to the House committee and the Results of Robert Yerkes army intelligence tests, and its letters page carried a choreographed sequence of contributions from eminent eugenicists including one from Henry Fairfield Osborn of the Museum of Natural History.

The scientific racialists did not, of course, entirely monopolize the public debate, but the fact that opposition to them was mainly voiced by Jews and Catholics actually strengthened their hand. There had long been a strong current of anti-Semitic and anti-Catholic feeling in American nativism, which Grant and the immigration restrictionists were happy to exploit. Grant understood that his strongest card was scientific authority, and he played it over and over again. Even so, there were some who were not fooled by his trick. F. Scott Fitzgerald wrote *The Great Gatsby* between 1922 and 1925, the period when the immigration debate was at its height. Early in the novel there is a telling exchange between Tom Buchanan, a brutal, old-moneyed WASP, and Nick Carraway, the book's narrator:

'Civilization's going to pieces,' broke out Tom violently. 'I've gotten to be a terrible pessimist about things. Have you read "The Rise of the Colored Empires" by this man Goddard?'

'Why, no,' I answered, rather surprised by his tone.

'Well, it's a fine book, and everybody ought to read it. The idea is if we don't look out the white race will be – will be utterly submerged. It's all scientific stuff; it's been proved.'[29]

The 1924 Act ushered in the 'Great Pause' in US immigration, leaving Emma Lazarus's 'golden door' only slightly ajar. The Act remained in force right up until the middle of the 1960s. In large part contrived and driven through the political process by biologists, zoologists and anthropologists, who were the main popular interpreters of evolutionary theory in their day, the Act incorporated into American law an unproven idea from Charles Darwin concerning the superiority and inferiority of races. The relative evolutionary backwardness Darwin had ascribed to tribesmen he had seen on the shore in Tierra del Fuego – which he had later been given cause to doubt – was now being ascribed to Italians, Greeks, Spaniards and Jews. Among those who would be kept out by the strict quotas were some of the tens of thousands of Jews trying to escape Nazi Germany – where exactly the same ideas about racial superiority and inferiority would be applied in unimaginably barbaric form.

# CHAPTER SIX

The basis of Hitler's political beliefs was a crude Darwinism.

Alan Bullock

Art criticism, as a genre, was banned by the Nazis. It was not enough to censure art itself as un-German, or 'Jewish-Bolshevist' in spirit – particularly the work of artists like Kirchner, Beckmann, Chagall, Picasso and Matisse; even just to write about such art, to mention it in the press at all, became a crime. At the notorious *Entartete Kunst* exhibit that began its eleven-city tour in Munich in 1937, one entire gallery was devoted to the work of Jewish artists (or those artists presumed Jewish by the Nazis; in fact, only six of more than a hundred artists held up for mockery in this show were actually Jewish), its walls emblazoned with slogans nearly meaningless in their sarcastic rage. 'Revelation of the Jewish racial soul' shrieked one; 'The ideal – cretin and whore' sneered another; and 'In Germany the Negro becomes the racial ideal of degenerate art'. Modernism, with its physical distortions and complex psychology, was self-evidently degenerate; and if modernism was Jewish, then anti-modernism conformed, in Nazi Germany, with anti-Semitism. To publish opinions about such art, good or bad, was to give it a credibility it must not have, and to keep it in the public mind. Hence the edict banning art writing issued by Goebbels in 1936.

The Führer himself, of course, remained at liberty to declaim his own aesthetic pronouncements, of which the most notorious was his statement that 'anyone who sees and paints a sky green and fields blue ought to be sterilized' – an injunction that immediately evokes the language of eugenicists such as Harry Laughlin. And aptly so, for no society has more blatantly or aggressively practised eugenics than the Third Reich, where it was known as race-hygiene. One of the first steps Hitler's government took, on coming to power in 1933, was to pass a 'Law for the Prevention of Hereditarily Diseased Offspring' based on Laughlin's model statute. Three years later, the University of Heidelberg awarded Laughlin an honorary degree for what were cited, in a phrase as redolent of the Balkan future as of the American past, as his 'services to racial cleansing'.[1]

Darwin's ideas were more enthusiastically adopted in Germany in his own day than perhaps in any other country – partly perhaps because German culture paid a respect amounting to deference to science and scholarship; partly, no doubt, because Darwin's theory chimed with the secularist and anti-Catholic spirit among liberals that found expression in the *Kulturkampf*; and certainly because of the opportunism and energy of Ernst Haeckel. There may be many other reasons why the Germans were so receptive to Darwin – the direction that liberal Protestant theology and biblical criticism had taken, and the popularity of historicism and positivism within the German academy among them; but maybe we should leave it there, for as the American historian William Hesseltine observed, attempting to trace the course of intellectual history is like trying to nail jelly to a wall. Suffice to say that the Germans were so quick on the uptake that three years before Francis Galton even coined the word 'eugenics', the German zoologist Robby Kossman was already calling for a ruthless, state-sponsored negative-eugenics programme. 'The Darwinian world view must look upon the present sentimental conception of the value of the life of a human individual as an overestimate completely hindering the progress of humanity,' Kossman declared in 1880. 'The human state', he continued with what the Nazis would later term ice-cold logic, 'must reach an even higher level of perfection, if the possibility exists in it, through the destruction of the less well-endowed individual . . . The state only has an interest in preserving the more excellent life at the expense of the less excellent.'[2]

The political scientist Leo Strauss, father of neo-conservatism, once coined the term *reductio ad Hitlerum* to mock the sloppy but common form of reasoning that goes like this: 'Adolf Hitler and Heinrich Himmler were both vegetarians; therefore, vegetarianism must be unspeakably evil.' More recently, Mike Godwin, general counsel for the organization that publishes Wikipedia, formulated what he called Godwin's Law, which – roughly paraphrased – holds that as any comment thread on the Internet grows longer, the probability that someone will invoke Hitler or the Nazis to bolster their argument approaches 1. Both these formulations are salutary in – and indeed reflective of – a culture that invokes the Holocaust far too glibly and frequently. However, the evidence that Darwin's evolutionary theories had a significant influence in shaping the ideology of National Socialism, and was even at the root of its genocidal practices, is so abundant and well attested that to ignore it would be perverse.

A host of writers from Hannah Arendt to Richard Weikart and nearly all of Hitler's respected biographers have made some form of Hitler–Darwin connection, though none has set out the case quite so pithily as David Klinghoffer. 'The key elements in the ideology that produced Auschwitz', Klinghoffer says, 'are moral relativism aligned with a rejection of the sacredness of human life, a belief that violent competition in nature creates greater and lesser races, that the greater will inevitably exterminate the lesser, and finally that the lesser race most in need of extermination is the Jews. All but the last of these ideas may be found in Darwin's writing.'[3]

Historically, eugenicists in both Britain and the United States frequently voiced their frustration at being constantly restrained by outdated religious ideas and by the timidity of God-fearing politicians. One might imagine a society in which they would have been happier: where biologists and evolutionary scientists were unshackled; where they did not need to concern themselves with the prattling of prelates; where they were free of the ethical restraints of sentimental humanitarianism, and where there was no cause to make the kinds of fudges and compromises that a pluralist, democratic society imposes; a society in which they could remake public policy along rational, scientific lines and according to the most up-to-date thinking in their field. But there is no need to imagine such a place. Nazi Germany made it a reality.

That Hitler should have been influenced by Darwin's thinking is not at all surprising or shocking. Karl Marx, Charles Darwin and Sigmund Freud all made a huge impact on the ideas of the generations that grew up in the second half of the nineteenth century and the first half of the twentieth. All Western philosophy and religion have been shaken by the implications of Darwin's work, most particularly perhaps by the idea that humans are simply a more complex kind of animal. According to some interpretations, this idea undercuts the work of all previous philosophers perforce, as well as the teachings of the world's great religions. If mankind is just another part of the animal kingdom, it is no longer obvious upon what rational basis any notion of human dignity and the sacredness of human life could be founded.

None of the serious thinkers who have chosen to emphasize Darwin's influence on Hitler has said that he was the only influence. Insofar as he was any kind of intellectual at all, Adolf Hitler was a synthesizer, selecting an eclectic mix of ideas to inform what became an inconsistent and barely coherent ideology. Hitler was not, after all, a political philosopher; he was a practical politician. It would therefore be a mistake to examine his intellectual influences in the same way that students of the history of ideas trace the influence of one thinker upon another. Ideas have quite a different function for the man of realpolitik than they do for the philosopher or the political science professor. The politician will, consciously or subconsciously, tend to take a more instrumentalist approach. Sometimes he may not himself know whether he espouses a particular view because he believes it to be true, or because it is expedient to appear to do so.

Hitler was exposed to evolutionary thinkers other than Darwin, such as Ernst Haeckel; and to racialist theoreticians, such as Houston Stewart Chamberlain, an English botanist who, inspired by Richard Wagner's music, wrote in 1899 a bestselling work – *The Foundations of the Nineteenth Century* – preaching Teutonic supremacism, before marrying the composer's daughter Eva, and ultimately joining the Nazi Party.

Chamberlain believed that what caused sap to rise in plants was a mysterious inner vital force; that most celestial bodies were covered in ice; that all Jewish women were prostitutes and that the Aryans were the master race. Both Hitler and the Nazi ideologue Alfred Rosenberg took Chamberlain and his ideas very seriously indeed.

It is arguable that much of what might be identified as 'Darwinist' in Hitler's outlook was received second hand, filtered through the thinking of the eugenicists. Whatever evolutionary biologists may say today, it is a fact that all the early eugenicists identified Darwin as the inspiration of their discipline and most of the leading figures in evolutionary science in the early decades of the twentieth century supported eugenics to some degree. During this period eugenics *was* science. Eugenics featured in all the main scientific journals, and in the 1920s more than three hundred academic courses involving eugenics were taught in American universities, including the most prestigious.

The claim made by moderate commentators on the Darwin–Hitler issue is not a determinist one – that Darwin's thinking led inexorably to the Holocaust. Those who see some value in exploring the connections between Darwinism and Nazism do not do so to discredit the scientific discoveries of Darwin, and certainly not to indulge in some childish blame game that casts Charles Darwin, that gentle and amiable soul pottering about his garden at Down House, as either immoral or amoral. But it seems more than likely that some of Darwin's followers have misinterpreted his work, have taken his ideas into areas where they do not belong, have claimed for them implications that cannot legitimately be claimed, or have applied them without morality. It is also possible that in some areas, beyond the scope of his meticulous accumulation of empirical evidence, Darwin himself got some things wrong. His ideas about the extent that evolutionary processes can satisfactorily explain human social behaviour and ethics for example, surely remain more speculative than factual.

Perhaps the best starting point in an investigation of the motives for mass murder is to look at what view the perpetrators took of human life and whence they derived that view. Charles Darwin, like Oliver Wendell Holmes, thought that man tended to have too high an opinion of himself. 'Man in his arrogance thinks himself a great work, worthy of the interposition of a deity,' Darwin wrote in his notebook. 'More humble and, I believe, true to consider him created from animals.'[4] A gentle and modest reflection on the part of a modest man. Holmes, by contrast, his emotional sensibility coarsened in the American Civil War, makes essentially the same observation, but in terms of it not mattering a damn whether mankind, like a nest of ants, is burned to death with kerosene. The same idea can take people of differing temperament in radically different directions; though just as often ideas can bring the oddest couples together. The urbane Madison Grant, a hunting companion of President Roosevelt, a chum of Herbert Hoover, at ease discussing politics high and low over the second magnum, concluded that 'life is valuable only when it is of use to the community or race',[5] a view with which Adolf Hitler, incarcerated in Landsberg prison, concurred; though Hitler used the word *Volk* rather than community.

Darwin's champions are never slow to point out that he personally was too soft-hearted to qualify as a social Darwinist. He recoiled from the idea of abandoning the unfortunate to suffer and die. He wrote: 'The aid which we feel impelled to give to the helpless is mainly an incidental result of the instinct of sympathy, which was originally acquired as part of the social instincts.' And, 'Nor could we check our sympathy, even at the urging of hard reason, without deterioration in the noblest part of our nature.'[6] But those who see this as absolving Darwin from any responsibility for social Darwinism miss the point. He may have had qualms about leaving the unfit to their fate, but plenty of others have had no such compunction and would dismiss as sentimental all references to the nobility of human nature. And Darwin himself has, in the first part of what he says above, handed them their licence to differ. By insisting on a purely naturalistic explanation for the origin of ethics, Darwin slams the door shut against the possibility of any universal or absolute morality.

Oliver Wendell Holmes, one of the generation immediately post-Darwin, the first generation which really had to grapple with the philosophical implications of Darwinism during their own intellectual formation, arrived at the same conclusion as many thousands of others in the years to follow. Holmes, in the words of the political scientist Daniel J. Mahoney, 'disparaged all moral preferences as arbitrary choices akin to the choice of coffee with or without milk.'[7] Once again, Darwin himself has much the same thought, but puts it far more delicately: 'A man who has no assured and ever-present belief in the existence of a personal God, or of a future existence with retribution and reward, can have for his rule of life, as far as I can see, only to follow those impulses and instincts which are the strongest or which seem to him the best ones.'[8] The catastrophe is that people sometimes commit abominable crimes while following those impulses and instincts that seem to them the best. Even Hitler's shade might claim to have *meant well*.


First they came for the feeble-minded. 'A state which, in the epoch of race poisoning, dedicates itself to the cherishing of its best racial elements, must some day be master of the world,' Hitler had written in *Mein Kampf*, in his grandiloquent style, denouncing weakness of body and brain. He also made a specific commitment to eugenic sterilization. 'He who is not physically and mentally healthy and worthy must not perpetuate his misery in the body of his child.'[9]

In 1934 Germany established a nationwide system of eugenic courts to decide who should be sterilized. Some of the courts introduced IQ tests as a means of assessment. At the same time every family doctor was ordered, on pain of a substantial fine, to inform the racial-hygiene authorities of any patient on their books with a genetic defect, a hereditary disease or the appearance of being feeble-minded. As in the United States, feeble-mindedness – in itself such an infirm term – was both loosely and punitively interpreted, and in Germany appears to have included a large number of alcoholics. After 1935, with the passage of the Nuremberg Laws, the same courts would arbitrate race cases, deciding who should be allowed to marry whom. In all, four hundred thousand Germans were sterilized, about half of them in the first four years of operation of the racial-hygiene system.

To begin with, the eugenic courts operated in a racially neutral manner. Hitler had, however, very firm views on the genetic perils of miscegenation. 'Any crossing between two beings of not quite the same high standard produces a medium between the standards of the parents,' the Führer wrote, souding rather like Charles Davenport or Harry Laughlin. 'That means: the young one will probably be on a higher level than the racially lower parent, but not as high as the higher one ... such a mating contradicts Nature's will to breed life as a whole towards a higher level.'[10]

In the Rhineland there was a small mixed-race population, around five hundred in number, who were fathered by French colonial troops, stationed there during the occupation after the First World War, and born to local German women. For both the obvious reasons, the Nazis regarded these teenagers as symbols of national shame. The Gestapo hunted them down and sent them to be sterilized.

By the late 1930s, German medical professionals were well used to receiving forms and questionnaires that had to be completed and returned to racial-hygiene bureaucrats, so it did not strike anyone as being particularly sinister when, in the summer of 1939, a body calling itself the 'Committee for the Scientific Treatment of Severe Genetically Determined Illness' wrote asking doctors and midwives to send them details of any children under three years of age exhibiting Down's syndrome, spina bifida, missing or malformed limbs, spasticism and a range of similar conditions. The registration forms were sent to Berlin, where a panel of doctors sifted through them writing either a plus or minus sign on each.

In October, those children whose files had been marked with a plus were collected from their parents and taken to special paediatric clinics. There they were put to death. Some clinics used cyanide gas, others administered an overdose of morphine. In one clinic where, presumably, the doctors were anxious about the legality of what they were being asked to do, the children were simply left to starve to death. The physicians need not have been so concerned about themselves: the Führer signed a secret order exempting participating medical staff from prosecution and backdated it to September so that even the pioneers of child-murder would be covered.

Later the same form requesting patient details was sent round the family doctors again: this time asking about children in the next age bracket. The process would be repeated until the state had identified, abducted and murdered all handicapped children up to the age of seventeen. The whole operation was carried out in secret, and referred to only by the cryptonym Aktion T4 – after the street address of the mansion at Tiergartenstrasse 4 where the directing staff was based.

Meanwhile, preparations were being made to exterminate all Germany's mental patients and the adult handicapped. In January 1940, Karl Brandt, Hitler's personal physician, visited a psychiatric hospital at Brandenburg to witness a horrible demonstration. A prototype gas chamber had been constructed, disguised as a communal shower room. Approximately twenty inmates of the asylum were led naked into the room. After the door was closed, a doctor then turned on a supply of carbon-monoxide gas, which dispersed into the room through small holes in what otherwise looked like water pipes. Six minutes later, the room was cleared of gas and a team of SS men took the bodies to the hospital crematorium. Karl Brandt expressed his satisfaction and ordered that, as in this case, qualified doctors must carry out all future exterminations.

Robert N. Proctor, who has written a detailed study of medicine under the Nazis, points out that 'Doctors were never *ordered* to murder psychiatric patients and handicapped children. They were *empowered* to do so, and fulfilled their task without protest, often on their own initiative.'[11] This is more than a legal nicety. Darwinian ideas, eugenics, and its ugly sister eugenic euthanasia were broadly accepted by the mainstream of the medical profession. Indeed, so convinced were the staff of the clinic at Kaufbeuren-Irsee in Bavaria that they were doing the right thing that even after Germany's surrender in 1945, following the impulses and instincts that seemed best to them, they carried on killing adults and children under American occupation, until a horrified US Army officer, who had found out about it, led a squad of GIs to the hospital and ordered them at gunpoint to desist.

Between January 1940 and August 1941, seventy thousand handicapped adults were murdered in six main killing centres equipped with gas chambers. Thereafter the responsibility for the euthanasia programme was decentralized and became simply part of the routine in local hospitals. No complete records exist of the numbers killed thereafter, but they are likely to have run into the tens of thousands. The Nazis' euthanasia programme merged seamlessly with the Holocaust. Ninety of the specialist personnel who took part in Aktion T4 were transferred to the east to operate the death camps at Belzec, Sobibor and Treblinka. The killing centre at the mental hospital at Hadamar in Hessen was reassigned for the murder of healthy Jewish children from 1943.

In today's world it is those with a racialist political outlook who are thought of as knuckle-dragging primitives from one of those cartoons illustrating the Darwinian idea of the ascent of Man. When we read passages from Madison Grant or Hitler's *Mein Kampf*, lauding the intrinsic superiority of the Nordic over the Slav, the Mediterranean and the Jew, we find it hard to believe that anyone really thought like that. If we did not know the story had such a tragic ending, we might find them laughable. Fortunately, some of the scientific racialists' contemporaries did laugh. Grant, along with Harry Laughlin, was frequently lampooned in American magazines.

Many people in many countries, however, took these laughable ideas seriously and tried to apply them in their societies, but only Adolf Hitler took the idea of the struggle for survival between the races and made it the organizing principle of national policy. He made his view plain, in the pages of *Mein Kampf*, that humans were just like any other animal, knowing only one law: the survival of the strongest. In such a worldview there was no room for compassion: '. . . there will never be found a fox which, according to its inner nature, would perhaps have humane tendencies as regards the geese, nor will there be a cat with a friendly disposition towards mice,' Hitler observed. Like Charles Darwin, Hitler anticipated a time when the lesser races would be annihilated – 'All who are not of good race in this world are trash' – so that the 'higher development of organic living beings' could continue.[12]

The Holocaust would not have happened without hundreds of years of Christian persecution and anti-Semitism. 'The Christian said *You cannot live among us as Jews*,' Raul Hilberg wrote in *The Destruction of the European Jews*, 'but the Nazis said, *You cannot live*.'[13] Charles Darwin made genocide a fact of life, a law of nature, or, at least, left it open to being interpreted that way. In his published writings, he coldly envisaged the extermination of Australian aborigines and in his private correspondence took an equally sanguine view of the destruction of other races. 'I could show fight on natural selection having done and doing more for the progress of civilisation than you seem inclined to admit,' Darwin wrote to William Graham in 1881. 'Remember what risks the nations of Europe ran, not so many centuries ago of being overwhelmed by the Turks, and how ridiculous such an idea now is. The more civilised so-called Caucasian races have beaten the Turkish hollow in the struggle for existence. Looking to the world at no very distant date, what an endless number of the lower races will have been eliminated by the higher civilised races throughout the world.'[14]

# CHAPTER SEVEN

The evolution of humanity will take a leap forward when we have around us only fine and beautiful young people, all of whom have been conceived, carried and born in true homes by conscious, powerful and voluntary mothers.

Marie Stopes

In August 1935, two weeks before the Nuremberg race laws were promulgated, the National Socialists had hosted an international conference on population science in Berlin. The event was given a high level of political backing. No fewer than seven Reichsministers sat on the conference committee, and the interior minister, Wilhelm Frick, delivered the opening address. Roland Freisler, later to become notorious for vicious and humiliating treatment of defendants in show trials before his 'People's Court', represented the Justice Ministry at the conference. The chairman of the plenary sessions was Eugen Fischer, recently installed by Adolf Hitler as the rector of Berlin's Friedrich Wilhelms University, an institution whose worldwide academic reputation had been somewhat tainted since Joseph Goebbels presided over the ceremonial burning of twenty thousand 'degenerate books' from the university's library.

A member of the Nazi Party almost from its inception, Fischer, a professor of medicine and anthropology, played a leading part, alongside the geneticists Erwin Bauer and Fritz Lenz, in providing a scientific underpinning to National Socialism's racial ideology through his physiological studies of the various racial types. The moving spirit of the population conference, however, was another doctor, Ernst Rüdin, professor of psychiatry at Munich University. Rüdin, too, was an early member of the party. At Munich, he supervised the studies of Joseph Mengele, later to become infamous as the 'Angel of Death' at Auschwitz, teaching his young charge that 'inferior' human lives were worthless. Together with his one-time brother-in-law, Alfred Ploetz, Rüdin had founded the racial hygiene movement in Germany. Looking back on this period from the perspective of 1943, Rudolf Ramm, a Nazi member of the Reichstag, who worked closely with Rüdin on implementing Germany's eugenics programme, would confirm that 'biology and genetics' were 'the roots from which the National Socialist worldview has grown'.[1]

Clarence G. Campbell of the Eugenics Research Institute and Wickliffe Draper represented the American eugenics movement at the Berlin population conference. Draper was a rich businessman and amateur anthropologist, who funded the 1927 expedition to the southern Sahara that discovered Asselar Man, early human remains dating from the early Holocene. Draper would later establish and endow the Pioneer Fund, which continues to subsidize much of the research throughout the world into racial differences in intelligence.

Campbell made an effusive speech paying tribute to some of the leaders in racial doctrine, naming among others Francis Galton, Leonard Darwin, Charles Davenport, Madison Grant,

Lothrop Stoddard, Eugen Fischer and Ernst Rüdin. 'From the synthesis of the work of all these men', Campbell went on, 'the Führer of the German nation, Adolf Hitler ... has been able to draw forth a far-reaching racial policy of evolving and improving the population ... which promises to become epochal in racial history.' Campbell told the conference that the 'difference between the Aryan and the Jew was as insurmountable as that between black and white' before concluding his address with a stiff-armed Nazi salute.[2]

From the outset, eugenics had been an international movement with especially close collaboration between its leading figures in Britain, the United States and Germany. Ernst Rüdin had been proposed by Charles Davenport to be his successor as president of the International Federation of Eugenics Organizations at the Third International Eugenics Conference at the Museum of Natural History in New York in 1932, and the motion was unanimously passed. Lothrop Stoddard was especially welcomed by the Nazi regime, and was even invited to sit as a judge in one of the eugenic courts where he recommended the sterilization of an 'apelike' man who was married to a Jew. Stoddard spent four months in the Reich as late as 1940, enjoying access to senior Nazis such as Heinrich Himmler and Hitler himself, and visiting Eugen Fischer and the geneticist Fritz Lenz. Stoddard reported back from this visit that the Jewish question was 'already settled in principle and soon to be settled in fact by the physical elimination of the Jews themselves from the Third Reich'.[3]

Sitting in the audience as Clarence Campbell heaped fulsome praise upon the Führer, were the UK delegates to the Berlin conference, the eugenicist D. V. Glass (who would later become a professor of sociology at the LSE), and Marie Stopes.

In addition to her doughty campaigning for birth control, Stopes was such a passionate and forceful speaker at meetings of the Eugenics Society in London that Leonard Darwin complained to colleagues that he was unable to control her.

Stopes's mother had been a cold and rather distant figure, and as a child Marie spent as much time as she could in the company of her paleontologist father. Through him, she was introduced at a very early age to some of the leading botanists and geologists of the day. A precocious child, she read Charles Darwin's *Origin* at an unfeasibly early age. She won a scholarship to study Botany and Geology at University College, London, where she was awarded first-class honours, before going swiftly on to become the youngest woman ever to receive a doctorate.

Marie Stopes became an internationally known figure when copies of her book *Married Love*, first published in England in 1918, were impounded by US customs. The book remained suppressed in the United States on grounds of obscenity until 1931, when the ban was revoked by Judge John Woolsey, the same judge who overturned the embargo on James Joyce's *Ulysses*. In Britain, Marie Stopes seemed an unlikely person to be the author of a sex manual, particularly one that contained such a vivid, even lyrical description of female orgasm. She had only recently had her marriage to Reginald Ruggles Gates annulled on grounds of non-consummation, and as far as her reading public were concerned, remained a virgin. Possibly so, but Marie Stopes had studied part of the time for her doctorate at the Botanical Institute in Munich, where she fell in love with the Japanese botanist Kenjiro Fujii, who was married. Nevertheless, Stopes followed Fujii back to Japan, presumably hoping he would leave his wife. When he failed to do so, Stopes returned to Britain via Canada, marrying Ruggles Gates on the rebound.

In the event, the embarrassed Ruggles Gates did the decent thing, allowing the divorce court to proceed on the basis that the marriage was unconsummated; though when his private papers were eventually released they contained a complaint that his wife had been 'super-sexed to a degree which was almost pathological'.[4] After the divorce, Stopes, always keen to be close to nature, set up a tent on a beach and spent her time taking notes of her own feelings of arousal and the intervals between them, which she assembled into a 'Tabulation of Symptoms of Sexual Excitement in Solitude'. This became the basis of *Married Love*, which contained charts presenting women's sexual feelings as cyclical and scientifically predictable.

In her book *Radiant Motherhood*, published in 1920, Stopes revealed the extent of her commitment to eugenics. It contained the same deadening litany of the dangers presented to the future of the race by degenerates, imbeciles, and the feeble-minded as the speeches of Leonard Darwin and the writings of Harry Laughlin. 'These produce less than they consume', Stopes complained and are 'ever weakening the human stock.' She called for legislation to sterilize unfit males by surgery and unfit women by irradiation with X-rays, calling upon the Labour Party, all progressives, and enlightened Conservatives to support her. Stopes added some further pseudo-scientific observations of her own. The circumstances of coition, she believed, were all important. The children of the working class, she averred, owed their sickliness and unattractiveness to the unplanned and frequently drunken couplings of their parents. For those of the 'highest type' she prescribed that intercourse should take place in rooms bedecked with copious bunches of flowers, or preferably *al fresco*, as nature intended. Children should be conceived, she advised, in spring or early summer – in accordance with nature's rhythms. A properly eugenic, healthy baby, she believed, would only be born to good-looking parents. In Marie Stopes's world, sex was not for the plain.[5]

When she set her will upon something, few found it possible to withstand Marie Stopes's forceful determination. She persuaded the University of London to allow her to take her degree after only two years; she had the rules changed in Munich to be allowed to gain her doctorate; and she broke the embargo on women teaching science at Manchester University. Outside her own immediate family, possibly the only person who ever successfully stood up to her was Scott of the Antarctic. Between his *Discovery* expedition and his ill-fated attempt to reach the South Pole, Marie Stopes had given Robert Scott lessons in fossil recognition, all the while badgering him to take her along on his forthcoming journey to Antarctica. Scott did not refuse, promised to see what he could do, but at the last moment found a convenient excuse to leave her behind. In 1920, when Stopes began lobbying for birth control, the prime minister, David Lloyd George, found himself under similar pressure. The Welsh Wizard, as he was nicknamed, was, however, a man of great guile. He refused to give Stopes any public support for her project until she had met a challenge he set. 'The subject of birth control is disreputable. Your problem is to change all that,' Lloyd George told the importunate Stopes.[6]

Of course, Stopes accepted the challenge and began campaigning at meetings all over the country. With financial help from her new husband, Humphrey Roe, she opened the first of a chain of birth-control clinics in Holloway, North London in 1921. In line with her eugenic purpose, the clinics were aimed at restricting the birth rate of the working class, not liberating the middle class. Despite, or perhaps because of her own experiences, Stopes strongly disapproved of sex outside marriage and her clinics had a policy of only treating married women.

Aside from her birth-control work, Marie Stopes enjoyed literature and the theatre, mixed with eugenically minded writers such as George Bernard Shaw and H. G. Wells, and took an interest in the careers of young poets. She sent a copy of her own anthology of love poems to Adolf Hitler in 1939, along with a covering letter commending them to him, and inviting the Führer to share them with the German people. Her son Harry Stopes-Roe later said that she made this gesture not out of any Unity Mitford-like passion for the German dictator, but because of her general megalomania.

At the height of his campaign against eugenics, G. K. Chesterton composed a spoof featuring a good eugenicist who, when his fiancée falls off her bicycle, breaks off the engagement for the sake of the race. So strong were Marie Stopes's views on eugenics, that she demonstrated in her personal life that Chesterton's squib bore a closer relation to reality than anyone could ever have guessed. When her own son announced his plan to marry the attractive and intelligent daughter of Barnes Wallis, the inventor of the Upkeep bouncing bomb used by the Dam Buster squadron, his mother, fearing that Mary Wallis's short-sightedness might be passed on to a grandchild, insisted the young man break off the engagement. When he refused to do so, Marie Stopes cut her son out of her will, and when she died in 1958, the bulk of her fortune, including the Marie Stopes clinic business, was left to the Eugenics Society.

In 1999, readers of the *Guardian* voted Marie Stopes the 'Woman of the Millennium', beating the scientists Marie Curie and Rosalind Franklin, and the feminist icons Sylvia Pankhurst, Mary Wollstonecraft and Queen Elizabeth I. In 2008, the Royal Mail included a Marie Stopes postage stamp in a series marking 'Women of Achievement'. When the postage stamp was announced, a number of commentators asked whether Marie Stopes was an appropriate person to be so honoured, given her unsavoury association with eugenics, and whether some other birth-control pioneer should not have taken her place. The truth is that the birth-control movement was, from the outset, a eugenics-driven enterprise and continued to be so for a startlingly long time. To list the leading figures in the field is almost to make a roll call of the Eugenics Society. Lady Denman, first chairman of the Family Planning Association, Margaret Pyke, Denman's successor at the FPA and Helen Brook, founder of the Brook Advisory Centres, were all Eugenics Society fellows or served on the society's council. Even Marie Stopes's direct contemporaries, members of the vanguard of the birth-control movement, Stella Browne and the American Margaret Sanger, were members of the Eugenics Society too.

It is an iron law of nature that all supposedly scientific social interventions carried out by progressively minded people will produce unintended and unwanted consequences. The cause of eugenic birth control has proved no exception. Today it is Marie Stopes's beautiful people of the 'higher type' – young, middle-class professional women – who make proportionately greater use of birth control, delay having children, and produce fewer offspring over their lifetimes. Those the eugenicists have traditionally regarded as a genetic threat – the poor, the unemployed, the unskilled – continue to breed at a faster rate. The class divide in fertility is mirrored in a class divide in the use of contraceptives.

In the years after the Second World War, the eugenics movement had to confront the damage done to its reputation by its close association with the Nazi regime. It also faced new political realities in which the continued public denigration of the poor would win them few political friends. The adjustment proved relatively easy on both sides of the Atlantic, where a new leadership had taken control. In the United States, Frederick Osborn, who had founded the Office of Population Research at Princeton, had emerged as the acceptable public face of eugenics. Osborn understood that members of races or social classes did not take well to be being branded 'inferior'. He proposed a new, below-the-radar approach to securing eugenic ends, one he termed 'voluntary, unconscious selection'. Osborn told his friends in the American Eugenics Society that, 'eugenic goals are most likely to be attained under a name other than eugenics'.[7]

In Britain a similar process of renewal was taking place. Even before the war the Eugenics Society had begun to switch its focus towards population studies and birth control under the leadership of its general secretary Carlos Blacker and the influence of Julian Huxley. Blacker, one of Huxley's former pupils, and a psychiatrist at the Maudsley Hospital, had taken over the administration of the Eugenics Society in 1931. He then fought and won something close to a civil war within the organization against an old guard, represented by the Cambridge statistician Sir Ronald Fisher. Blacker wanted to wind down the society's campaigning for sterilization and devote more of its resources to advancing contraception for eugenic ends, and also keep the society's thinking in line with the latest developments in genetic science. Some of his opponents, however, accused him of wanting to dilute the eugenics movement's traditional strong-hereditarian outlook, and paying too much regard to environmental factors. In fact, Blacker was, at heart, a fairly orthodox Galtonian and Darwinist, but one with enough political nous to understand that the eugenics movement had to change with the times.

A long, slow process of rebranding took place throughout the global eugenics community. Wherever possible 'genetics' would be preferred to 'eugenics'. In Britain, the *Annals of Eugenics* was renamed the *Annals of Human Genetics*, and London University's Galton Professor of Eugenics henceforth occupied the chair of Human Genetics; while in the United States, *Eugenics Quarterly* became *Social Biology*. (Oddly, the mother-organizations were slow to change their own names: the American Eugenics Society did not transform itself into the Society for the Study of Social Biology until the early 1970s, and it was not until 1989 that the Eugenics Society in Britain changed its moniker to the Galton Institute.)

The new strategy of 'crypto-eugenics', as it was termed privately by the eugenicists themselves, called for new ways of working. The Eugenics Society decided not to lobby Parliament in its own name, rather to secure whatever legislative changes it wanted by acting through other organizations. Henceforth, the Society would interest itself in five main areas: population, birth control, abortion law reform, advocacy of euthanasia, and mental health.

The campaign to liberalize the abortion laws, which culminated in David Steele's 1967 Abortion Act, offers an extraordinary case study of crypto-eugenics in action. Like the agitation for the 1913 Mental Deficiency Act, the various campaigns for eugenic sterilization in Britain, the US and Scandinavia, and the 1924 Johnson–Reed immigration restrictions in the US, it involved concerted political action by adherents of an ideology derived from Francis Galton and Charles Darwin to win a legislative change that they believed would boost the future evolution of the human race. This time, however, the involvement and aims of the eugenicists themselves would not be foregrounded.

At a meeting at the House of Commons on 27 October 1992 to celebrate the Act's twenty-fifth anniversary, Lord Steele paid tribute to the important role of the Abortion Law Reform Association (ALRA) in getting his bill through. Three women, Stella Browne, Janet Chance and Alice Jenkins, had founded the ALRA in the mid-1930s. They co-opted onto their committee Frida Laski (the wife of Harold Laski) and Dora Russell (the wife of Bertrand Russell). All five were either at the time, or would subsequently become, associated with the Eugenics Society.

By the early 1960s, the Society was providing the ALRA with funds and office accommodation. It also supplied the campaign group with its new president, the law professor Glanville Williams. In the run up to the 1967 Bill, the ALRA was chaired by Vera Houghton, who had the advantage of being married to the chairman of the Parliamentary Labour Party. Houghton had long been associated with the International Planned Parenthood Federation, set up by Margaret Sanger. Carlos Blacker sat on the IPPF's board. David Steele's two medical advisers during the passage of the Bill were Malcolm Potts and Peter Diggory. The former was already a Eugenics Society Fellow, while the latter joined a couple of years later, was elected to its council in 1971, where he remained for some twenty years, twice serving as vice-president. Add to this web of connections the relationship between the eugenics movement and the large birth-control organizations campaigning for the bill – the Marie Stopes Clinic was actually owned and operated by the Eugenics Society at this time – and a conspiracy theorist could knock up a case in a trice that eugenicists legalized abortion all on their own.

They did not, of course. The 1967 Abortion Act needs to be seen in the context of a much broader shift in public attitudes towards sex and morals in the 1960s. Besides, Parliament is not easily manipulated by pressure groups – even those as tactically dexterous and politically savvy as the ALRA showed itself to be as the bill made its progress through its various legislative stages. The involvement of the Eugenics Society *by proxy*, however, shows how even an utterly discredited ideology can stage a comeback if its adherents master the art of political stealth. The involvement of quite so many eugenicists in bringing about a change in Britain's abortion law is extraordinary and unexpected and is bound to make people wonder how and why they pulled off the trick of effectively managing a national political campaign while remaining under the media radar.

Worldwide, abortion appears to be providing some, but not all, of what many of the eugenicists wanted all along, but failed to achieve either through positive eugenics, sterilization or contraception. Abortion has had a greater impact in reducing births among the economically disadvantaged than the middle class, and is proportionately more frequently carried out on women from racial minorities in the United States. Coercive abortion in China and the developing world, with pregnant women being grabbed by vigilantes off the street and dragged to abortion clinics, could also be seen as stemming the 'rising tide of colour' that so worried Lothrop Stoddard. 'Birth control and abortion are turning out to be great eugenic advances of our time,' remarked Frederick Osborn after the United States Supreme Court decision in *Roe vs. Wade*, which effectively legalized abortion throughout the United States. 'If they had been advanced for eugenic reasons it would have retarded or stopped their acceptance.'[8]

The law of unintended consequences, however, continues to work its effects. Although a large number of foetuses with genetic defects are aborted – meeting the eugenic objective – the number of children born with Down's syndrome in England and Wales rose during the 1990s and the early years of the twenty-first century, in spite of a threefold increase in pre-natal screening. The most likely reason for this is that women with careers, and easy access to abortion in their twenties, have put off having children until later in life, when the risk of Down's syndrome increases markedly. The various screening processes themselves are far from perfect, providing false positives leading to the abortion of unaffected children or by stimulating miscarriage. One recent survey estimated 'that current screening practice in England and Wales reduces annual live births of babies with Down's syndrome by around 660 and leads to the losses of 400 babies without Down's syndrome.'[9] Those opposed to abortion consider this to be an outrageous and unwarranted destruction of human life, but even ice-cold eugenic logic would have to consider it a high price for a small gain. If indeed there is any eugenic gain at all. Since children born with Down's syndrome do not in any sense pollute the gene pool, it is unclear what benefit eugenicists see in aborting them, except for the small saving the taxpayer may make for not having to provide resources for them. Or is it that eugenicists consider defective lives are not worth living?

The reason the eugenics movement was involved in helping to liberalize the abortion law was essentially the same reason it interested itself in contraception. The ultimate aim was – as it has always been – to improve the genetic quality of future generations. Having failed to persuade the professional classes to increase their fertility, or the poor to exercise reproductive restraint, and having found it impossible to persuade politicians to allow them to sterilize anyone with a genetic defect, promoting contraception and abortion appeared to be methods of securing eugenic ends at arm's length. People would act according to their own motives, but the net result would be fewer children born with defects and – if only society behaved in a rational manner – fewer children born to that social class that eugenicists deem problematic.

Although this may seem a softer, gentler eugenics – arguably softer and kinder than compulsorily sterilizing the unfit, or marshalling the mentally ill into lethal chambers – what remains worrying is that, in terms of fundamental outlook, the eugenicists have not really changed at all. The same victims – the 'underclass' and the disabled – remain the target groups. Moreover, the same false assumptions, drawn from Galton and Darwin – that like breeds like, and that the quality of the gene pool is constantly degenerating because of the differential birth rate between the social classes – appears to be what continues to drive eugenics. Had the eugenicists been right all these years, we should have seen society progressively deteriorate, become ever stupider, sicker, more feckless and depraved. Perhaps, that is indeed how they perceive what has become of us over the past hundred years?

In the US, pre-natal screening for hundreds of conditions has markedly reduced the number of disabled children being born. As more genetic markers are found for inherited conditions, this tendency will continue. Currently, in some states 80 per cent of Down's syndrome foetuses, and 95 per cent of those with cystic fibrosis are aborted. Fear of malpractice suits for what is termed as 'wrongful birth' leads to physicians steering parents towards abortion when even relatively minor defects such as deafness or bowed legs are predicted. Sometimes parents are merely presented with the mathematical odds of their child being born different from others. Told that they have a 1 in 40, or a 1 in 500 chance, they do not know what to do.

This kind of defensive medicine is fostering a culture in which parents of children with dwarfism, congenital blindness, or even almost cosmetic defects such as harelip are accused of being unfeeling or selfish for having brought an imperfect child into the world. Some doctors report that the pressure to terminate is now frequently coming from the parents. An obstetrician at Mount Sinai Hospital in Manhattan reported in 2004 that one of his patients demanded an abortion when the foetus was found to have an extra finger on one hand during an ultrasound scan. The same patient returned some time later with a second pregnancy, and once again insisted on termination when the same defect was spotted. It turned out that the mother herself had been born with an extra digit, which had been removed by a simple and painless operation in early childhood. Although she herself had had a happy and fulfilled life in spite of this trivial hereditary defect, she was adamant that she would not settle for anything less than a perfect baby. The early eugenicists would certainly have considered this progress; and it may be that the new, more highly evolved ones do too.

Sex-selection by infanticide is commonly associated with cultural backwardness in developing countries. Sex-selection by abortion, however, is practised on the Upper East Side of Manhattan. Dr Mark Engelbert told the *New York Times* he had performed an abortion on a woman who was carrying a girl, but wanted a boy. 'She's not doing anything illegal,' Engelbert said, 'and it's not for me to decide.'[10]

In his dissenting opinion in *Roe vs. Wade*, United States Supreme Court Justice Byron White spelled out the implications of the court's decision in these words: 'During the period prior to the time the foetus becomes viable, the Constitution of the United States values the convenience, whim, or caprice of the putative mother more than the life or potential life of the foetus.'[11] The United Kingdom Parliament too took viability into account, originally restricting abortions over twenty-eight weeks of pregnancy to situations where there was a grave risk to the mother's life. In 1990, the law was amended, reducing the viability point from twenty-eight weeks' gestation to twenty-four weeks', but permitting abortions after that time if the child would be born with a serious handicap. Unlike the American judges, the UK legislators did not otherwise leave total discretion to the pregnant woman. The 1987 Act required two doctors, acting in good faith, to certify that at least one of the criteria set out in the Act making an abortion lawful applied in any particular case. Most abortions before the viability point are carried out on the basis that 'the continuance of the pregnancy would involve risk . . . of injury to the physical or mental health of the pregnant woman or any existing children of her family', a condition that though extremely liberally interpreted in practice, falls short of an unfettered right to choose, and was certainly not intended to indulge whim or caprice.[12]

Although sex-selection by abortion is prohibited in the UK, there are signs of whim and caprice creeping into eugenic, or medical abortion, even those after twenty-four weeks' gestation. When Parliament was debating amendments to the Abortion Act in 1990, two Oxford law professors, John Finnis and John Keown, provided David Alton MP with an opinion that some doctors would interpret 'serious handicap' as including 'hare lip and cleft palate'.[13] The Labour MP Frank Doran described this warning as 'pure scaremongering', David Steele called it a 'a gross calumny on the medical profession', while the Government's Solicitor General, Harriet Harman, said that the two lawyers 'ought to be reported to the Law Society or to the Bar Council'.[14]

After 1990 there was a huge increase in the number of abortions carried out because of some observed or predicted defect, both before and after twenty-four weeks' gestation. Again, eugenicists would consider this casual disposal of human life a blessing for future generations, but Joanna Jepson, a young Church of England curate who had herself been born with a cleft palate that had been corrected by surgery, sought judicial review of the police's failure to prosecute the two doctors who had signed off on an abortion performed in December of the previous year of a twenty-eight-week foetus diagnosed with a cleft lip and palate. Jepson believed the doctors' action amounted to unlawful homicide. After the police reopened the case, however, the Crown Prosecution Service said no charges would be brought, the doctors having acted in good faith. Since the medical evidence is effectively sealed, for reasons of patient confidentiality, no one who was not privy to the case can know how serious the condition really was.

The case generated tremendous public support for Jepson's stand. It also mobilized disability groups to demand that the law be looked at afresh. One point made time and again by disabled people themselves was that eugenic abortion made the worth of their own lives contestable. Not everyone agrees. The bioethicist Peter Singer says that the desire not to bring a disabled child into the world does not necessarily have any implications for the moral worth of disabled people already living, citing the US Surgeon General's health warning advising women not to drink during pregnancy 'because of the risk of birth defects', which is stuck on every bottle of liquor sold in the United States.

Singer approaches the issue of eugenic abortion from a fairly standard Darwinist position. 'I do not think that a foetus is the kind of being that has a right to life,' he says. 'Hence it is not hard to justify terminating a pregnancy.'[15] Indeed, he goes further, arguing that it is not wrong to kill disabled children even some time after they are born. The notion that human life is sacred is one he considers hokum. 'That a being is a human being, in the sense of a member of the species Homo sapiens, is not relevant to the wrongness of killing it,' Singer wrote in his book *Practical Ethics*, 'it is, rather, characteristics like rationality, autonomy, and self-consciousness that make a difference. Infants lack these characteristics. Killing them, therefore, cannot be equated with killing normal human beings . . .'[16] Although it is startling to see such views expressed so baldly, they are by no means unusual among evolutionary scientists. As long ago as 1973, scientists were reported to have proposed the idea that children might not be legally declared alive until three days after birth in order to allow the killing of those found with previously undiscovered defects. The Nobel laureate Francis Crick concurred. 'No new-born infant should be declared human until it has passed certain tests regarding its genetic endowment,' Crick said. 'If it fails these tests it forfeits the right to live.'[17]

The United States Supreme Court, in deciding *Roe vs. Wade*, and the UK Parliament, in passing the 1967 Abortion Act, both ended up making the same practical compromise in set-tling upon viability as a criterion. They found this compromise necessary because they did not know for sure when human life begins. 'When those trained in the respective disciplines of medicine, philosophy, and theology are unable to arrive at any consensus,' Justice Blackmun, writing for the majority, declared frankly, 'the judiciary, at this point in the develop-ment of man's knowledge, is not in a position to speculate as to the answer.' This modest admission of ignorance of one of life's great mysteries also rather let them off the hook of having to consider at any length what moral rights might or might not convincingly be asserted on behalf of the unborn child.

At the beginning of 2009, Pope Benedict XVI approached an old fight from a new flank, warning of a resurgence of the 'hateful practice' of eugenics. 'Every human being is much more than a singular combination of genetic information that is transmitted to him by his parents,' the Pope told a confer-ence on genetics. 'The generation of man can never be reduced to the mere reproduction of a new individual of the human species, as is the case with all other animals . . . If we want to enter into the mystery of human life, then it is necessary that no science isolate itself, pretending to have the last word.'[18] The judges and the politicians may have left it to the scientists, philosophers and clerics to fight out, but eventually this fundamental question must come back to the courts and the politicians to decide.

# CHAPTER EIGHT

If we have to give up either religion or education, we
should give up education.

William Jennings Bryan

What looked like a forced resignation on the part of Michael
Reiss as director of education at the Royal Society, Britain's
national academy of science, in the autumn of 2008, brought
a remarkably civil dialogue between religion and science in
English life to an abrupt and brutal end. The affair signalled a
new militancy in the science camp and gave the British public
a taste of the acrimony and intolerance that has poisoned the
debate on the teaching of evolution in schools in the United
States.

To anyone without a dog in this fight, the savaging of Reiss
by his scientific colleagues, including three Nobel Prize winners, seemed undeserved, even bizarre. Reiss had been asked
to address a meeting at the British Association's Festival of
Science in Liverpool. In his talk, he brought up the problems
that classroom teachers sometimes face when explaining
evolution or the big bang theory to fourteen- to sixteen-year-
olds who are among the estimated 10 per cent of people in the
UK who believe that the earth is only some ten thousand years

old, who accept as literal truth the stories of man's origins in the Bible or the Koran, and who might feel that scientific cosmology challenges their religious conception of the universe.

'There is much to be said for allowing students to raise any doubts they have,' Reiss said, pointing out that this was 'hardly a revolutionary idea in science teaching'.[1] Reiss was careful to make clear that he was not advocating teaching creationism as a plausible or valid alternative to evolution, nor that it should be given equal time or equivalent treatment. He was merely proposing that teachers took a respectful approach to their pupils' worldviews and cultural traditions and tried to engage them in a discussion in which they might learn some science instead of sitting in sullen and suspicious silence with their arms folded defensively against the lesson the teacher was trying to impart.

Two weeks before Reiss's remarks became public, John McCain, the Republican candidate in the US presidential election, had picked the Governor of Alaska, Sarah Palin, as his running mate. In the United Kingdom, media attention focused on her folksy, down-home style, her problem teenage daughter and her views on abortion and creationism. The latter does not usually provoke much interest in Britain, but for the moment, at least, creationism was news.

To begin with, the Royal Society gave Reiss its unequivocal backing. Responding to media enquiries, a spokesman said: 'Michael's views are the views of the Royal Society. Our position is that if young people put forward a creationist perspective in the classroom, it should be discussed.' But Phil Willis MP, chairman of the Commons Innovation, Universities, Science and Skills Committee, took a markedly tough line. 'I am at the Royal Society on Wednesday and I will be raising this very issue,' he told *The Times*, 'I was horrified to hear these views and I reject them totally. They are a step too far and they fly in the face of what science is about.'[2] It seems likely that Willis had not known for sure what Reiss had actually said and was relying on misleading media reports or an unreliable precis. 'I think if his views are as mentioned, they may be incompatible with his position,'[3] Willis warned, sounding rather pompous and illiberal for a Liberal Democrat. One might have expected a man of his political tradition to rush to support the principle of academic freedom, even had Reiss claimed that the earth was flat, or the fixed centre of the planetary system around which the sun revolved, or pretty much any kind of foolishness short of Holocaust denial. Instead he came across like a little martinet in liberal clothing, using the authority of his select committee chairmanship to make what seemed like a threat.

After taking his PhD in animal behaviour and evolutionary biology at Cambridge, Michael Reiss pursued post-doctoral research in the same field before training to be a teacher. He taught science in schools and later re-entered academic life as an educationalist specializing in how science is learned and researching ways to improve how it is taught. This background, one might think, more than adequately qualified him to discuss the challenges of teaching evolution. There was, however, something else in his curriculum vitae that made some leading members of the Royal Society mighty suspicious. For Michael Reiss turned out to be an ordained priest of the Church of England.

A few days after Reiss's talk had been reported in the newspapers, Sir Richard Roberts, who won the Nobel Prize in Medicine in 1993, wrote to the president of the Royal Society on behalf of himself and two other Nobel laureates urging that Reiss step down, or be asked to step down, as soon as possible. 'We gather Professor Reiss is a clergyman, which in itself is very worrisome,' Roberts said. 'Who on earth thought that he would be an appropriate Director of Education, who could be expected to answer questions about the differences between science and religion in a scientific, reasoned way?'[4]

The bald assumption that no clergyman could take an objective, rational line on evolution or big bang theory is itself worrisome. After all, Charles Darwin himself trained for the Anglican priesthood as a young man, and the big bang was first proposed by Monsignor Georges Lemaître, a Roman Catholic cleric and professor of physics at the Catholic University of Leuven. The implication of Roberts's letter, however, is that nowadays only someone who subscribes to a narrowly naturalistic worldview can really be trusted to represent the Royal Society. There are very few ordained ministers of religion working at a senior level in British science, so it will probably be some time before a comparable case arises. Nevertheless, the incident does leave the impression that a Methodist lay-preacher, or even an ordinary churchgoing believer, might also be regarded with suspicion, might possibly even be discriminated against by employers or passed over for admission to learned societies, and that if one wants to pursue a successful career in science, it is altogether smarter to be an atheist.

Harry Kroto was one of the other Nobel laureates calling for Reiss to be sacked. Kroto is an atheist and has been since the day when, during a period of fasting among the Jewish community, young Harry sneakily scoffed a croissant with butter. No divine retribution ensued, so Kroto concluded 'there was nothing there'.

According to an autobiographical essay posted on the Nobel Prize website, he is 'a supporter of ideologies which advocate the right of the individual to speak, think and write in freedom and safety (surely the bedrock of a civilised society)'.[5] However, when asked to explain why he thought Michael Reiss should be sacked, he said: 'The thing the Royal Society does not appreciate is the true nature of the forces arrayed against it and the Enlightenment . . .'[6] Kroto is by no means the first person to seek to hound a man from his position for a minor departure from the prevailing ideological line, but it is certainly unusual to do so in the name of the Enlightenment. Equally puzzling is his reference to mysterious 'forces' arrayed against it. Unlike in the United States, in England there is no well-funded lobby calling for the teaching of creationism as a scientific alternative to evolution in science lessons. Moreover, Parliament has legislated for a common, national curriculum, and the government has issued guidelines to teachers to prevent the teaching of creationism. As it happens, one of those involved in drafting those guidelines was Michael Reiss.

The beleaguered educationalist stepped down a few days later. In its public statement the Royal Society said that Reiss's words had been 'open to misinterpretation'.[7] This much was true – at least two newspapers had printed their accounts of Reiss's talk under headlines that gave the misleading impression that he had called for the teaching of creationism alongside evolution, but as any politician's press aide will attest, the only sure way to proof a public statement against misinterpretation by Fleet Street headline writers is to say nothing substantive at all. The society also claimed that Reiss's words had 'damaged its reputation'. However Lord Winston, professor of science and society at Imperial College,

London, and a religiously observant Jew, said he feared 'that the Royal Society has only diminished itself' by failing to give Michael Reiss its backing.[8]

Lord Winston had spoken at the Festival of Science in Liverpool, using the occasion to condemn the current wave of books by writers such as Richard Dawkins, Daniel Dennett and Christopher Hitchens that appealed to scientific authority to advance an argument for atheism. He had previously accused Dawkins of 'a science delusion' in claiming that evolutionary biology and religious belief were necessarily inimical. 'What Dawkins says is, "if you don't believe in the fact that religion is a nonsense then you're deluded". I think that is a very dangerous message because I think actually it is irresponsible. I think it poo-poos other people's views of a universe about which none of us knows clearly or absolutely.'[9]

Right in the middle of the brouhaha over Reiss's remarks, and showing a spectacularly poor sense of timing, the Church of England issued a public apology to Charles Darwin. Following the example of Pope John Paul II's statement of regret for the Catholic Church's persecution of Galileo, the Church of England felt the need to express contrition for the intemperate criticism of Darwin's *Origin* by some churchmen, including Samuel Wilberforce, the then Bishop of Oxford. It chose to do so in a statement addressed directly to the naturalist himself, even though Darwin had been dead for a hundred and twenty-six years. Clearly, the Church of England, unlike Darwin, has not entirely abandoned its belief in the afterlife. The apology, posted on the Lambeth Palace website, where the great naturalist's spirit, wherever it might currently reside, could no doubt see it, said: 'Charles Darwin, 200 years from your birth the Church of England owes you an apology for misunderstanding you and, by getting our first reaction wrong, encouraging others to misunderstand you still.'[10] Darwin's great-great-grandson, Andrew Darwin, reportedly professed himself bemused by the gesture, which he regarded as pointless. A great-grandson through another line pointed out that the Church had buried his illustrious forebear in Westminster Abbey, which he considered apology enough.

The question of what should and what should not be taught in schools about evolution has been at the root of one of the longest and most bitter controversies in the United States. During the time that Americans have been squabbling about this issue they have solved others that looked much more intractable. A vast immigrant population from all parts of Europe has been successfully integrated (though the full integration of other immigrants from closer to home and farther afield remains a work in progress); the descendants of slaves have obtained equality and civil rights; America has emerged as the world's pre-eminent superpower and has created wealth and prosperity on a scale the earth has never before seen. But Americans are still conducting their disagreements over evolution in the same intemperate manner they did when William Jennings Bryan and Clarence Darrow clashed in 1925. Outsiders look on bemused.

If anyone deserves an apology from posterity, it is William Jennings Bryan. Insofar as he is remembered at all, it is, particularly by political liberals, as an old fool of a Christian fundamentalist, a prototypical Pat Robertson perhaps, who got a deserved comeuppance when he was humiliated at the hands of Clarence Darrow during the Scopes Monkey Trial in Dayton, Tennessee.

In fact, Bryan was three times the Democratic Party's candidate for the presidency of the United States and was by some way the most politically radical Democrat ever to receive his party's nomination – and that includes Franklin D. Roosevelt and Barack Obama. The scourge of Wall Street bankers and big business, Bryan argued for a minimum wage, progressive labour laws, subsidies for poor farmers and government guarantee of bank deposits. He demanded the nationalization of key industries such as railroads, and the telegraph and telephone services; he called for the establishment of minimum prices for agricultural produce and a cap on the profits of middlemen. His appeal was to the masses, and his enemies were the establishment. The historian Garry Wills has accurately described Bryan's campaigns as the most leftist in American history.[11]

William Jennings Bryan was by far the most gifted political orator of his time. He had tremendous faith in the good sense of ordinary people, and was greatly loved in return. Nicknamed the Great Commoner, he was a 'populist' before that term acquired its current pejorative flavour – Bryan did not appeal to the lowest instincts of the common people, but always to the finest. Since he lost all three of his presidential elections, and only briefly held high office – as Secretary of State under Woodrow Wilson – Bryan had to earn his own living, chiefly through his rhetoric. Few politicians in any age or nation could have prospered by charging admission to their rallies or speeches, but in the year 1907 alone, three hundred thousand Americans, mostly from hardscrabble rural districts, paid to hear the Great Commoner speak. Though he never reached the White House himself, he had an enormous effect on the Democratic Party, moving it from support for the gold standard, from a fiscally cautious, limited-government outlook to become one in which populism fused with progressivism to create a party of social reform on the side of the most marginalized. If there were any justice in the apportioning of political reputation, today's liberal Americans would have prepared a magnificent shrine for Bryan in their Pantheon; instead he occupies just a small corner in their demonology. That is because, towards the end of his life, Bryan resolved to take on the Darwinists.

For most of us who live outside the United States, almost everything we think we know about the Scopes Monkey Trial turns out, upon closer acquaintance with the facts, to be false. As each bubble of popular mythology is pricked, we start in surprise, in much the same way we do when we first discover that Senator Joe McCarthy never held any hearings investigating Communist activity in Hollywood.[12] A combination of popular culture and lazy journalism have provided us with a set of less than wholly truthful accounts of a number of episodes in US history. Sometimes we may even pass on the faulty memes to our offspring, and they inherit the myth.

With regard to the Scopes trial, a composite picture of typically received impressions from books, films and glancing mentions, would look something like this:

> *An earnest and high-minded young schoolmaster called John T. Scopes, who reads widely and keeps abreast of intellectual progress, decides to teach his pupils about Darwin's theory of evolution by natural selection, which is by now more than sixty years old and is accepted by biologists as a scientific fact. Scopes is motivated chiefly by a commitment to the welfare of the young minds in his charge:*

*he is determined to give them the best education he can, one founded on truth, not superstition; one that will give them a sure foundation for life in the modern world. He obtains a set of the most up-to-date textbooks and starts teaching evolution. The pupils are gripped. They want to learn more.*

*However, Scopes's initiative falls foul of a fusty, outdated law that forbids the teaching of evolution and requires him to teach the creation story set out in the Bible, which Scopes knows to be wrong because fossil evidence, combined with what he has read in Charles Darwin's book, proves that the world is many millions of years older than a literal reading of the Book of Genesis allows. Scopes is also up against powerful vested interests – politicians and clergymen of reactionary disposition who have a lot at stake – Darwin's work being radically subversive of their sources of authority and power.*

*Scopes makes a brave and noble stand. The issues at stake are academic freedom, freedom of speech, the separation of Church and state, the claims of scientific truth, and Scopes's own professional integrity. The case comes to court, where a thrilling duel of wits ensues between two of the finest trial attorneys in the land. For the defence – Clarence Darrow, who looks just like Spencer Tracy, or perhaps Jack Lemmon, represents the new world of science and progress. For the prosecution stands William Jennings Bryan, the very epitome of a fast-fading old order, who bears a passing resemblance to both Fredric March and George C. Scott. To begin with, it seems the prosecutor has the edge. The jury are simple country folk, and he plays to their natural conservative prejudices. Darrow, by contrast is a big city boy, his slick urbanity elicits the jury's suspicion.*

*Meanwhile, outside the courthouse, the media have arrived – radio journalists and newspapermen from all across America. The case has become a national splash. Back inside the court, the tables have been turned. Bryan had hoped to put Darwin on trial, but the wily Darrow has put the Bible on trial instead. Not only that, he has put the prosecutor on the stand. The old man makes an almighty fool of himself trying to explain how God made the world in six days and created every animal individually. Why did God give men nipples? He has no answer to that. Finally, in a moving summing up for the defence, the silver-tongued Darrow persuades the jury to acquit. As the young schoolmaster comes blinking into the sunlight to face the newsmen, his young pupils swarm around him. Now they can go on to become research chemists or geneticists. Heck, the geeky one with the specs might even win the Nobel Prize.*

The truth is much more gripping. John Thomas Scopes was not altogether frank. He had no special commitment to his pupils, and was not planning on staying in Dayton very long. He was not even a full-time science teacher; he was the high school's football coach, though he did teach mathematics and, very rarely, science when the regular teacher was away. Scopes's own college degree had been in law. He probably never really taught his class about evolution. He himself gave a number of conflicting accounts – that he did teach the lesson; that he set a chapter of a textbook as homework, but never taught evolution in the classroom; and, most credibly, that he had made the whole thing up. Scopes was not called as a witness at his trial for precisely this reason. Had he given testimony on oath he would either have had to lie, risking a jail term for perjury, or he would have had to tell the truth – in which case the trial would have collapsed in embarrassing ignominy.

The trial itself was a cynical contrivance. The plot was hatched around a table in Fred Robinson's Dayton drugstore by a group of local businessmen. One of them had spotted a small-ad in a city newspaper placed by a pressure group wanting to find a community willing to challenge the law forbidding the teaching of evolution. The small-town boosters saw it as a commercial opportunity. A big trial would make Dayton famous, pulling in visitors from miles around, who would probably spend more dollars in local shops, hotels and restaurants every day the trial was in progress than local residents spent in a month. They replied to the advertisement and made their plans.

John Scopes was invited to meet the business leaders on 5 May 1925. They made their pitch. He was a young man, twenty-four years old, with nothing to lose. He could become famous. They would see to it that whatever the outcome, no harm would come to him. He would be doing the whole community a favour. Scopes agreed, saying that he disapproved of the law anyway. Arrangements were made for the young teacher to confess to teaching a class about evolution in breach of Tennessee law.

The relevant statute, known as the Butler Act, was not a fusty old one. It was brand new, having been signed into law by the Governor on 23 March, less than two months previously. The Tennessee House of Representatives had passed the bill by seventy-one votes to five; the state Senate endorsed it twenty-four to six. These margins reflected the Butler Act's enormous popularity among the people of Tennessee. In 1925, the nationwide eugenics campaign was at its height. In the rural areas of Tennessee folks may not have had a sophisticated grasp of Darwinian science, but they knew the eugenicists who preached Darwinism in the cities despised country people, called them 'imbeciles' and 'defectives' and would sterilize them if they got the chance. They knew they despised God and the Bible too. Now they wanted to teach children that grandpa was descended from an ape. But America was a democracy, and that meant that simple people, if they made their views plain, could fight back.

The book John Scopes pretended to have used to teach his class about evolution was the standard biology text that had been in service in Tennessee schools before the Butler Act. No one had yet got around to withdrawing George William Hunter's *A Civic Biology*, a work that was consistent with the scientific orthodoxy of its day – that is to say, it was strongly influenced by scientific racialism and eugenics. Hunter noted Dugdale's study of the Jukes, but unlike Dugdale himself, attributed immoral behaviour, alcoholism and criminality to heredity. Families like the Jukes, the book said, were parasites. 'If such people were lower animals, we would probably kill them off.' The book informed schoolchildren that mankind was divided into five races, with, as usual, the African at the bottom of the evolutionary scale and the white man at the highest level. Hunter's book had been published two years before Madison Grant's racial classification appeared, so it employed the term 'Caucasian' rather than 'Nordic', but the underlying attitudes and sentiments were the same as those of the mainstream eugenicists and racial theorists.[13] Certainly no public-school teacher would allow such a book in her or his classroom today.

William Jennings Bryan had three reasons for taking part in the Scopes trial. One was political. He saw himself as a defender of democracy, believing the trial was a contrivance on the part of a middle-class elite to cheat the ordinary citizens of Tennessee out of a law that they very much wanted and that their elected representatives had voted for by large margins. In short, the legal system was being used to frustrate democracy.

Bryan had a profound faith in the good sense of the masses, and his populist instinct rebelled against any attempt, however well intentioned, to second-guess the will of the majority. He also relished the idea of a courtroom battle over evolution. For years he had been on a personal crusade against Darwinism and had been instrumental in getting it banned from being taught in fifteen states. He had toured the country giving speeches, published books on the subject and carried on a debate in the *New York Times* and other newspapers against the biologist E. G. Conklin and the paleontologist Henry Fairfield Osborn, both advocates of eugenics. Thirdly, Bryan was a devout Presbyterian and knew that the defence was planning to use the trial to insult his most cherished religious beliefs.

Scopes travelled to New York City before the trial for a series of briefings organized by the American Civil Liberties Union. He also visited Henry Fairfield Osborn at the Museum of Natural History, who promised to solicit a letter of support from his friend Leonard Darwin. George Rappleyea, one of the businessmen behind the plot, wanted the English novelist and science writer H. G. Wells to lead the defence team. A puzzled Wells refused, but Clarence Darrow, who had become well known for defending the Chicago 'thrill killers' Leopold and Loeb, offered his services for free. In the Chicago case, Darrow had succeeded in getting his clients off the death penalty, arguing in the case of one of them that 'this terrible crime was inherent in his organism, and it came from some ancestor'.[14]

A couple of nights before the trial began, Scopes was seated at dinner next to William Jennings Bryan. The two had met before. Scopes came from Bryan's hometown in southern Illinois and the Great Commoner had given a commencement address at his school. Scopes admired the old man, calling him 'the greatest man produced in the United States since Thomas Jefferson.'[15] Nothing in this case was entirely straightforward.

As the town's business leaders had hoped, the trial did pull in thousands of visitors. The area around the courthouse soon began to resemble a funfair or a carnival. Visitors arrived in 'Monkeyland' dressed in bizarre costumes. Fundamentalist ranters stood on soapboxes prophesying doom, while a troupe of live monkeys cavorted on the lawn. More than two hundred journalists turned up, two of them all the way from England. Not all the publicity was good publicity for the townsfolk of Dayton. The writer H. L. Mencken came to cover the trial for a Baltimore newspaper. He was a supporter of eugenics and wrote a series of articles contemptuous of the ignorant hicks and hillbillies he perceived the country people of Tennessee to be, but over at Fred Robinson's drugstore no one was complaining as the dollar bills piled up.

Inside the court, Darwinian evolution was not on trial. In fact, all evidence relating to whether evolution was true or false was ruled inadmissible from the outset. The issue of the separation between Church and state was quickly disposed of too. In 1925, this constitutional doctrine was seen as applying only to the federal tier of lawmaking and individual states were free to do as they liked. Two pupils were called to testify at the trial that Scopes had taught them evolution. They had been coached by the defence and given *Civic Biology* to mug up before they gave evidence. Since the defence admitted that Scopes had breached the statute, the only real line they had left to pursue was whether the biblical version of the creation story was in the least bit plausible. Darrow had a team of scriptural advisers, including a Baptist, on hand to help him frame questions showing the Book of Genesis was logically incoherent.

Neither party comes out well from the set-piece confrontation between Clarence Darrow and William Jennings Bryan. Both men played to the public gallery for cheap laughs and frequently traded insults, requiring the judge to intervene and restore order. However, the occasion was not the total humiliation of Bryan that posterity remembers. Although Bryan was a Christian fundamentalist, his answers demonstrated that even fundamentalism has its shades of grey. Darrow was evidently surprised by the answers he got when he pressed Bryan on key points relating to the age of the world and the time taken to create it.

Q – Have you any idea how old the earth is?

A – No.

Q – The book you have introduced in evidence tells you, doesn't it?

A – I don't think it does, Mr Darrow.

Q – It says BC 4004?

A – That is Bishop Ussher's calculation.

Q – That is printed in the Bible you introduced?

A – Yes, sir . . .

Q – Would you say that the earth was only 4,000 years old?

A – Oh, no; I think it is much older than that.

Q – How much?

A – I couldn't say.

Q – Does the statement 'The morning and the evening were the first day' and 'The morning and the evening were the second day' mean anything to you?

A – I do not think it necessarily means a twenty-four-hour day.

Q – You do not?

A – No.

Pressed further on this, Bryan went on to say that the word 'day' was used elsewhere in Genesis to mean an indeterminate period of time and that he did not think it mattered from the Christian point of view whether a person believed it took God six days, six million years or six hundred million years to create the earth. His answer showed that even someone who regarded the Bible as literal truth could allow some room for interpretation, while at the same time refusing to go as far as regarding the Genesis story as mere metaphor. For the court, this meant that Darrow's inquisition had no real evidential value and the judge swiftly brought it to a close. The jury took only nine minutes to reach their verdict: John Scopes was guilty.[16]

It would be another forty-three years before the United States Supreme Court ruled that laws forbidding the teaching of evolution were unconstitutional. In the meantime, all but two states, Arkansas and Mississippi, had voluntarily abolished them. Even Tennessee repealed the Butler Act in 1967. After the Scopes trial some states, fearing a repeat of the monkey trial on their own turf, had quietly dropped their hostility to evolution. Most of the mainstream Churches found that, so long as the idea was kept within bounds, there was no necessary incompatibility between evolution and religious belief. The Soviet Union's launch of the Sputnik satellite in 1957 turned political attention to the importance of science teaching and its role in the nation's Cold War effort. The 1958 National Defense Education Act prompted a review of science teaching and evolution confirmed its place on the curriculum clutching the coat-tails of a new determination to make American science the best in the world.

The case that ended the ban, *Epperson vs. Arkansas*, also involved a schoolteacher. In 1964, Susan Epperson had started work in a Little Rock high school and began teaching her tenth-grade class from the textbook authorized and provided for use in public schools. Epperson discovered that the book had a chapter covering evolution. She was in a dilemma. She wanted to teach it, the topic was there in the book, but she knew the law said she could be fired for teaching it. She sought clarification; but getting no comfort from state officials, asked for judicial clarification from the Arkansas Chancery Court. Eventually the case went to the Supreme Court. Justice Fortas delivered the final decision. Finding for Susan Epperson, he said, 'Government in our democracy, state and national, must be neutral in matters of religious theory, doctrine, and practice. It may not be hostile to any religion or to the advocacy of nonreligion; and it may not aid, foster, or promote one religion or religious theory against another or even against the militant opposite. The First Amendment mandates governmental neutrality between religion and religion, and between religion and nonreligion.'[17]

Now the tables were turned and a long legal and political struggle would begin – one that continues in the present day – to get any Bible-based alternative to evolution taught in American schools. An attempt to establish 'creation science', and give it equal treatment in the classroom, was attempted in Arkansas in 1981. Bill Clinton, who had been Governor of the state since 1979, had been ousted by a Republican challenger and would not return until 1983. Clinton was a supporter of evolution, but his successor, Frank White, signed into law a statute mandating equal treatment for creation science, whose principles it defined as:

the scientific evidences for creation and inferences from those evidences. Creation science includes the scientific evidences and related inferences that indicate:

1. Sudden creation of the universe, energy and life from nothing.
2. The insufficiency of mutation and natural selection in bringing about development of all living kinds from a single organism.
3. Changes only with fixed limits of originally created kinds of plants and animals.
4. Separate ancestry for man and apes.
5. Explanation of the earth's geology by catastrophism, including the occurrence of worldwide flood.
6. A relatively recent inception of the earth and living kinds.

Perhaps with an eye to a Supreme Court test of the law's validity, the Arkansas legislators included within the wording of the act a set of legislative 'findings of fact' that amounted to a defence of their measure. Pointing out that only evolution-science was presented to students in courses discussing the subject of origins, the legislators complained that 'Public schools generally censor creation-science and evidence contrary to evolution. Evolution-science is not an unquestionable fact of science, because evolution cannot be experimentally observed, fully verified, or logically falsified, and because evolution-science is not accepted by some scientists.'[18]

Moreover they argued that public-school presentation of evolution alone 'abridges the Constitution's prohibition against establishment of religion, because it produces hostility toward many Theistic religions and brings preference to Theological Liberalism, Humanism, Nontheistic religions, and Atheism, in that these religious faiths generally include a religious belief in evolution.'

The Arkansas law was subsequently struck down by the Supreme Court, which took the view that creation science had 'no scientific merit or educational value as science'.[19] Five years later, in 1987, the court also struck down a Louisiana law that did not require schools to teach either evolution or creation science, but did require any school teaching evolution to teach creation science alongside it.

Notwithstanding this and many other legal setbacks, creation science continued to flourish throughout the 1990s and into a new century, becoming an enormous industry publishing thousands of books, pamphlets and films. The young-earth creationists have developed a complete, alternative story explaining away fossils and other evidence for evolution. In 2007, a $27-million Creation Museum opened in Kentucky. A kind of anti-Darwin Disneyland, it featured animatronic dinosaurs going two by two into Noah's Ark.

However, creation science was clearly no longer a viable instrument for challenging the teaching of evolution in schools. During the 1990s, a new movement emerged, advocating intelligent design (ID). It proposed that there are some features of the universe that cannot be satisfactorily explained by undirected processes such as natural selection and which suggest the existence of a designing intelligence. By not identifying this designer with any particular god, or even stating that he is a god at all, ID's proponents believed they could get round the US Constitution's Establishment clause. ID, it was maintained, was secular and scientific. To its opponents, however, ID was merely creationism in disguise.

Intelligent design has an appeal well beyond the tiny minority of young-earth creationists and Christian fundamentalists who were identified with creation science. It is not necessarily incompatible with what is genuinely known as fact in evolutionary science. For some, it expresses a vague idea they have long held but never articulated: that though evolution explains how the world has changed and developed, God must have set the process in motion in the beginning. ID tended to focus on areas where the Darwinian explanation was weakest or most speculative. It discussed gaps in the fossil record, which appeared to lack the transitional forms one would expect to see as one ancient creature supposedly slowly changed into another. ID wondered aloud how a complex physiological feature like the eye – requiring an optic nerve and a dedicated part of the brain to process the images it captured – could conceivably have evolved bit by bit over thousands of years by tiny gradual changes. And it asked where the mechanism of evolution itself, DNA, with its highly ordered structures and complex processes, could have come from in the first place.

Some of the objections cited by ID (such as the eye) are hoary enough to have been discussed in Darwin's day. Others such as 'irreducible complexity' adduced by one of the ID movement's professional scientists, the biochemist Michael Behe, were novel and sufficiently interesting to engage people who would never have given old-fashioned creationism a second glance. Exponents of orthodox neo-Darwinism have not had much trouble swatting away the objections, but in doing so they have often had to abandon the sure ground of

what is known and proven and stray into hypothesis and speculation. There is absolutely nothing wrong with scientists
doing this, science would never progress without it, but it can
give the impression to the watching lay public that the whole
of evolution science is speculative, hypothetical, still 'just a
theory'.

By broadening the base of potential support to non-funda-
mentalist believers, ID also gave the creationist movement the
chance to become a political force. In Pennsylvania and Kansas
the ID movement tried using school boards to get ID taught in
science lessons alongside evolution. Americans like and value
their system of local control of schools. There is no national
curriculum and locally elected representatives, sitting on
school boards, have the major say in what is taught and how
resources are allocated. There are great advantages in this
arrangement – schools are genuinely community institutions
and are responsive to local needs; the citizens of the county feel
they own them and the innumerable disadvantages of a state
or Federal education bureaucracy are for the most part
avoided. But like any democratic structure, they are susceptible to capture by well-organized and politically motivated
groups.

In 2004, the Dover Area School District, in Pennsylvania,
announced that teachers would be required to read this formal
statement to pupils in Dover High School's ninth-grade biology class:

The Pennsylvania Academic Standards require students to
learn about Darwin's theory of evolution and eventually
to take a standardized test of which evolution is a part.

Because Darwin's Theory is a theory, it is still being

tested as new evidence is discovered. The Theory is not a fact. Gaps in the Theory exist for which there is no evidence. A theory is defined as a well-tested explanation that unifies a broad range of observations.

Intelligent design is an explanation of the origin of life that differs from Darwin's view. The reference book, *Of Pandas and People*, is available for students to see if they would like to explore this view in an effort to gain an understanding of what intelligent design actually involves.[20]

This initiative gave rise to yet another lawsuit – *Kitzmiller vs. Dover Area School Board* – brought by parents with children at the school. The court found that intelligent design, like the old straightforward creationism, was essentially religiously motivated and therefore unconstitutional. In Kansas, instructions adopted by the state's school board to teach intelligent design were overturned by democratic means – four of the six board members behind their introduction lost their seats.

Nevertheless, despite these setbacks, hostility to Darwinism has become a significant factor in America's politics. Twenty-six per cent of the total US electorate is made up of white evangelicals. This demographic group has long been known to psephologists and pollsters as 'the Republican Party's black vote' – for the reason that just as the Democrats could not win an election without the African American vote, Republicans cannot win without white evangelicals. In fact, the Republicans are proportionally much more dependent on the evangelicals than the Democrats are on African Americans. In the Presidential Election of 2008, 40 per cent of those who voted for John McCain were white evangelicals, while only 23 per cent of Barack Obama's voters were black. Intelligent design has a strong appeal to the evangelical demographic – and beyond that can hope to appeal to a broad swathe of theists of other Protestant denominations, even those generally comfortable with the core science of evolution.

During the presidency of George W. Bush, even the old, unreconstructed creationists from the fundamentalist sects were able to gain a measure of political leverage from their place as part of the Christian Right. ID would appear to have even bigger prospects. A USA Today/Gallup poll in 2007 showed Americans are not just in two minds over the issue of creationism, many of them want to be on both sides at the same time. Sixty-six per cent of those surveyed said they thought that 'Creationism, that is, the idea that God created human beings pretty much in their present form at one time within the last 10,000 years . . .' was definitely true (39 per cent) or probably true (27 per cent). However, 53 per cent of the same sample also said they thought that 'Evolution, that is, the idea that human beings developed over millions of years from less advanced forms of life', was either definitely true (18 per cent) or probably true (35 per cent).

You could account for the overlap by saying that those respondents who voted for both propositions were plain stupid, or you might take the more charitable, and probably more realistic, view that they felt conflicted. The poll also asked them which they thought was 'definitely false' – 15 per cent said young-earth creationism, while 28 per cent said evolution. The only unambiguous result of this survey must surely be that what has been taught in American schools about evolution over recent decades has not been taught very convincingly.[21]

The idea that schools should simply 'teach the controversy', rather than teach ID as true, has emerged (with a little help from the ID movement's main think tank, the Discovery Institute) as a superficially attractive *via media* and has been given prominent endorsement by President George W. Bush and Sarah Palin among many others. That there is a controversy is undeniable – and many reasonable Americans would see no harm in teenagers discussing it, and some see potential benefits – of the kind that Michael Reiss identified – in doing so too. Besides, since other religions such as Islam and Hinduism are frequently discussed in religion lessons in Christian denominational schools, why should scientific heresies be banned from classroom discussion?

That idea is fiercely resisted by most mainstream scientists, who see 'teach the controversy' as a Trojan Horse or the thin end of a wedge whose broad end would bring biblical literalism back into the science class. Given the support for creationism revealed in the poll cited and a number of similar ones, it is easy to see why supporters of evolutionary science might be panicking. Scientists' own defensiveness, however, could be pushing more and more Americans into the opposing camp. Intelligent design already has its martyrs – a recent film, *Expelled: No Intelligence Allowed*, made by Ben Stein, the Hollywood actor, TV personality and former speechwriter for Richard Nixon and Gerald Ford, alleges that some pro-evolution zealots have been forcing academics and journal editors from their jobs for merely showing curiosity about ID, and have begun extending their dogmatic intolerance to anyone who believes in a personal God. Stein's film has proved an unexpected success.

The official position of many of the main Christian denominations – Catholic, Episcopalian, Methodist and Presbyterian

– has traditionally been to accept the scientific facts of evolution, while rejecting the materialist outlook contained in Darwin's work, and promoted by some of his boosters. These churches command the allegiance of vast numbers of Americans, who are becoming more and more alarmed by the shrill denunciations of religion by atheists within the science community. The advocates of intelligent design would dearly like to persuade these large churches into their camp. Writers affiliated with the Discovery Institute have recently been documenting instances where the teaching of evolution in schools goes well beyond the bounds of scientific fact and engages in proselytizing for a materialistic and atheist worldview. Before long we may see yet another Monkey Trial, this time with Darwinism itself accused of breaching the United States Constitution's Establishment clause by bringing the advocacy of 'nonreligion' into the classroom of some public school.

# CHAPTER NINE

> It seems on the whole fair to regard negroes as on aver-
> age inferior to white men, although for work in the
> tropics they are indispensable, so that their extermi-
> nation (apart from questions of humanity) would be
> highly undesirable.
>
> Bertrand Russell

During the high summer of 1971, Pat Buchanan, later to
become a presidential candidate, was working as a White
House aide for Richard Nixon. Aside from his other responsi-
bilities, Buchanan had been posted *en vedette* to keep an eye
on the media and give the president early warning of any
dangerous ideas that might be approaching. In late August,
Buchanan spotted something that led him to write an immediate memo to the president. He had found an article in
*Atlantic* magazine by a young Harvard psychologist arguing
that intelligence is largely inherited. The writer's name was
Richard Herrnstein. Twenty-three years later he would become
famous, and in some quarters infamous, as one of the authors
of *The Bell Curve*.

Buchanan saw that Herrnstein's article had momentous
political significance. 'Basically, it demonstrates that heredity,

rather than environment, determines intelligence – and that the more we proceed to provide everyone with a "good environment," surely the more heredity will become the dominant factor in their intelligence, and thus in their success and social standing,' he told the president. 'If correct, then all our efforts and expenditures not only for "compensatory education" but to provide an "equal chance at the starting line" are guaranteeing that we wind up with the intelligent ones coming in first. And every study we have shows blacks 15 IQ points below whites on the average.'[1]

Richard Nixon had not cut back the 'Great Society' programmes initiated by his predecessor, Lyndon Johnson, which were aimed at the elimination of poverty and racial injustice. In fact, he had expanded them, with federal spending on social welfare increasing from $55 billion in 1970 to almost $132 billion in 1975, alongside a massive boost for education.

Nixon had long had an interest in racial justice issues. In the 1950s he had been more of a supporter of civil rights than either John F. Kennedy or Lyndon Johnson. As vice-president, presiding over Senate debates, he took a tough line with those who tried to use filibusters to block civil rights measures, and when he became president, introduced a number of affirmative action policies. Executive Order No. 11478, issued by Nixon in 1969, introduced equal opportunity hiring in federal agencies, and Nixon's Philadelphia Plan required building contractors working on government projects in the construction industry to hire minority workers.

Neither the president's passion for big spending, nor what some saw as an unnecessary indulgence of America's African American community, commanded universal support in the Republican Party. There were plenty who argued that he should be balancing the budget and not using tax dollars for social engineering. What Buchanan had spotted was that if it became accepted that social and racial inequalities were determined by biology, then Nixon's social and racial justice policies were not just a waste of taxpayers' money, they might exacerbate social tensions.

On one level, Herrnstein's main point is not really controversial at all. It is a mathematical truth in the same way as two plus two equals four. Assuming that there is a meaningful concept called 'intelligence' and that it is partly a result of upbringing and partly the result of genetic inheritance, then the more you equalize the upbringing, the more, proportionally, heredity will account for any variation. If you could completely equalize the effects of upbringing, then heredity would explain all the variation. On the societal scale, the more you remove inequities such as racial discrimination, nepotism, the old-school-tie effect and unequal educational opportunities, then the more that will leave only people's own innate talents and their personal effort to explain their relative success or failure in the job market.

What was controversial, and remains so to this day, are the assumptions that there is a single factor for intelligence, that it is in significant part inherited, and that the racial differences in IQ, or those between social classes, have a hereditary rather than an environmental cause. The very idea that there is a biological basis to race is itself contested. The political left, particularly the Marxist left, had long sought to explain everything in human social affairs solely in environmental terms, barring the door to any consideration of inheritance at all. This was ideologically consistent: you cannot build a social utopia with equal outcomes if inherited differences threaten to skew those outcomes in favour of the genetically well endowed.

After the Second World War, all forms of social Darwinism were discredited by association with the Nazis. For the next forty years the prevailing model of human nature in the social sciences became that of the 'blank slate', where differing experiences explained all social and behavioural traits. Even gender was decoupled from the biological differences between the sexes, and masculinity and femininity declared merely 'social constructs'.

In some respects, this approach was emancipatory. Social class distinctions, for example, once believed to reflect real superiorities or inferiorities that were inherited, came to be seen as fairly arbitrary classifications deriving from the economic status one's parents enjoyed in a outdated and fast-fading social dispensation. Racial minorities no longer faced overt discrimination. Women, who had previously been thought unsuited to a whole range of occupations, or even to do paid work at all, once released from the tyranny of the XX chromosome entered the workplace in vast numbers and prospered in all kinds of jobs previously reserved for men. To suggest there were any real differences between men and women, beyond the obvious physiological ones – that men's and women's brains were 'wired differently', for instance – was absolutely taboo; and at Harvard it remains so.

Larry Summers, now President Barack Obama's chief economics adviser in the White House, was forced to resign from his job as president of Harvard University in 2006 for breaking this taboo. Summers had, ironically, been attending a diversity in the workplace conference, where he complained how hard he had found it to find women to fill professorships in mathematics and physics at Harvard. He speculated that innate differences between men and women might explain this. Recalling the event afterwards, Summers said he pointed out that fewer girls than boys have top scores on science and maths tests in late high school years. 'I said no one really understands why this is, and it's an area of ferment in social science . . . [but] . . . research in behavioral genetics is showing that things people previously attributed to socialization weren't due to socialization after all.'[2]

Summers understood that differences in the mean averages between boys' and girls' marks in maths or science might be thought irrelevant in discussing appointments to professorships at Harvard, where successful candidates would be drawn only from the top of the performance scale. He addressed this point directly. 'There is relatively clear evidence that whatever the difference in means – which can be debated – there is a difference in the standard deviation and variability of a male and female population,' he told the conference.[3] Effectively, what Summers was saying was that even if the average abilities of men and women are the same, there would be fewer women than men in the tiny group of high performers in maths and science suitable for a job at Harvard.

The conservative writer Dinesh D'Souza has advanced a similar argument in relation to IQ differences between men and women. 'Male and female IQ can be plotted on a bell curve. The mean score looks the same, but the bell curves look different. The female bell curve is taller and narrower; the male bell curve is shorter and flatter. This means that female performance tends to congregate about the mean, whereas among men there are many more geniuses – and many more dummies.'[4]

In his speech to the diversity conference, Larry Summers was clear that his concern was with the geniuses: 'if one is talking about physicists at a top twenty-five research university, one is not talking about people who are two standard deviations above the mean ... but ... talking about people who are three and a half, four standard deviations above the mean: in the one in 5,000, one in 10,000 class. Even small differences in the standard deviation will translate into very large differences in the available pool . . .'[5]

Somewhere around this stage in his talk, one of the women at the conference table got up and stormed out. 'If I'd stayed, I'd have either have blacked out or thrown up,' Nancy Hopkins, a Harvard graduate on the faculty of MIT, said afterwards. Many other women in the American academy shared Hopkins's outrage.[6] Open letters were drawn up, petitions signed and the year-long campaign to oust President Summers began.

In July 2008, a study by Janet Hyde of the University of Wisconsin-Madison was widely reported by news media across the United States under headlines such as 'Girls' Math Skills Now Measure Up to Boys''.[7] This was the largest study of its kind ever conducted and compared the test scores of seven million children across ten states in standardized tests. The results showed that there was no difference in the averages of boys and girls in high school, contradicting studies from twenty years ago that found that there were, and which gave rise to a 'boys are better at maths' stereotype. However, buried in the small print were the details of the variance the researchers had found, showing that at the extreme 'genius' end of the maths ability scale, four standard deviations from the mean, boys outnumbered girls by three to one. For Larry

Summers this vindication came eighteen months too late. By then he was working for the Obama campaign.

The Summers controversy has a social and political significance far beyond Harvard Quad. People are inclined to judge the efficacy of equal opportunities programmes by iconic or highly visible indicators such as how many women are in the boardrooms of the FTSE 100 companies, or holding leadership positions in particular organizations. For years women's groups have been trying to find ways to break through the 'glass ceiling' that stopped them reaching the highest leadership positions. The failure to break through, despite enormous changes in business culture and equal opportunities legislation over the past thirty years, is usually attributed either to residual sexism among males, or the fact that many women's career trajectories are interrupted when they have children. Now, however, an explanation based on real biological differences between the sexes, one that has not been taken seriously for a generation – the old 'wired differently' line – was back again, this time claiming fresh scientific endorsement.

Dr Paul Irwing, an organizational psychologist at Manchester University, went even further. In a 2005 survey based on IQ tests given to eighty thousand people, and a further study of twenty thousand university students, he said he found evidence of a significant intelligence gap between the sexes. If true, it could be large enough to explain away the glass ceiling and the gender pay gap. 'All the research I've done points to a gender difference in general cognitive ability,' Irwing says. 'There is a mean difference of about five IQ points ... There are twice as many men with an IQ of 120-plus as there are women, there are 30 times the number of men with an IQ of 170-plus as there are women.' Dr Irwing is uncomfortable with the political implications of his own research. He says that he has always approached the question of sex differences from a left-of-centre, egalitarian perspective and that his scientific findings challenge his personal worldview.[8]

Armed with evidence like Irwing's, some argue that the Harvard controversy shows that the hereditarians were right all along, and that biology matters: explaining inequalities of representation between men and women on the boards of banks or among the faculty at Harvard. The sexes may be equal, they say, but they are also different, and the physiological architecture built by genes equips men and women for different roles. Trying to shatter glass ceilings or deal with the gender pay gap, they go on, is a Procrustean approach; better to accept the inherent diversity in human nature and stop trying to equalize outcomes artificially. The old taboos are breaking down. Advances in genetic science, and the profile given to them in the media, along with the current fashion for evolutionary psychology, has come close to reversing the immediate, reflexive assumptions people make in this area. Where only a short time ago we would have been cautious about suggesting a genetic cause, it is increasingly the case that genes are the first things that we all point to when searching for an explanation to a social mystery.

Larry Summers is a good example of this tendency. Despite acknowledging that there was little if any difference between most men and women when it came to maths, his first line of speculation about the cause of a difference among a tiny number at the margin, was that it might be genetic. He even told a story about how he had bought his twin daughters toy trucks instead of dolls, but they gave them names – Daddy Truck and Baby Truck. It seems curious that Summers homed in on the perilously volatile genetic explanation when there were so many safer environmental ones to hand.

Given that the pupils in the study took their exams after their teachers had spent twenty years believing boys tended to outperform girls, then it is a fair bet that the brightest boys will have been more assiduously coached. Nancy Hopkins, the MIT professor who walked out on Summers's talk, afterwards directed reporters to studies that show that girls are so sensitive to environmental influences that they perform better in maths tests if there are fewer males in the room.

Charles Darwin, by contrast, took the hereditarian line. 'I am inclined to agree with Francis Galton', he said, 'in believing that education and environment produce only a small effect on the mind of any one, and that most of our qualities are innate.'[9] He was, of course, only able to speculate in the most general terms about the implications of that belief, referring only in passing to 'some inherited modification of the brain', and judging that 'the various parts of the brain must be connected by very intricate channels of the freest intercommunication'.[10]

However, whatever the cause, whether genetic or to do with upbringing, or the high or low expectations of teachers, for the present generation the difference in the numbers of men and women in the pool qualified to teach mathematics or physics at Harvard is a genuine fact. The university has an entire department dedicated to diversifying its faculty, and it is hard to believe that its public agonizing over a failure to recruit enough women and ethnic minorities is simply an elaborate charade put on to disguise latent sexism and racism.

This marked revival of genetics-based accounts of differences between people, one that has been growing steadily over the past fifteen years, has once again brought the observed differences in IQ between races – the phenomenon that so troubled Pat Buchanan in the early 1970s – back into view. The difference between the average test scores of African Americans and whites is generally given as one of fifteen IQ points, or one standard deviation from the mean. By contrast, East Asians and Ashkenazi Jews tend to have higher scores than whites, in the case of Ashkenazi Jews, between one half and one standard deviation. This means that there is considerable overlap between people of all races, but marked differences at the margins. The evolutionary psychologist Steven Pinker has spelled out the effects at the Harvard or MIT end of the scale. Where there are two groups of identical size, and the average of Group A tops the average of Group B by fifteen IQ points, or one standard deviation, then '. . . among people with an IQ of 115 or higher the As will outnumber the Bs by a ratio of three to one,' Pinker says, 'but among people with an IQ of 160 or higher the As will outnumber the Bs by a ratio of forty-two to one.'[11]

Interestingly, studies of high-IQ blacks have found several times as many females as males above the 120-IQ level. Black males and black females share the same genetic inheritance. That means, says the African American social commentator Thomas Sowell, we should be looking at family culture, upbringing, and the ways boys are taught in schools, rather than heredity.

Nevertheless, progress in genetic science compels us to take a fresh look at the whole subject of race and racial difference. One of the arguments traditionally mustered against the racial IQ gap is one that denies there is any biological reality to racial classifications at all. Many common racial generalizations turn out to be false. East Africa, for instance, has produced many champion level marathon runners. But you have to focus on a small number of tribal groups in Kenya and Ethiopia before you find being good at the marathon is a common trait. Other East Africans, West Africans, and African Americans do not possess this skill. By extension, almost any other trait to do with sporting ability, or musical performance – the notorious 'sense of rhythm' argument – turns out to be an unsupportable generalization too, when it is applied to a whole race. In the early 1970s this led the Harvard geneticist Richard Lewontin to declare that 'racial classification is now seen to be of virtually no genetic or taxonomic significance'.[12] Also, most social scientists regarded the races as an artificial set of categories based on mere superficialities such as skin colour or skull shape, but essentially another social construct. Many like to point out there is as much or more difference between individuals of the same race as between an individual of one race and an individual of another.

Perhaps the biggest contemporary challenge to this line of thinking is posed by the television series *CSI*. Given a tiny fragment of DNA left at a crime scene, Gil Grissom and his forensic scientists on the swing shift can tell you with remarkable rapidity the race of the person who left it. They could also say with a reasonable degree of certainty whether his ancestors were Ashkenazi Jews, Finns, Scotch-Irish, or from the Basque country. According to some commentators, this technology broadly confirms traditional racial classifications. 'If a sample of people from around the world are sorted by computer into five groups on the basis of genetic similarity, the groups that emerge are native to Europe, East Asia, Africa, America and Australasia – more or less the major races of traditional anthropology', wrote Armand Marie Leroi on the *New York Times*'s op-ed page.[13]

Moreover, genetic scientists have been exploring a whole other dimension of human difference. It may not be merely a question of which genes we inherit that accounts for racial characteristics, but how those genes express themselves. Scientists comparing the action of the same genes in a sample of white Europeans and another of Asians, found that a quarter of the genes studied varied markedly in their expression levels – in the case of one Caucasian gene, at twenty-two times the intensity of its Asian equivalent. The causes of this variation was tracked down to one-letter changes in DNA, called single nucleotide polymorphisms, SNPs or *snips* for short, in the stretches of DNA that promote and regulate the gene's transcription. This means that though individuals from different races may appear almost identical in terms of the genes they carry, differences between them previously ascribed to environmental factors may turn out to be caused by yet-to-be-understood epigentic mechanisms.

Some scientists are immensely cautious about what they say about race and intelligence, others less so. James Watson suddenly had to abandon a lecture tour of Britain in the autumn of 2007 after he was suspended from his job at, as it happens, the Cold Spring Harbor laboratory, after some remarks he made in an interview with the *Sunday Times*. He told the newspaper he was 'inherently gloomy about the prospect of Africa' because 'all our social policies are based on the fact that their intelligence is the same as ours – whereas all the testing says not really'.[14]

The public denunciations of Watson were reminiscent of the outrage occasioned in the mid-1990s after the publication of Charles Murray and Richard Herrnstein's *The Bell Curve*. Writing in the *New York Times*, Bob Herbert described the book as 'a scabrous piece of racial pornography' and 'just a genteel way of calling somebody a nigger'. Herbert offered his own explanation of the black–white IQ gap. He argued that the African American experience of slavery; poverty; inadequate healthcare, nutrition, housing and education; unemployment; together with casual racism, all contributed to an understandable relative underperformance in intelligence test scores.[15]

This comprehensive environmental account was one many other critics of *The Bell Curve* voiced as well – prompting the book's supporters to ask what catalogue of relative disadvantages white Americans might compile to explain their IQ deficit relative to East Asians and Ashkenazi Jews. In fact, the authors of *The Bell Curve* had relatively little to say about race, their main subject being how America was developing a new class structure based on cognitive ability. They sought to show how low IQ had a close correlation with a range of social problems including criminality, unemployment, family break-up and welfare dependency.

The furore over *The Bell Curve* exemplified the same pattern of political alignment over intelligence that has existed since the 1960s. What has made the issue of the race gap so politically charged is the question of to what extent intelligence is inherited. By and large, the Left has tended to account for observed racial differences in IQ by pointing to social and environmental factors. The Right, by contrast, argues that genes play a substantial part in determining intelligence – but leaves room for environmental factors to play a part too. People in the centre either insist that it is as yet impossible to know one way or the other, or look for a compromise between the hereditarian end environmental positions, distrusting both extremes, which they see, with some good cause, as reflecting wider ideological agendas.

The left-wing assumption that innate abilities are equally distributed across groups has been the dominant one in public policy in both Britain and America for thirty years. Policy approaches to combating discrimination in employment; the way schools are organized, and what is taught and how; and affirmative action programmes – all rest on this assumption being true. A rigid code of political correctness has tended to stifle any questioning of the assumption itself. When outcomes defy the model – with organizations unable to meet their diversity targets, or education standards failing to rise – the Left tends to demand further government intervention.

'Elites throughout the West are living a lie, basing the futures of their societies on the assumption that all groups of people are equal in all respects,' wrote *The Bell Curve*'s co-author Charles Murray in the aftermath of the Larry Summers controversy. 'It is a lie because so many elite politicians who profess to believe it in public do not believe it in private.'[16]

One of George W. Bush's first announcements on becoming president was the No Child Left Behind plan for schools. Extra federal funding was provided for education, but schools were required to meet performance targets. A common standard of achievement tests was introduced, and pupils tested for their progress at key stages of development. It was broadly similar to the target-driven, SATs monitored system introduced in Britain by Tony Blair's Labour government. One of the requirements of the Bush plan was that schools had to demonstrate progress in closing the racial achievement gap (which fairly closely mirrors the IQ gap). Schools that failed to close the gap faced penalties and could be deemed to be failing. This requirement, which critics saw as an attempt to compensate for biology by government fiat, caused many dysfunctional distortions. A vivid illustration of the pressures schools were put under was given in the television series *The Wire*, where imaginative and promising approaches designed to engage some of Baltimore's teenage street-corner drug dealers with their schoolwork in maths and English had to be abandoned to cram them for the tests, otherwise the school would lose funding. In middle-class areas some schools were accused of trying to ethnically cleanse their school rolls by excluding poor black kids on the slightest pretext, so that their race gap figures would look better. The lesson was that minority pupils were actually being harmed by a policy that was supposed to help them.

Britain has a similar race gap to the United States, though it is seldom mentioned in public. Politicians here dissemble in much the same way as they do across the Atlantic, seeing it as necessary to prevent the lower achieving groups being generally stigmatized. In England, the East Asian community is mostly made up of people of Hong Kong Chinese extraction. They outperform all other groups in English at age eleven, even when significant numbers of them do not have English as a first language when they enroll in primary school. At GCSE (aged sixteen) they leave white British pupils trailing by more than 20 percentage points in achieving a minimum of five passes at grades A*–C, including maths and English. British Chinese males are four times as likely (and Indian males three times) to achieve three or more science A-levels than the general population, and Indian and Chinese girls show a strong preference for science at A-level compared with other ethnic groups, leading to a disproportionately high representation of these two ethnic groups among science graduates.

Insofar as politicians or the media ever mention the British Chinese and Indian success stories, it is usually with a somewhat patronizing rider about how their families value education more highly than other groups do. Under the prevailing protocol it is seen as acceptable to make broad generalizations about cultural difference, but no genetic influence may be hinted at. British achievement patterns though would give all-out genetic determinists some problems too. Indian pupils do well, while Pakistani and Bangladeshi pupils – from the same race, but living in markedly different social conditions – do badly. Fewer than a quarter of Afro-Caribbean boys gain five top-grade GCSE passes compared with 36 per cent of boys overall, though girls do much better.

The understandable reluctance not to talk too much about group differences in intelligence, some part of which many people beyond the psychometrics industry now at least privately acknowledge to have some basis in inheritance, may, like well-intentioned but bungled education policies, be harming precisely the people it is supposed to help. The refusal of liberals to engage in debate means that some people are left feeling that there is a truth being kept from them by a conspiracy of political and media elites. There are plenty of crackpots and charlatans on the Internet willing to fill in the gaps with a distorted account of what the real science shows. There is already a tendency for people to form, on the basis of a passing acquaintance with a few facts, broad generalizations such as 'black people are stupider than white people'. As a result, black people may be seen primarily as members of a group rather than individuals and suffer more casual discrimination than would be the case if the complexities of the issue were more widely aired. Steven Pinker, who is unusual in being a political liberal but a convinced hereditarian, proposes a different way of looking at equality that takes account of group difference. 'Equality is not the empirical claim that all groups of humans are interchangeable,' Pinker avers, 'it is the moral principle that individuals should not be judged or constrained by the average properties of their group.'[17]

Another danger of persisting with evasion and denial is that society may be ambushed by scientific progress. One discovery in genetic science could overnight leave the political establishment floundering. Not only are scientists scouring the genome day and night in the hope of finding genes influencing intelligence, evolutionary psychologists are moving on to explore new areas of racial difference. Jonathan Haidt of the University of Virginia has been monitoring research into the inheritance of character or behavioural traits normally seen as arising out of upbringing – aggressiveness, docility, the ability to delay gratification and so on. He predicts that the discovery of racially linked genetic variations in people's propensity to acquire what are often seen as virtues or vices will be an explosive scientific event. 'I believe that the "Bell Curve" wars of the 1990s, over race differences in intelligence, will seem genteel and short-lived compared to the coming arguments over ethnic differences in moralized traits,' Haidt says. He predicts the detonation will take place between 2012 and 2017.[18]

This prediction makes it all the more urgent for society to get to the bottom of the many riddles and unresolved controversies in the study of intelligence. Two of the most problematic areas concern the existence of a general factor of intelligence called 'g', and the possibility of assessing heritability. The various elements of intelligence tests – verbal reasoning, spatial awareness, mathematical ability and so on – correlate positively with one another. Psychometricians employ a statistical technique called factor analysis and derive this general factor 'g', which appears highly heritable. If 'g' is real, and represents something that *can be* inherited – a 'general intelligence' that equips people to perform well in a range of different tests – then the case for intelligence being largely genetic is bolstered.

Scientists working in the field of intelligence testing almost universally accept the reality of 'g'. Factor analysis, though it has gone through a number of (perhaps significant) changes, has been employed in this field since the beginning of the twentieth century. Some experts in statistical methodology, however, say that the system of factor analysis that psychometricians use inevitably throws up a factor that looks like 'g'. According to them, 'g' is an inevitable product of the tool being used, a mere statistical quirk. 'Factor analysis', says Cosma Shalizi of Carnegie Mellon University, '*always* says that there is a general factor whenever there are only positive correlations. The appearance of *g* is a trivial reflection of that correlation structure.' [19]

A phenomenon thrown up simply as a result of statistical methodology is not something that can be inherited. The implication of this criticism is that there may be no single 'general intelligence' but a range of particular skills, each of which may be partly inherited and partly governed by environment. Moreover, in each case the percentage of the variation explained by either inheritance or the environment will probably be different.

The notion of 'heritability' also causes misunderstanding.

Heritability is properly a measure of how much of the variation (with regard to a particular trait) between individuals in a population is influenced by genetic factors. It cannot not tell you, for instance, what proportion of an individual's 'intelligence' is caused by genes, or what proportion by the environment. Some critics argue that the statistical methods customarily used in intelligence research tend to produce exaggerated estimates of the heritability of IQ.[20]

Even if 'g' is a mathematical mirage, that does not mean IQ tests are pointless. They clearly measure *something*, even if only a collection of different skills. That can be useful in predicting who is more likely to go to Oxford or Cambridge, or who is more likely to wind up unemployed or in jail. But the doubts surrounding the validity of much IQ research should make us sceptical about the broad claims made about group differences and their significance. Indeed, until scientists can say which genes influence intelligence, and how they are differently distributed among particular groups, most of what they say should perhaps be regarded as merely speculative.

If the methodology of research into group differences in IQ is suspect, so is its provenance. A large proportion of the best-known researchers in the field during the past fifty years have received grants to assist their work from the controversial Pioneer Fund, which many outsiders regard as a tainted source. When the organization came under fire from critics in the late 1990s, its then president said that the fund had been founded by a group of individuals 'interested in genetics and evolution as the keys to understanding human nature'.[21] In fact the fund was established in 1937 by Wickliffe Draper, the multi-millionaire who had attended the Berlin population conference two years previously along with Clarence Campbell. Since his

1927 expedition to Africa that discovered Asselar Man, Draper had fancied himself as an amateur anthropologist. However, he had long been a devotee of the writings of Madison Grant and, being somewhat obsessed with what he saw as the dangers of miscegenation, had personally paid for Charles Davenport's 1929 study of racial crossing in Jamaica.[22]

The Pioneer Fund was, from its inception, a project intended to advance eugenics and scientific racialism. Its founding directors included Harry Laughlin, Frederick Osborn (the secretary of the American Eugenics Society) and John Marshall Harlan, a lawyer who was later appointed to the United States Supreme Court. To anyone familiar with the work of Madison Grant and Lothrop Stoddard, the name 'Pioneer' was itself a giveaway. Indeed, there was nothing clandestine about the fund's purposes at the time: its articles of incorporation unambiguously spelled out its commitment to encouraging the propagation of people 'descended predominantly from white persons who settled in the original thirteen states prior to the adoption of the Constitution of the United States'.[23] In other words, the ideal New England pioneer type whom Grant and Stoddard believed to be more highly evolved than the rest of the American population. In his preface to Grant's *The Passing of the Great Race*, Frederick Osborn's uncle, the paleontologist Henry Fairchild Osborn, articulated an idea based on the writings of Charles Darwin, which would become the organizing principle of both scientific racialism and the Pioneer Fund. 'Race implies heredity,' Osborn wrote, 'and heredity implies all the moral, social, and intellectual characteristics and traits which are the springs of politics and government.'[24]

The intervention of the Second World War forced the new

Pioneers to put their project on hold. Harry Laughlin had retired from the Eugenics Record Office, and his close association with the Nazi regime made him unsuitable for sensitive war work. Wickliffe Draper, however, went off to serve as a military intelligence officer, and Frederick Osborn took charge of the US Army's propaganda effort, ending up as a major general. This experience doubtless gave him an excellent preparation for his post-war role as the godfather of 'crypto-eugenics'.

By the 1950s, however, Draper had returned to his obsessions. He funded an alarmist campaign to racially segregate donated blood, based on the theory that transfusing negro blood into whites might put the recipients in danger of contracting alien diseases. He also set up an enormous slush fund that operated in parallel with Pioneer to fight the desegregation of schools after the US Supreme Court's 1954 landmark decision in *Brown vs. Board of Education*. Draper subsidized the publication of books and pamphlets, mounted an extensive political lobbying campaign aimed at blocking the Civil Rights Act of 1964, and bankrolled legal challenges to *Brown*.

As well as this more or less overt political work, Draper also funded a more clandestine effort to amass 'scientific evidence' that purported to show that blacks were inferior to whites and that their political and economic plight was a result of their own biological shortcomings. As well as paying the research and publication costs of scientists likely to produce the right sort of evidence, Draper helped establish the 'Human Genetics Fund' as a front organization for distributing grants and, on the sly, endowed a chair in genetics at Wake Forest University in North Carolina. It later emerged that four or five leading scientists had throughout the 1960s received an annual cheque from Draper (worth $5,000 in today's money) as a 'Christmas gift'.

Draper was also closely involved with a new journal, launched in 1960, entitled *Mankind Quarterly*. Even by the already pitifully low standards of eugenics and scientific racialism, this project attracted a particularly unsavoury roster of editors and contributors. Its editor in chief was Robert Gayre, who became an ardent advocate of apartheid in South Africa because he believed the system offered the potential of 'evolutionary advance'.[25] Elsewhere, Gayre insisted, 'the negro . . . is breeding like rabbits because all his natural predators have been removed'.[26] *Mankind Quarterly*'s associate editor was the cytologist Reginald Ruggles Gates, whom we last encountered shamefacedly slinking off after the annulment of his marriage to Marie Stopes on grounds on non-consummation. The unfortunate Gates, whose academic career had suffered numerous setbacks, had developed an unpopular theory that the races of mankind were, in fact, five separate species – a view that Charles Darwin had once briefly entertained, but swiftly rejected. Gates had also developed a consuming hatred for Jews, whom he blamed for terminating his fellowship at Harvard and having him blackballed from the leading scientific journals. When he died in 1962, Gates's successor at *Mankind Quarterly* was Corrado Gini, a former scientific adviser to Benito Mussolini.

During the 1970s, *Mankind Quarterly* was taken over by an Englishman, Roger Pearson. A member of the British Eugenics Society, Pearson had moved to the United States in the 1960s, where he wrote for a series of magazines with a neo-Nazi and strongly anti-Semitic flavour. By 1971, however, he had transformed himself into a respectable-seeming academic and became head of the department of anthropology at the University of Southern Mississippi. There he attracted the first of a series of grants from the Pioneer Fund (he would receive well over a million dollars in subsequent years), before moving to Washington DC, where he has been associated with a number of right-wing think tanks. Through the 1970s, 1980s and 1990s, *Mankind Quarterly* published papers by a number of the leading authorities in the study of intelligence in general, and racial differences in particular, most of whom have themselves been grantees of the Pioneer Fund. There is evidence to suggest that Pioneer had a definite end in mind even after Wickliffe Draper died in 1972. Draper refused point-blank to pay for research that might produce results that ran counter to his own racial prejudices. Some of those Draper entrusted with managing his legacy seem to have felt some fiduciary obligation only to provide grants that the old man would have approved. Consequently, projects that would help portray the African American, or black people in general, as biologically inferior would stand a very good chance of attracting funding. Those that might point to environmental factors being at the root of observed group differences in IQ would not. To what extent this policy may have skewed the science remains an open question.

Among the best-known scholars whose research has been at least part-funded by Pioneer have been: Arthur Jensen, William Shockley, Thomas J. Bouchard (the Minnesota Twins Study), Richard Lynn, Robert A. Gordon, Linda Gotfredson, Hans Eysenck and J. Phillipe Rushton (who is now Pioneer's president). Although he was never a Pioneer grantee himself, Richard Herrnstein's work was reprinted and widely popularized by the Foundation for Human Understanding, an organization that was in receipt of substantial sums of Pioneer money. Some of these eminent scientists whose projects received grants from the fund may well have been only dimly aware of the circumstances and purposes of the Pioneer Fund's founding, or of the ideological aims and racist attitudes of Wickliffe Draper and his close associates. Or they may have chosen to ignore them. Plenty of scholars, after all, are happy to receive money from the Ford Foundation despite Henry Ford's own record of virulent anti-Semitism. However, the Pioneer Fund's activities in other areas of the race debate, such as its funding of anti-immigration groups in the early 1990s, tend to reinforce the conviction held by many critics that not just the Pioneer Fund itself, but the whole field of IQ research too, is irredeemably contaminated.

# CHAPTER TEN

It is as if man had been suddenly appointed managing
director of the biggest business of all, the business of
evolution . . .

Julian Huxley

ANDi proved something of a disappointment to the media. He
was not green and did not glow. Back in 2001, newsrooms
across the world had high hopes of the first transgenic primate. Picture editors rubbed their hands in anticipation of the
money-shot, or, as some called it, the monkey shot: a green,
fluorescent rhesus macaque, under a UV light, preferably
eating a banana. But though he carried the jellyfish gene that
had been inserted into his mother's ovum during IVF, ANDi –
*i-for-inserted DNA* backwards – just would not glow. His twin
siblings glowed nicely, exhibiting fluorescent hair follicles and
toenails. Sadly, they had miscarried at seventy-three days and
no one wants to look at pictures of two dead monkey foetuses.

The scientific community, however, received ANDi rather
more enthusiastically. He provided evidence that a primate egg
could develop normally after genetic manipulation. Rhesus
macaques are natural pioneers. Both NASA and the Russians
have shot them into outer space, and months before ANDi

arrived, another rhesus monkey named Tetra became the first primate produced by cloning. Seven years later scientists finished sequencing the genome of the rhesus macaque, finding that the rhesus monkey 'differs by approximately seven percent from that of humans, while chimpanzees are just one to two percent different'.[1]

By 2006, it was fluorescent pigs that were hogging the limelight. Another team of genetic researchers had cloned three pigs, while inserting the same kind of jellyfish gene that failed to express itself in ANDi. Not only did these animals glow, but two years later one of them gave birth to a litter, of which two little porkers glowed fluorescent green from snout, trotters and tongue. These results, the researchers claimed, showed that not only could genes be successfully inserted into a cloned animal, they could be co-opted by the genome and passed on to future generations.

Although so far such experiments have only been conducted in laboratory animals, scientists have been discussing the theoretical aspects of human germ-line engineering since before the millennium. The first-ever symposium on engineering the human germ line – changing human sperm or egg cells, or very early embryos – was held in Los Angeles in March 1998 at the UCLA Center for the Study of Evolution and the Origin of Life. Delegates promised to eradicate cancers, halt the ageing process and discussed germ-line enhancement – creating designer babies. As ever, James Watson, from Cold Spring Harbor, eschewed the usual euphemistic language. 'If you could cure a very serious disease, *stupidity*,' Watson said, 'that would be a great thing for the people who otherwise would be born seriously disadvantaged.'[2] Watson was adamant that politicians should not try to interfere with the development of the emerging genetic technologies by erecting regulatory frameworks. That, he said, would be 'a complete disaster', though he did concede that: 'If there is a terrible misuse and people are dying, then we can pass regulation.'[3]

Anyone who thought the eugenic impulse had flagged somewhat during the 1980s and 1990s was mistaken. Before human germ-line engineering arrived to offer new hi-tech opportunities, eugenicists had continued plugging away with the old ways of breeding superior people. In 1980, Robert Graham, a millionaire philanthropist who had made a fortune manufacturing impact-resistant spectacles, opened the Repository for Germinal Choice in Escondido, California. More popularly known as the 'Nobel sperm bank', the repository originally planned to supply only the sperm of Nobel laureates. Up to five prizewinners ejaculated into plastic containers and handed their seed to Graham, but the only one to admit doing so publicly was William Shockley, who won his laurels for physics but became better known to Americans for his controversial research on racial differences in IQ. Nobel sperm, it soon transpired, tended to be rather too geriatric for the purpose, characterized by low counts and impaired motility. Reluctantly, Graham had to lower his sights, settling for sperm from lesser-known academics, successful physicians and even the occasional Olympic athlete, but was confident enough about his product to warrant that it had a triple-A rating for cognitive ability.

More than two hundred babies were born with help from the Nobel sperm bank between 1982 and the end of the 1990s. Although the Repository for Germinal Choice was run on the basis of strict confidentiality, David Plotz, the editor of *Slate* magazine, subsequently tracked down many of the children for his book *The Genius Factory*. 'To answer the obvious question: no, they are not all geniuses,' Plotz says. 'Some are dazzling. But the kids are spread in a bell curve, slid a bit to the right of average.'[4] Plotz adds, however, that although the repository did not live up to Robert Graham's original aspirations, it did alter the terms of trade for Americans wanting to acquire donor sperm and ova. Where once people had to accept gratefully whatever sperm their doctor or clinic offered, the Nobel sperm bank stimulated a competitive market where patients could specify desired traits, and hard-up Harvard and Yale students could help pay their way through college by becoming donors.

Just as the Repository for Germinal Choice was winding down, an hour and a half's drive up Highway 15, the Engineering the Human Germline Symposium was getting underway. Among the speakers was Gregory Stock, the director of the Program on Medicine, Technology, and Society at UCLA's School of Medicine, and since then the author of an influential book, *Redesigning Humans: Taking Charge of Our Own Heredity*. Stock believes that mankind currently has the opportunity to 'write a new page in the history of life, allowing us to seize control of our evolutionary future'.[5] Stock foresees a future in which individuals may choose, if they can afford it, to endow their children with an enhanced personality, higher intelligence, physical beauty and long life. Underpinning this way of thinking is a conviction that Mother Nature has not done such a bad job through evolution, albeit in a fairly random and amateurish way; but now it is time for her to stand aside and allow the professionals to speed the process along and give it some proper direction.

Since Stock, like many other evolutionary scientists, perceives a big role for genes in influencing human behaviour, the future he envisions would presumably allow shy parents to have confident daughters, congenital liars to have scrupulously truthful sons and irritable parents to have easy-going offspring. 'Our genes account for anywhere from 40 to 60 percent of the variation in personality among us,' Stock says. 'This includes our level of extroversion and self-involvement, our emotional stability and reaction to stress, our conformity and dependability, our friendliness and likableness, and our general openness and curiosity. Even whether a person says that religion is important in his or her life is about 50 percent heritable.'[6]

Many of the studies that support this outlook are highly suspect. They employ questionable methods of statistical analysis that may give quite misleading results, in the same way as the analysis of IQ sometimes does. Estimates of the heritability of traits like religious belief may well be complete hokum. Those who go even further, misunderstanding heritability as a measure of how much of an individual's religiosity is attributable to his or her genes are straying way off the true path. Besides, attributing 50 per cent of being religious to genes, and 50 per cent to environmental influences is to be 100 per cent determinist, ignoring what is likely to be one the most significant factors of all, individual volition. Man's behaviour is more than the sum of nature and nurture, or any interplay between them. Of course, the religious person's own answer – that their faith is a supernatural gift from the Holy Spirit – is ruled inadmissible by evolutionary scientists because it is not naturalistic. Here is the crux of the current, seemingly insuperable problem between evolutionary science and religion. The religious person might with good reason reply that 'of course it isn't naturalistic, we're discussing the supernatural. You are out of bounds.' But the evolutionary scientist recognizes no bounds, and admits of no supernatural. For him, religious faith is, like everything else, a product of evolution.

The Princeton microbiologist Lee M. Silver is possibly even more gung-ho for taking the controls of human evolution than Gregory Stock. Silver imagines a utopia/dystopia where what he calls 'The Gen-Rich', a genetically engineered 'modern-day hereditary class of genetic aristocrats' would form a political, economic and media elite.[7] In time, the Gen-Rich and the poor 'naturals' might become two distinct species. It may sound like science fiction, but Silver is professor of public policy at the Woodrow Wilson School of Public and International Affairs, and in the thick of the political arguments and culture wars over reprogenetics. His former Cold Spring Harbor colleague James Watson has for a long time given religious objections to germ-line intervention short shrift. 'People say we are playing God,' Watson has said. 'My answer is: "If *we* don't play God, who will?"'[8] Silver takes more or less the same view. He is also impatient with arguments against germ-line engineering that cast it as 'unnatural' and therefore wrong. Silver is on strong ground here. The conflation of what is natural with what is right – the confusion of *is* with *ought* – has long been identified as a fallacy. Besides, such an argument assumes too rosy a picture of nature. The British geneticist J. B. S. Haldane famously quipped, 'If there is a Creator, He must have an inordinate fondness for beetles.' Nature surely shows a similar partiality towards mosquitoes and viruses.

Both Lee M. Silver and Gregory Stock think the advent of human germ-line engineering is inevitable. Any technology that *can* proliferate, *will* proliferate. Pandora's box is already open. The choice may be between simply allowing genetic technology to evolve by natural selection, with all the random chance that process involves, or taking charge of the techniques of artificial selection and bending it to a well-thought-out purpose. Silver warns that if an alliance of religious groups and what he terms 'post-Christian organic food devotees', persuades politicians to erect regulatory barriers in the West, then genetic technology will go East, where, unlike our monotheistic culture, 'every spirit is transcendent, eternal, self-determining and self-evolving'.[9] One has to wonder if Silver has ever met a Chinese Communist bureaucrat.

Such schemes to tweak the human germ line, and possibly create a new species in the longer run, have mainstream secular critics too. 'We do not have to accept any of these future worlds under a false banner of liberty, be it that of unlimited reproductive rights or of unfettered scientific inquiry,' writes Francis Fukuyama. 'True freedom means the freedom of political communities to protect the values they hold most dear, and it is that freedom that we need to exercise with regard to the biotechnology revolution today.'[10] Fukuyama dismisses the threat to take the technology East, pointing to what he regards as reasonably effective international controls on weapons of mass destruction and the trade in human body parts.

The insistence by scientists on the inevitability of a genetically engineered future is reminiscent of the old Marxist declaration of the inevitability of the victory of the proletariat in the class struggle. Many of those who believed it was inevitable saw no reason to help it come sooner rather than later. There is no moral imperative to swim with the current of history rather than against it. It was a perfectly coherent intellectual position for the bourgeois to believe that though socialism would eventually come, he, for the sake of his own and his children's happiness, would do his best to delay its arrival for a generation or two.

Though unlikely to cut much ice with the Darwinists, the religious man should at least try to plead his better claim to the successor generations. With his stake in eschatology, he can plausibly assert a greater investment in the future than can the Darwinist, who – seeing life as meaningless and purposeless – need not really care if the rest of the human race survives him or not. He may worry about his children's welfare, but since he regards his own feelings for his offspring as nothing more than an instinct, an adaptive trait picked up somewhere in the hunter-gatherer period, he should quickly be able to ratiocinate himself out of any compelling sense of obligation on that score.

The politician, who must decide in the end whether human germ-line engineering should be lawful, would be naive to imagine that he can be an honest broker between the rival camps. There are no limits to the Darwinist's territorial imperialism. Not only does he believe that religious sentiment can be explained by evolution, but he believes political outlook can be as well. Robert Yerkes, the man behind the army intelligence tests, was convinced that the propensity to have either a liberal or conservative outlook was significantly heritable.

Nowadays there are a variety of evolutionary accounts of the origin of political attitudes. Some are slightly adapted version of the familiar Alpha Male primate stories – all about dominance hierarchies in the Pleistocene. The politics of envy, we are assured, had its origins in the zero-sum economy of the hunter-gatherer period, where goods were allocated according to status. However, conditions were harsh and we began to share goods as an insurance against lean times – hence the welfare state. On the other hand, the Pleistocene endowed us with genes that make us indignant about sums expended on the welfare dependant and disinclined to vote for higher benefits. And so it goes on, mostly expressed in the standard Darwinist language of concepts. As Ernst Mayr has acknowledged, while in the physical sciences theories are based on laws, 'in evolutionary biology ... theories are largely based on concepts such as competition, female choice, selection, succession and dominance .'[11]

We do not need to believe all this guff. Most of it is entirely speculative, and a good deal is downright specious. No one really has much detailed knowledge of what went on in the early Holocene (10,000 years ago) in terms of human social organization, let alone the late Pleistocene (the 150,000 years before that). Nor do we need to believe most of what turns up relentlessly in the media attached to topical matters of political concern. Recently, when the issue of obesity came on the agenda, there was a sudden rush of evolutionary anthropologists telling us that it was all to do with a switch in our diets 2 million years ago. Those were the very earliest days of the genus *Homo*. Can it be true that our digestive systems have not evolved since then?

If our political outlook is rooted in the Pleistocene, then what of our moral sentiments? Did they continue to evolve, or are they still largely stuck in the time when tribes cheerfully committed genocide against one another? Darwin thought they went on evolving, but from the evidence of the twentieth century, it is hard to tell. Unlike other branches of science, evolutionary science is trying to compile an explanation of what happened a long time ago. This makes it more like history than physics or chemistry. And, as with history, sometimes the facts have to be imagined to fill the gaps in the narrative.

The contrast between what is known and what is imagined is particularly striking in the countdown to human germ-line engineering. Lee M. Silver says that the technology is more or less in place. He is straining at the leash. His graduate students have been practising gene therapy on mice for years, and a mouse embryo looks very like a human embryo under a microscope. But though thousands of geneticists across America know *how* to insert strings of DNA into the genome, they still have little idea which bits to put where. Nobody has the slightest clue where the genes for our extroversion or self-involvement, emotional stability, reaction to stress, our conformity, dependability, friendliness, likeableness, or our general openness and curiosity sit on the genome. They do not know which genes influence intelligence, or where the genes that decide if we are liberal or conservative belong. They do not know if the same allele for religiosity, expressed to a lesser or greater intensity, makes a Scottish Presbyterian and a whirling Dervish of the Sufi persuasion, or whether two quite different ones are required. They do not know where the genes for envy are in our DNA, nor even the location of the Pleistocene one that makes us resent increases in social security benefits.

Evolutionary scientists can and do tell us that the tendency for conservatives to take an organic view of society, be fond of institutions and defend hierarchies is innate. They say that liberal preferences for rights, autonomy and social justice are also innate. But they cannot say even in which chromosome those genes are lurking, nor how the political gene produces a leftist firebrand in late adolescence and then does a one hundred and eighty degree flip once he acquires a house, a mortgage and has kids in school. They do not know what tiny mutations account for the tweedy young fogey in his twenties, or the shabby Trotskyite in late middle age.

On the other hand they probably do know that a single gene cannot govern any one of these complex behaviours, and that many genes are required to interact, or they may be coming to suspect that genes are beside the point, and epigenetics is the new frontier. Some Darwinists may even be wondering whether the vast amount of genetic information required to govern those behaviours that are uniquely human – and remember we have not got on to altruism, the ability to spot cheats, men's propensity to rape, a woman's preference for pink, or the incest taboo yet – is ever going to fit into what is left of the 2 per cent gap between our genome and the chimpanzee's, once the more obvious physiological differences are accounted for. But assuming they resolve that, and they might – tiny differences in genes and gene expression can have huge effects on the phenotype – then they have to think what form an 'enhancement' to any one of these traits might involve, both technologically, and indeed conceptually. After all, the Labour Party could squabble for another decade over whether it is Tony Blair's or Gordon Brown's genome that represents Nature's last word.

Though we all know in our hearts that when the earnest young geneticists go before the parliamentary committees with their PowerPoint presentations and their charts, that these people are no more ready to take the controls of human evolution than a two-year-old infant is to fly a high-performance jet fighter, it will nevertheless be hard to stop them. Our legislators tend to proceed on the basis of precedent rather than principle in these matters, and we have already in Britain permitted the creation of hybrid embryos, so it may be a little late to be raising the *principles* of human nature and human dignity, though perhaps not too late to save the substance.

As we have seen, Darwin's legacy has turned into something of a monstrous hybrid itself over the past 150 years: part science – that we should not quarrel with – but also part ideology. The ideology has caused considerable social harm in the past, and the notable lack of contrition exhibited by its adherents today offers little reassurance that the threat has passed. Indeed, all the signs are that evolutionary science has failed to learn from the mistakes of its own history and is bent on repeating them. History, observed the French historian of philosophy, Etienne Gilson, is the only laboratory we have to test the consequences of thought. Repeated attempts to re-order society along scientific lines, made by successive generations of evolutionary scientists, have been proved in the laboratory of history to be pernicious. We should bear the results of these experiments in mind when, as a society, we decide what measure of scepticism to apply to the boasts and promises of contemporary evolutionary scientists, and what level of deference we pay to them in our national conversation.

If we were to imagine that another branch of science – inorganic chemistry, say – had proved dangerously unreliable over 150 years, then we would have long ago marked its card. When inorganic chemists pressed forward promoting public policy prescriptions based on their researches, we would be justified in setting the bar of acceptance a little higher than we would for scientists from other disciplines. In nearly all its applications in the social and political field, evolutionary science has proved dysfunctional and disruptive. Moreover, the gap between what evolutionary science claims to be true and what it can demonstrate to be true is larger than is the case in most other scientific disciplines. Its claim, for instance, to be able to offer a genetic explanation for *all* social behaviour before it has succeeded in identifying a genetic mechanism controlling *any* non-pathological social trait, would be considered somewhat rash by those working in more conservative branches of science. We are, therefore, justified in taking precautions.

We would be wise to maintain a high level of scepticism in the face of evolutionary science's current cultural triumphalism. On a practical level, evolutionary science poses numerous problems for the smooth running of democratic politics, while on a theoretical or philosophical level it poses a serious threat to our system of liberal democracy itself and the values that underpin it. Both these threats – the practical and the philosophical – are demonstrated by the way today's evolutionary scientists behave in the public square.

Traditionally, scientists were happy to work on the basis that science is about facts, not values. When the facts were in, their work was done. They might invent a nuclear weapon, but the decision whether or not to use it would be one for the politician to make, for politics *is* about values. The politician, in such a situation, would most probably consult others who are in the values business – political thinkers, philosophers, ethicists, priests. Scientists would view such an arrangement as perfectly legitimate, acknowledging that there are many different kinds of truth about the human condition, and that the best public policy decisions are those informed by a range of intellectual traditions. Moreover, in complex multicultural democracies, such as the UK, this inclusive approach is necessary in order to assemble a coalition of support for any particular proposal, one that can bring together in a common cause people with markedly different views of the world. In this pluralist model of society, differences between individuals or groups do not have to be resolved out of existence, but they do have to be accommodated.

The growth of evolutionary science has, however, been accompanied by a parallel growth in scientism – the view that science can offer a natural explanation for everything in life, and that the scientific method of establishing knowledge or truth should trump all other ways of doing so. This narrowing of epistemological authority either relegates to the second rank, or dismisses as entirely delusional, those truths previously seen as recuperable from other traditions, philosophical, religious, humanistic or literary. Critics of scientism, such as the economist and political philosopher F. A. Hayek, have seen it as a form of trespass. The disciplines of scientific method and deductive reasoning are tools suitable to the specific purpose of interpreting the natural world; trying to use these tools outside the natural sciences is foolish and sometimes dangerous. Using scientific methodology to describe phenomena in the social realm is to employ the wrong tool, like using a screwdriver to do the job of a spirit level. Hayek wanted to stem the intrusion into economics and the social sciences of methodological approaches derived from biology and physics, an intrusion he thought had already begun in Charles Darwin's day. '. . . In the hundred and twenty years or so, during which this ambition to imitate Science in its methods rather than its spirit has now dominated social studies, it has contributed scarcely anything to our understanding of social phenomena,' Hayek wrote in his essay 'Scientism and the Study of Society'.[12]

For many scientists, however, the methodology they employ every day in their work becomes more than a tool, it becomes a way of looking at the world beyond the laboratory; for some the *only* legitimate way of looking at the world. The development of the scientific method itself is seen as part of social progress, marking a rite of passage into man's adulthood. Other systems of thought are held to belong, like superstition, to mankind's infancy. Thus, the historian of science, Michael Shermer, puts a positive spin on the word 'scientism' in contrast to the pejorative sense in which the word is more frequently used. 'Scientism', Shermer says, 'is a scientific worldview that encompasses natural explanations for all phenomena, eschews supernatural and paranormal speculations, and embraces empiricism and reason as the twin pillars of a philosophy of life appropriate for an Age of Science.'[13]

In the political context, scientism is a conversation stopper. Empiricism and reason are seldom adequate to the task of mobilizing political action. Appeals to emotion and idealism, however disreputable to the person of scientistic bent, are vital ingredients of liberal democratic politics. Denying the validity of the supernatural basis of religious values, and trying to clear any consideration of them out of the public square, offends against the canons of pluralism and tolerance upon which modern democracy depends.

Although much of the current militancy of atheistic scientism is rooted in a reaction to the terrorist attacks of 9/11, scientism and political Islamism have more in common with one another than either has with the liberal democratic mainstream. Both begin the conversation with a flat-out rejection of the premises of their opponents' arguments. One asserts the absolute, trumping authority of the Koran; the other asserts the absolute, trumping authority of the scientific method. One can no more negotiate the rights and wrongs of reproductive cloning with someone who insists his science proves that human life should be afforded no more special value than the lives of pigs and monkeys than one can negotiate peace in the Middle East with someone who insists his scriptures tell him that Jews are no better than pigs and monkeys.

If you think this comparison is far-fetched, you would do well to study the rhetoric and actions of the biologist Paul Myers. Working in the field of evolutionary developmental biology, Myers is probably the world's pre-eminent expert on the zebrafish. He is also a writer and public intellectual who wishes to banish religion from government and public life. One of his platforms is the website Pharyngula, which was ranked as the top science blog of 2006 by the scientific journal *Nature*. This is a significant accolade. *Nature* was founded in 1869 and was closely associated with Thomas Henry Huxley's X-Club, a group of friends and supporters of Charles Darwin that included Herbert Spencer and the botanist Joseph Hooker. In July 2008, Paul Myers posted an article on Pharyngula under the title 'The Great Desecration'. It described how he had obtained a host or wafer used in the Catholic sacrament of the Eucharist and drove a rusty nail through it. 'I hope Jesus's tetanus shots are up to date,' Myers quipped, mocking the Catholic belief that the consecrated host becomes the body and blood of Christ. Myers went on to attach the defiled Eucharistic wafer to some pages torn from a copy of the Koran, and threw the montage into the rubbish bin along with some used coffee grounds and a banana peel to express his 'unconcerned contempt'. He also photographed the desecration and posted the resulting picture on his blog. [14]

Except in cases of unthinking hooliganism, acts of desecration such as vandalizing graves, urinating on or burning national flags, scrawling graffiti on buildings, are essentially acts of political communication. By doing actual violence to a revered symbol, what they communicate is hatred or contempt. In Myers's case, the message was all the more vicious because the Catholic Eucharist was chosen precisely because it is held to be more than a symbol. Myers's action prompted numerous copycat desecrations. Within a few days of the Pharyngula posting a host was stolen from the London Oratory and desecrated online. In the months afterwards a series of similar desecrations were posted on YouTube. Those who take part in such actions, and those who condone them, whether they are BNP skinheads, radical Islamists or evolutionary scientists, set themselves apart from the moderate mainstream in the political conversation and deserve to be regarded as extremists. Surprisingly, Paul Myers's attitude appears to be broadly representative of that of evolutionary scientists in general. There has been no high profile condemnation of his action by his academic peers; instead he was roundly applauded on many science websites. Professor Richard Dawkins wrote an article calling for people to 'rally round and show support' for Myers when complaints were made to the authorities of his university.[15]

It would be a mistake to think that the present spat between evolutionary science and organized religion is something that non-religious people can safely ignore. It is worth attending to because essentially the same kinds of argument deployed against religion have also been deployed by evolutionary scientists against more secular targets such as commonly shared ethical values and the existence of human rights. Though there is always a risk in extending a metaphor too far, the simile that joins evolutionary fundamentalists with the Islamist variety has hopefully enough elasticity in it for one last stretch, permitting us to consider how, as a democratic society, we deal practically with an intolerant ideology that does not respect the rules of cultural pluralism.

Anjem Choudary is a former solicitor who now describes himself as a judge of the Sharia Court of the UK and a principal lecturer at the London School of Sharia. However sceptical we may be about the importance, or even the existence, of these two institutions, we can be fairly certain that Choudary knows more about Islamic law than most of us ever will. Choudary has spoken in support of the Islamic radical Omar Bakri Mohammed, who has been declared persona non grata in Britain by the Home Office after giving deliberate and studied offence on an even greater scale than Paul Myers. One of Anjem Choudary's more outlandish policy proposals is that all British women, whether Muslim or not, should be made to wear the full burka.

After a number of false starts, British society now knows how to handle people like Anjem Choudary. No longer restrained by political correctness or cultural relativism, we have regained sufficient confidence in our own Western values to label Choudary an extremist and pay little attention to what he says. We should perhaps adopt broadly the same approach when an eminent geneticist like Richard Dawkins tells us that religion is 'a virus of the mind' and we should therefore close down all our faith schools.[16] These schools are the ones that tend to perform best, and their closure, or transfer to a secular authority, would surely impoverish our state schools system. For that reason – and because we believe in the right of parents to decide how their children are brought up – we are entitled to reject Dawkins's proposal as foolish and extreme, as we do Choudary's. Obviously, any comparison between Dawkins and Choudary should not be taken too far: neither miltant atheists nor evolutionary scientists belong to a broader ideological movement some members of which are given to violent extremism or even terrorism. Any such thing would doubtless horrify Richard Dawkins, and quite possibly Anjem Choudary too. However – as we have seen – some evolutionary scientists in the past have shown as few moral scruples about killing people as the more bloodthirsty type of radical Islamist. Certainly, when evolutionary scientists press to be allowed to undertake human reproductive cloning, or demand unregulated access to the controls of human evolution and unfettered freedom to re-engineer the human genome, we should recover sufficient confidence in our Western values to label them as extremists too. Not many of us want to live under an Islamic theocracy, but very few want to live in a scientistic dystopia either.

Our political system, however, suffers from two weaknesses that make us vulnerable to an importunate Darwinism. The first is chiefly a matter of custom, and is relatively easily changed. Our politicians are far too deferential to science and to scientists. Oblivious to Hayek's warnings of how little good and how much harm the inappropriate application of scientific methodology to the social realm can do, we have moved steadily in the direction of making government a technocratic business, with buzz phrases such as 'evidence based policy'. In measuring everything, setting benchmarks, and establishing targets accordingly, we have fallen into the very trap that Hayek predicted: we have come to place too much value on what can be measured, at the expense of the truly important things that cannot be quantified. Our SATs-driven education system is a good example of this tendency.

The public, by contrast has demonstrated a healthy distrust of experts in general, and scientists in particular. In the mid-1990s they heard ministers at the dispatch box assuring them that weight of scientific opinion held that Bovine Spongiform Encephalopathy (BSE) could not jump species. When new-variant CJD appeared, they knew how much weight to attach to the 'weight of scientific opinion' in the future. During the BSE crisis, when controls on British beef were at their most stringent ever, and when scientists could rationally argue that it had never been safer, the public displayed a gloriously perverse refusal to eat it, despite the Agriculture Secretary, John Gummer, feeding a hamburger to his daughter to set us all a good example. The public remains steadfast in its suspicion of genetically modified foods, however many scientific endorsements Monsanto provides; and refuses in significant numbers to allow its children to be given the MMR jab, despite the 'weight of scientific opinion' insisting there is no associated risk of autism.

The British public has little trust for politicians at the best of times, but it trusts them even less when they hide behind scientific authority. The risks associated with genetic science dwarf all previous dangers and voters will look to politicians to be robustly sceptical of the siren claims of cures for serious diseases or even social ills (supporters of new genetic technologies are already touting the promise of identifying and interdicting the 12 per cent of the male population responsible for 50 per cent of violent crime). Just as the Americans have a built a constitutional wall of separation between church and state, all democracies will soon need to begin to create a wall between science and state, drawing clearer distinctions between the proper domains of facts and values.

The second weakness is one that will prove harder to resolve. As liberalism has become progressively disconnected from its roots in European Christian civilization (the Enlightenment was an artefact of that civilization too, we should not forget) we have become less and less certain about what our values are based upon. The claim that all men are equal in the eyes of God, or President Kennedy's insistence that human rights are God-given and not man-made, struggle for traction in a self-consciously secular and culturally plural society. Increasingly we find that rights are shrilly asserted rather than reasoned and we are coming slowly to the discomforting realization that we have been living off the accumulated cultural capital of our Christian past to sustain not just our ethical and moral precepts but our political values as well.

Just at this moment of generalized cultural uncertainty, where people tend to know how they should behave, what they truly treasure, but are not absolutely sure why, our society finds itself suddenly assailed by a raucous and impatient scientism demanding its Year Zero, the jettisoning of consolations, the remaking of the world along scientific lines, everything to be decided by ice-cold logic. Fortunately, we can say no thank you. We prefer not.

'Up until the age of thirty . . . poetry of many kinds, such as the works of Milton, Gray, Byron, Wordsworth, Coleridge and Shelley, gave me great pleasure,' Charles Darwin wrote in his autobiography. 'But for years I cannot endure to read a line of poetry: I have tried lately to read Shakespeare, and found it so intolerably dull that it nauseated me. I have also almost lost any taste for pictures or music.'[17]

One imagines that such an atrophy of the sensibility writ large is what life would be like in a society dominated by the scientistic mindset. And if it would be a spiritual dust bowl, it would surely be a political dystopia too. The Darwinist ideology simply cannot supply the moral and ethical basis for the democracy we want to live in. Evolved moral sentiments offer an inadequate foundation for a system of universal human rights, or for minorities to assert their rights against a tyrannical majority. They cannot supply the demands of justice; and can provide no grounding for human dignity in the face of runaway genetic technology. A little altruism here, a touch of reciprocity there and the odd example of cooperation for good measure is not enough when there is no compelling reason why the strong should not oppress the weak for their own satisfaction or amusement.

Besides, we have seen the threatened future in the past. This is the worldview that coldly put Ota Benga in a cage, locked Kathleen Bradley away for twenty years because she was sick; forcibly sterilized Carrie and Doris Buck; slammed shut America's Golden Door in the faces of desperate refugees; and pushed disabled Germans into a shower room and turned on the poison gas. And now this philosophy tells us *we* should live more rationally? It took nearly a century to sort out the chaos left by Marx and Freud, and to bring their ideas back within reasonable intellectual bounds; but the task of clearing up after the great revolutionary thinkers of the nineteenth century will not be complete until Darwin has been put back in his box.

# Select Bibliography

Alschuler, Albert W., *Law without Values: The Life, Work, and Legacy of Justice Oliver Wendell Holmes* (University of Chicago Press, 2000)

Bagehot, Walter, *Physics and Politics: Thoughts On the Principles of Natural Selection and Inheritance to Political Society* (Ivan R. Dee, Chicago, 1999)

Barrett, Gautrey, et al. (eds.) *Charles Darwin's Notebooks* (Cornell University Press, 1987)

Berenbaum, Michael, Peck, Abraham J., *The Holocaust and History*, United States Holocaust Memorial Museum (Indiana University Press, 2002)

Bradford, Phillips Verner, Blume, Harvey, *Ota: The Pygmy in the Zoo* (St Martin's Press, New York, 1992)

Briant, Keith, *The Life of Marie Stopes* (W. W. Norton, 1962)

Brigham, Carl Campbell, *A Study of American Intelligence* (Princeton University Press, 1923)

Carnegie, Andrew, *Autobiography of Andrew Carnegie* (Constable, London, 1920)

Chesterton, G. K., *Avowals and Denials* (Dodd Mead & Co., New York, 1935)

Chesterton, G. K., *Eugenics and Other Evils: An Argument Against the Scientifically Organized State*, (ed.) Michael W. Perry (Inkling Books, Seattle, 2000)

Crook, Paul, *Darwinism, War, and History* (Cambridge University Press, 1994)

Dalhbom, Bo, *Dennett and His Critics: Demystifying Mind* (Blackwell, 1993)

Darwin, Charles, *Autobiographies* (Penguin, London, 2002)

Darwin, Charles, *On the Origin of Species*, (John Murray, London 1859)

Darwin, Charles, *The Descent of Man and Selection in Relation to Sex* (John Murray, London, 1871 & revised second edition 1882)

# SELECT BIBLIOGRAPHY

Darwin, Charles, *The Life and Letters of Charles Darwin Volume II*, (ed.) Francis Darwin (Adamant, Boston, 2000)

Darwin, Charles, *Voyages of the Adventure and Beagle: Narrative of the surveying voyages of His Majesty's Ships Adventure and Beagle between the years 1826 and 1836, describing their examination of the southern shores of South America, and the Beagle's circumnavigation of the globe. Journal and remarks. 1832–1836*, Vol. III (Henry Colburn, London, 1839)

Davenport, Charles B., *Eugenics* (H. Holt & Co., New York, 1910)

Davenport, Charles B., Steggerda, Morris, *Race Crossing in Jamaica* (Carnegie Institution, Washington, 1929)

Dawkins, Richard, *A Devil's Chaplain* (Weidenfeld & Nicholson, London, 2003)

Dennett, Daniel C., *Darwin's Dangerous Idea: Evolution and the Meanings of Life* (Penguin, London, 1996)

Desmond, Adrian, Moore, James, *Darwin's Sacred Cause: Race, Slavery and the Quest for Human Origins* (Allen Lane, London, 2009)

D'Souza, Dinesh, *Letters to a Young Conservative* (Basic Books, 2002)

Dugdale, R. L., *The Jukes* (Putnam, 1877, reprinted by Arno Press, New York, 1970)

Estabrook, Arthur H., *The Jukes in 1915* (Carnegie Institution of Washington, 1916)

Estabrook, Arthur, 'The Tribe of Ishmael', in *Eugenics, Genetics and the Family*, Vol.I, Second International Congress of Eugenics, New York (Williams & Wilkins Co., Baltimore, 1923)

Ferri, Enrico, *Socialism and Positive Science* (Independent Labour Party, London, 1905)

Franks, Angela, *Margaret Sanger's Eugenic Legacy* (McFarland, North Carolina, 2005)

Fukuyama, Francis, *Our Posthuman Future: Consequences of the Biotechnology Revolution* (Profile Books, London, 2002)

Gallagher, Nancy L., *Breeding Better Vermonters: The Eugenics Project in the Green Mountain State* (University Press of New England, 1999)

Galton, Francis, *Memories of My Life* (Methuen, London, 1908)

Ghent, William J., *Our Benevolent Feudalism* (Macmillan, New York/London, 1902)

Gilmore, Grant, *The Ages of American Law* (Yale, 1977)

Goddard, Herbert Henry, *The Kallikak Family* (Macmillan, New York, 1913)

Gould, Stephen Jay, *The Flamingo's Smile* (W. W. Norton & Company, New York, 1985)

Grant, Madison, *The Passing of the Great Race* (Charles Scribner & Co., New York, 1916)

Haeckel, Ernst, *Freedom in Science and Teaching* (Appleton, New York, 1879)

Haeckel, Ernst, *The Wonders of Life* (Harpers, New York, 1904)

Haldane, J. B. S., *The Inequality of Man* (Chatto, London, 1932)

Hayek, F. A., *The Counter-Revolution of Science: Studies On the Abuse of Reason* (Liberty Fund, Indianapolis, 1980)

Hilberg, Raul, *The Destruction of the European Jews* (Holmes & Meier, 1985)

Hitler, Adolf, *Mein Kampf* (Houghton Mifflin Co., Boston 1941) Searchable e-edition, Universal Digital Library call no. 35176, www.archive.com

Hofstadter, Richard, *Social Darwinism in American Thought* (Beacon Press, Boston, 1992)

Hogben, Lancelot, *Genetic Principles in Medicine and Social Science* (Williams & Norgate, London, 1931)

Holmes, Oliver Wendell, Posner, Richard A., *The Essential Holmes: Selections from the Letters, Speeches, Judicial Opinions, and Other Writings of Oliver Wendell Holmes, Jr.* (University of Chicago Press, 1997)

Hornaday, William T., *The Minds and Manners of Wild Animals*, 1922. Project Gutenberg e-book # 6052, 2004

Howard, Ted, Rifkin, Jeremy, *Who Should Play God?* (Dell, 1981)

Howe, Mark DeWolfe (ed.), *Holmes-Laski Letters* (Harvard University Press, 1953)

Humphrey, Seth K., *Mankind: Racial Values and the Racial Prospect* (Scribner, New York, 1917), reissued as *The Racial Prospect* (Scribner, 1920)

Hunter, George William, *A Civic Biology: Presented in Problems* (American Book Co., New York, 1914)

Jennings, Herbert Spencer, *The Biological Basis of Human Nature* (W. W. Norton, New York, 1930)

Kevles, Daniel J., *In the Name of Eugenics* (Harvard University Press, 1999)

Krammick, Isaac, Sheerman, Barry, *Harold Laski: A Life On the Left* (Allen Lane, Penguin, 1993)

Kropotkin, P., *Mutual Aid: A Factor in Evolution* (William Heinemann, London, 1902). Project Gutenberg e-text no. 4341

# SELECT BIBLIOGRAPHY

Kühl, Stefan, *The Nazi Connection* (Oxford University Press US, 2002)

Laughlin, Harry H., *Eugenical Sterilization in the United States* (Psychopathic Laboratory of the Municipal Court of Chicago, 1922)

Lewis, C. S., *Of Other Worlds: Essays and Stories*, (ed.) Walter Hooper (Harcourt Brace & World, New York, 1967)

Lindsay, A. D., *Karl Marx's Capital: An Introductory Essay* (Oxford University Press, 1925)

Lombardo, Paul A., *Three Generations, No Imbeciles: Eugenics, the Supreme Court, and Buck V. Bell* (Johns Hopkins University Press, 2008)

MacDonald, J. Ramsay, *The Social Unrest* (T. N. Foulis, London & Edinburgh, 1913)

Marks, Jonathan M., *Human Biodiversity: Genes, Race, and History* (Aldine Transaction, New Jersey, 1995)

Marx, Karl, Engels, Friedrich, *Marx/Engels Collected Works*, Volume 41 (Lawrence & Wishart, London, 1985)

Nietzsche, Friedrich, *The Will to Power* (trans. Anthony M. Ludovici), Vol.II, Book III, in *The Complete Works of Friedrich Nietzsche*, (ed.) Oscar Levy (T. N. Foulis, Edinburgh, 1910), Vol.15

Noll, Steven, *Feeble-Minded in Our Midst* (UNC Press, 1996)

Oudes, Bruce (ed.), *From the President: Richard Nixon's Secret Files* (HarperCollins, 1990)

Paul, Diane B., *The Politics of Heredity* (SUNY Press, New York, 1998)

Pearson, Karl, *The Life, Letters and Labours of Francis Galton*, Vol.IIIA (Cambridge University Press, 1930)

Pernick, Martin S., *The Black Stork: Eugenics and the Death of 'Defective' Babies in American Medicine and Motion Pictures Since 1915* (Oxford University Press US, 1999)

Pinker, Steven, *The Blank Slate* (Allen Lane, London, 2002)

Proctor, Robert N., *Racial Hygiene: Medicine Under the Nazis* (Harvard University Press, 1988)

Rosen, Jeffrey, *The Supreme Court* (Times Books, 2007)

Rühle, Otto, *Karl Marx: His Life and Work* (Viking Press, New York, 1929)

Sanger, Margaret, *The Pivot of Civilization* (1922). Project Gutenberg e-text 1689.

Scott Fitzgerald, Francis, *The Great Gatsby*, (ed.) Ruth Prigozy (Oxford University Press, 1998)

# SELECT BIBLIOGRAPHY

Silver, Lee M., *Remaking Eden: Cloning and Beyond in a Brave New World* (Avon Books, New York)

Singer, Peter, *Practical Ethics* (Cambridge University Press, Cambridge, 1993)

Slater, John, Köllner, Peter (eds.), *The Collected Papers of Bertrand Russell, Volume 11 – Last Philosophical Testament 1947–68* (Routledge, London, 1997)

Spencer, Herbert, *Social Statics* (John Chapman, London, 1851)

Spiro, Jonathan Peter, *Defending the Master Race: Conservation, Eugenics, and the Legacy of Madison Grant* (University Press of New England, 2008)

Stoddard, Lothrop, *The Rising Tide of Color Against White World-Supremacy* (Charles Scribner's Sons, New York, 1921)

Stone, Dan, *Breeding Superman* (Liverpool University Press, 2002)

Stopes, Marie Carmichael, *Radiant Motherhood* (Putnam, London, 1920)

Sumner, William Graham, *The Forgotten Man and Other Essays* (Ayer Publishing, Manchester NH, 1969)

Stock, Gregory, *Redesigning Humans: Our Inevitable Genetic Future* (Houghton Mifflin Harcourt, 2002)

Tucker, William H., *The Funding of Scientific Racism* (University of Illinois Press, 2002)

Vaux, Kenneth L., *Birth Ethics: Religious and Cultural Values in the Genesis of Life* (Crossroad, New York, 1989)

Warner, Amos G., *American Charities* (Thomas Y. Crowell Co., New York, 1908)

Webb, Sidney, *The Decline of the Birth Rate*, Fabian Tract 131 (Fabian Society, London 1907)

Weikart, Richard, *From Darwin to Hitler* (Palgrave Macmillan, 2006)

Wheen, Francis, *Karl Marx* (Fourth Estate, London, 1999)

Wills, Gary, *Under God: Religion and American Politics* (Simon & Schuster, 1990)

Wills, Gary, *Head and Heart: American Christianities* (Penguin Press, London, 2007)

Wintle, A. D., *The Last Englishman* (Michael Joseph, London, 1968)

Yerkes, R. M., *Almost Human* (Century Co., New York, 1925)

Yerkes, R. M., *Chimpanzees: A Laboratory Colony* (Johnson Reprint Corporation, New York, 1943/1971)

# SELECT BIBLIOGRAPHY

## ARTICLES

Armytage, W. H. G., 'The Social Context of Eugenic Thought IV', Galton Institute Newsletter, March 1996

Beveridge, William, 'The Problem of the Unemployed', Sociological Papers, Vol.III (Macmillan, London, 1907), pp.323–41

Buckley, F., Buckley S. J., 'Wrongful Deaths and Rightful Lives – Screening for Down Syndrome', Down Syndrome Research and Practice, Vol.12, Issue 2, October 2008, p.79–86

Danielson, Florence H., Davenport, Charles B., The Hill Folk, ERO Memoir No.1, Cold Spring Harbor, New York, 1912

Dennett, Daniel, 'Darwin's Dangerous Idea', The Sciences, May/June 1995, pp.34–40

Goddard, Dr H. H., 'The Intelligence of Immigrants', Journal of Heredity, 1917; 8: 554–6

Gould, Stephen Jay, 'Carrie Buck's Daughter', Natural History 93 (July): 14–18

Hodgson, Geoffrey M., Social Darwinism in Anglophone Academic Journals, Journal of Historical Sociology, Vol.17 No.4, December 2004

Hyde, Janet, et al., 'Gender Similarities Characterize Math Performance', Science 25 July 2008 Vol.321. no.5888, pp.494–5

Kenny, Michael G., 'Towards a Racial Abyss: Eugenics, Wickliffe Draper and the Origins of the Pioneer Fund', Journal of History of the Behavioral Sciences, Vol.38(3), 259–283 Summer 2002. p.279

Leonard, Tim, Origins of the Myth of Social Darwinism, Department of Economics, Princeton, November 2007

Lewontin, R. C., 'The Apportionment of Human Diversity', Evolutionary Biology 6: 381–98

Lombardo, Paul A., 'Carrie Buck's Pedigree', The Journal of Laboratory and Clinical Medicine, 138:278–82 (2001)

Lombardo, Paul A., 'Involuntary Sterilization in Virginia: From Buck v. Bell to Poe v. Lynchburg', Developments in Mental Health Law, 3 (July–September 1983)

Lombardo, Paul A., 'Taking Eugenics Seriously', Florida State University Law Review, Number, 30 (Winter 2003)

# SELECT BIBLIOGRAPHY

Lombardo, Paul, 'Eugenic Sterilization Laws' (University of Virginia), Eugenics Archive, Dolan DNA Learning Center, Cold Spring Harbor Laboratory: www.eugenicsarchive.org

Lombardo, Paul A., 'Pioneer's Big Lie', *Albany Law Review*, Vol.66, p.1137

Mackay, G. W., 'Leucotomy in the Treatment of Psychopathic Feeble-minded Patients in a State Mental Deficiency Institution', *Journal of Mental Science*, 94: pp.834–41

Murray, Charles, 'The Inequality Taboo', *Commentary*, September 2005

Nikoukari, Mondana, 'Gradations of Coercion: The Plight of Women of Color and Their Informed Consent in the Sterilization Debate', *Connecticut Public Interest Law Journal*, Vol.1, No.1. 2001, p.52

Paul, Diane, 'Eugenics and the Left' *Journal of the History of Ideas*, Vol.45, No.4, October–December 1984, p.574

Shermer, Michael, 'The Shamans of Scientism', *Scientific American*, June 2002

Singer, Peter, 'Shopping at the Genetic Supermarket', in *Asian Bioethics in the 21st Century*, (eds.) S. Y. Song, Y. M. Koo & D. R. J. Macer (Tsukuba, 2003), pp. 143–56

Stack, D. A.,The First Darwinian Left: Radical & Socialist Responses to Darwin, 1859–1914, *History of Political Thought*, Vol. XXI, No.4, Winter 2000

Ward, Robert de C., 'The Immigration Problem Today', *Journal of Heredity*, 1920; 11. p.323

Weikart, Richard, 'Darwinism and Death: Devaluing Human Life in Germany 1859–1920', *Journal of the History of Ideas*, Johns Hopkins University Press, Volume 63, Number 2, April 2002, pp.323–44

West, John G., 'The American Eugenics Movement and the Tyranny of Scientific Expertise', Seattle Pacific University, a paper prepared for the 'Science and Democratic Culture', Panel at the Southwestern Political Science Association Annual Meeting, March, 2005, New Orleans

Whitney, Glayde, 'Reproduction Technology for a New Eugenics', a paper for The Galton Institute conference 'Man and Society in the New Millennium', September 1999, *Mankind Quarterly*, Vol.40, No.2, 1999, pp.179–92

# Notes

CHAPTER ONE

1 New York Times, 10 September 1906.
2 The Minds and Manners of Wild Animals, William T. Hornaday, 1922. Project Gutenberg e-book # 6052, 2004. Ch.1.
3 Ibid. Preface.
4 Ibid. Ch.5.
5 The Wonders of Life, Ernst Haeckel (Harpers, New York, 1904), p.56–7.
6 The Descent of Man and Selection in Relation to Sex, Charles Darwin (John Murray, London, 1871), Vol.1, p.201.
7 New York Times, 11 September 1906.
8 New York Times, 'The Scandal At the Zoo' by Mitch Keller, 6 August 2006. See also Ota: The Pygmy in the Zoo, Phillips Verner Bradford & Harvey Blume (St Martin's Press, New York, 1992), p.183.
9 New York Times, 12 September 1906.
10 Religion and Politics, Pew Forum on Religion and Public Life, Washington DC. 24 August 2006.
11 'Darwin's Dangerous Idea', Daniel Dennett, The Sciences, May/June 1995, pp.34–40. See also: Darwin's Dangerous Idea: Evolution and the Meanings of Life, Daniel C. Dennett (Penguin, London, 1996).
12 'Is There a God', Bertrand Russell (commissioned – but not published – by Illustrated Magazine in 1952). The Collected Papers of Bertrand Russell, Volume 11 – Last Philosophical Testament 1947–68, (eds.) John Slater, Peter Köllner (Routledge, London, 1997), pp.542–8. See also: A Devil's Chaplain, Richard Dawkins (Weidenfeld & Nicholson, London, 2003), pp.117–18.

13  *The Supreme Court*, Jeffrey Rosen (Times Books, 2007), p.199.

14  Website of the Zoological Society of London: http://www.zsl.org/

15  *Associated Press*, 26 August 2005.

16  *John F. Kennedy's Inaugural Address*, 20 January 1961, Department of State Bulletin, 6 February 1961.

17  *Descent* (1871), pp.100–1.

18  *The Need for Transcendence in the Postmodern World*, Vaclav Havel. Address delivered in the Independence Hall, Philadelphia, 4 July 1994.

19  Transcript: *Barack Obama's Inaugural Address*, www.nytimes.com/

20  www.dissentfromdarwin.org/

21  *Smoking and Health Proposal*, Brown & Williamson 1969. University of California, San Francisco, Legacy Tobacco Documents Library, Bates No. 680561778/1786.

22  *Project Steve*, National Centre for Science Education, 17 October 2008. www.ncse.org/

23  'Evolution of Human Races', Henry Fairfield Osborn, *Natural History*, Jan/Feb 1926. Reprinted in *Natural History* 89 (April 1980), p.129.

24  *Times Online*, 17 October 2007. Watson subsequently issued statements variously described as 'clarifications' and 'retractions' denying that he took the view that black people were less intelligent than white people – as the *Times* headline stated. Details of these can be found on his Wikipedia page.

CHAPTER TWO

1  *Autobiographies*, Charles Darwin (Penguin, London, 2002), p.72. (Details of Darwin's reading at this time are discussed in 'Darwin's Middle Road' in *The Panda's Thumb*, Stephen Jay Gould (W. W. Norton, 1992), citing 'The Origin of the Origin Revisited', Silvan S. Schweber, *Journal of the History of Biology*, 1977.)

2  Letter from Karl Marx to Ferdinand Lassalle, 16 January 1861, *Marx/Engels Collected Works*, Volume 41 (Lawrence & Wishart, London, 1985), p.245.

3  *Karl Marx: His Life and Work*, Otto Rühle (Viking Press, New York, 1929), p.365.

4 *Karl Marx's Capital: An Introductory Essay*, A. D. Lindsay (Oxford University Press, 1925), p.22.

5 *Karl Marx*, Francis Wheen (Fourth Estate, London, 1999), pp.364–8.

6 Letter from Charles Darwin to Karl von Scherzer, 26 December 1879, *The Life and Letters of Charles Darwin Volume II*, Charles Darwin, (ed.) Francis Darwin (Adamant, 2000), p.413.

7 *Freedom in Science and Teaching*, Ernst Haeckel (Appleton, New York, 1879), pp.90–1.

8 Letter from Karl Marx to Friedrich Engels, 18 June 1862, in *Marx Engels Collected Works*, Volume 41 (Lawrence & Wishart, London, 1985), p.380.

9 An *allele* is an alternative form of a gene (one member of a pair) that is located at a specific position on a specific chromosome. *Selection pressure* relates to the (usually environmental) factors that influence the direction of natural selection. Natural selection operates at the level of the organism, causing, say, giraffes with shorter necks to die more quickly than those with longer necks, because they cannot reach the available food.

Over time, the alleles giving rise to longer necks will become more common within the giraffe population than those giving rise to shorter necks. In this example, the frequency of long-neck alleles has increased in response to a selection pressure brought about by high-growing leaves and the absence of sufficient vegetation at ground level.

10 *Physics and Politics: Thoughts On the Principles of Natural Selection and Inheritance to Political Society*, Walter Bagehot (Ivan R. Dee, Chicago, 1999), pp.40–1.

11 *Mutual Aid: A Factor in Evolution*, P. Kropotkin (William Heinemann, London, 1902), Project Gutenberg e-text no. 4341.

12 *The Principles of Biology*, Herbert Spencer (D. Appleton & Co, New York, 1898), Vol. 1 pp. 444–5.

13 *Social Statics*, Herbert Spencer (John Chapman, London, 1851), p.323–5.

14 Ibid. pp.380–1.

15 *Descent* (1871), p.168.

16 Darwin adds this rider:

> The aid which we feel impelled to give to the helpless is mainly an incidental result of the instinct of sympathy, which was orig-inally acquired as part of the social instincts, but subsequently

rendered, in the manner previously indicated, more tender and more widely diffused. Nor could we check our sympathy, if so urged by hard reason, without deterioration in the noblest part of our nature. The surgeon may harden himself whilst performing an operation, for he knows that he is acting for the good of his patient; but if we were intentionally to neglect the weak and helpless, it could only be for a contingent benefit, with a certain and great present evil. Hence we must bear without complaining the undoubtedly bad effects of the weak surviving and propagating their kind; but there appears to be at least one check in steady action, namely the weaker and inferior members of society not marrying so freely as the sound; and this check might be indefinitely increased, though this is more to be hoped for than expected, by the weak in body or mind refraining from marriage. (*Descent*, pp.168–9).

Nowadays considerable controversy rages about whether Darwin approved or condoned social Darwinism or eugenics. This passage clearly demonstrates his refusal to condone the 'hard' social Darwinism involved in refusing charitable assistance to the poor; but the solution he advocates is unquestionably a eugenic one. Darwin's exchanges with Francis Galton show that he was not unsympathetic to eugenics, and Alfred Russel Wallace noted Darwin was worried about the dysgenic effects of the differential birthrate:

In one of my latest conversations with Darwin he expressed himself very gloomily on the future of humanity, on the ground that in our modern civilisation natural selection had no play, and the fittest did not survive. Those who succeed in the race for wealth are by no means the best or the most intelligent, and it is notorious that our population is more largely renewed in each generation from the lower than from the middle and upper classes. (*Human Selection*, Alfred Russel Wallace, *Fortnightly Review*, Volume 48, September 1890.)

This supports the view that Darwin did support eugenics in principle, but may have had doubts about its practicability. Darwin was dead before eugenics had its heyday, so it is not possible to know for sure whether he would have condoned or approved particular eugenic practices. A number of Charles Darwin's own children became prominent in the eugenics movement. In other respects they were anxious to safeguard their father's legacy and reputation, so it seems unlikely they would have involved themselves in a project they did not think their father would have condoned.

17 *New York Times*, 12 June 1893.

18 *The Forgotten Man and Other Essays*, William Graham Sumner (Ayer Publishing, Manchester NH, 1969), p.225.

19 'Looking Backward', Adolph Read Jr., in *Left Hooks, Right Crosses* (eds.) Christopher Hitchens & Christopher Caldwell (Thunders Mouth Press/Nation Books, New York, 2002), p.79.

20 *Darwinism, War, and History*, Paul Crook (Cambridge University Press, 1994), p.14.

21 Quoted in *Social Darwinism in American Thought*, Richard Hofstadter (Beacon Press, Boston, 1992), p.45, citing *Our Benevolent Feudalism*, William J. Ghent (Macmillan, New York/London, 1902), p.29.

22 'The Concentration of Wealth: Its Economic Justification', William Graham Sumner, in *The Challenge of Facts and Other Essays*, William Graham Sumner (Yale University Press, 1914), Online Library of Liberty e-edition, www.oll.libertyfund.org/

23 *Times Online*, 'Sir Fred Goodwin's financial risk-taking might all be in the genes', Mark Henderson, 11 February 2009.

24 *Autobiography of Andrew Carnegie*, Andrew Carnegie (Constable, London, 1920), p.339.

25 *Socialism and Positive Science*, Enrico Ferri (Independent Labour Party, London, 1905), p.xi. Quoted in 'The Diffusion of Spencerism and its Political Interpretations in France and Italy', Naomi Beck, in *Herbert Spencer: The Intellectual Legacy*, (eds.) Greta Jones and Robert A. Peel (Galton Institute, London, 2004), p.53.

26 *Reuters*, 'Republicans Practise "Social Darwinism" ', by Barbara Liston, 11 December 2005.

27 Auvinen's manifesto was posted on YouTube, and has subsequently been removed. See www.oddculture.com/

28 *An Open Letter to Louisiana Legislators*, Darell Scott (Columbine Redemption, Littleton CO), 9 March 2004. www.columbineredemtion.com/

# NOTES

## CHAPTER THREE

1 *Memories of My Life*, Francis Galton (Methuen, London, 1908), p.288.

2 H. G. Wells, during a panel discussion at a meeting of the Sociological Society on 16 May 1904. Francis Galton and Karl Pearson were present. Reported in *The American Journal of Sociology*, Volume X, July 1904, No.1.

3 The society was called the Eugenics Education Society between 1908 and 1926, when it became the Eugenics Society. For the sake of simplicity, I have used the latter, better known, designation throughout, until the society again renamed itself as the Galton Institute in 1989.

4 *Daily Express*, 4 March 1910, cited in *Breeding Superman*, Dan Stone (Liverpool University Press, 2002), p.127.

5 *The Decline of the Birth Rate*, Sidney Webb, Fabian Tract 131 (Fabian Society, London 1907).

6 *Avowals & Denials*, G. K. Chesterton (Dodd Mead & Co., New York, 1935), pp.58–9.

7 *Eugenics and Other Evils: An Argument Against the Scientifically Organized State*, G. K. Chesterton, (ed.) Michael W. Perry (Inkling Books, Seattle, 2000), p.56.

8 Ibid. p.17. See also 'First Steps towards Eugenic Reform', Leonard Darwin, *Eugenics Review*, 4, 1912. pp.26–38.

9 *Hansard*, House of Commons Debates, 17 May 1912, Vol.38 cc1443–519. Letter: Darwin to Gray, 21 August 1862.

10 *The Social Unrest*, J. Ramsay MacDonald (T. N. Foulis, London & Edinburgh, 1913), p.3.

11 *Hansard*, 17 May 1912.

12 *Genetic Principles in Medicine and Social Science*, Lancelot Hogben (Williams & Norgate, London, 1931), p.210; cited in 'Eugenics & the Left', Diane Paul, *Journal of the History of Ideas*, Vol.45, No.4, October–December 1984, p.574.

13 Introduction by H. G. Wells to *The Pivot of Civilization*, Margaret Sanger (1922). Project Gutenberg e-text 1689.

14 *The Life, Letters and Labours of Francis Galton*, Karl Pearson, Vol.IIIA (Cambridge University Press, 1930), p.414.

15 *Eugenics Review*, 1.3, 1909, p.191.

16 *The Will to Power*, Friedrich Nietzsche (trans. Anthony M. Ludovici), Vol.II, Book III, in *The Complete Works of Friedrich Nietzsche*, (ed.) Oscar Levy (T.N. Foulis, Edinburgh, 1910), Vol.15, p.194.

17 'The New Outlook', Thomas Common, *Notes for Good Europeans (The Good European Point of View)*, 1.1, 1903, p.4; quoted in *Breeding Superman*, Dan Stone (Liverpool University Press, 2002), p.67.

18 *Of Other Worlds: Essays and Stories*, C. S. Lewis, (ed.) Walter Hooper (Harcourt Brace & World, New York), 1967, p.77.

19 'Leucotomy in the Treatment of Psychopathic Feeble-minded Patients in a State Mental Deficiency Institution', G. W. Mackay, *Journal of Mental Science*, 94: pp.834–41. See also *Edith and the Rampton Leucotomies*, www.psychosurgery.org, December 2006.

20 *The Last Englishman*, A. D. Wintle (Michael Joseph, London, 1968), p.7.

21 *The Inequality of Man*, J. B. S. Haldane (Chatto, London, 1932), p.251.

22 *Harold Laski: A Life On the Left*, Isaac Kramnick & Barry Sheerman (Allen Lane, Penguin Press, 1993), p.85.

23 *Human Biodiversity: Genes, Race, and History*, Jonathan M. Marks (Aldine Transaction, New Jersey, 1995), p.86. Richard Lynn identifies six Nobel laureates whom he claims at some point have accepted the scientific validity of eugenics: Alexis Carrel, Hermann Muller, Linus Pauling, Peter Medawar, Francis Crick and Joshua Lederberg. See: *Eugenics: A Reassessment*, Richard Lynn (Preager, 2001), p.42.

24 'The Problem of the Unemployed', William Beveridge, *Sociological Papers*, Vol.III (Macmillan, London, 1907), pp.323–41.

25 *Eugenics Review*, Vol.35, 1943, p.23.

26 'The Social Context of Eugenic Thought IV', Professor W. H. G. Armytage, Galton Institute Newsletter, March 1996.

27 'Reproduction Technology for a New Eugenics', Glayde Whitney, a paper for The Galton Institute conference 'Man and Society in the New Millennium', September 1999, *Mankind Quarterly*, Vol.40, No.2, 1999, pp.179–92.

## CHAPTER FOUR

1 'New Contraceptive Advances Freedom, Responsibility', Judy Mann, *Washington Post*, 12 December 1990.

2 *The Biological Basis of Human Nature*, Herbert Spencer Jennings (W. W. Norton, New York, 1930), p.203. Jennings was named after Herbert Spencer. According to his American Philosophical Society biography: 'His father was a physician and an evolutionist philosopher . . . His father's love for the works of Herbert Spencer, Charles Darwin, Thomas Henry Huxley, Tyndall, and the like was passed on to Herbert, his oldest son.' (http://www.amphilsoc.org/)

3 *In the Name of Eugenics*, Daniel J. Kevles (Harvard University Press, 1999), p.76.

4 'The New Decalogue of Science: An Open Letter from the Biologist to the Statesman', Albert Edward Wiggam, *Century Magazine*, March 1922. Further editions published by Blue Ribbon Books, New York, 1923 and Bobbs Merrill Co., Indianapolis, 1923. Reprint of *Century Magazine* article held at University of Albany, New York. e-version at Eugenics Archive :www.eugenicsarchive.org/ # 1349.

5 *Eugenics*, Charles B. Davenport (H. Holt & Co., New York, 1910), pp.31–2.

6 *Eugenical Sterilization in the United States*, Harry H. Laughlin (Psychopathic Laboratory of the Municipal Court of Chicago, 1922), pp.446–51.

7 See *Chimpanzees: A Laboratory Colony*, R. M. Yerkes (Johnson Reprint Corporation, New York, 1943/1971), p.11.

8 See *Almost Human*, R. M. Yerkes (Century Co., New York, 1925).

9 *The Passing of the Great Race*, Madison Grant (Charles Scribner & Co., New York, 1916), pp. 49-50.

10 *Descent*, Charles Darwin, Second Edition, (John Murray,1882), p.618.

11 *Birth Ethics: Religious and Cultural Values in the Genesis of Life*, Kenneth L. Vaux (Crossroad, 1989), pp.8–9. See also 'Gradations of Coercion: The Plight of Women of Color and Their Informed Consent in the Sterilization Debate', Mondana Nikoukari, *Connecticut Public Interest Law Journal*, Vol.1, No.1. 2001, p.52.

12 Quoted in *The Black Stork: Eugenics and the Death of 'Defective' Babies in American Medicine and Motion Pictures Since 1915*, Martin S. Pernick (Oxford University Press US, 1999), p.95.

13 *The Jukes*, R. L. Dugdale (Putnam, 1877, reprinted by Arno Press, New York, 1970), p.119.

14 Preface by Charles Davenport to *The Jukes in 1915*, Arthur H. Estabrook (Carnegie Institution of Washington, 1916), p.iii.

15 *The Kallikak Family*, Herbert Henry Goddard (Macmillan, New York, 1913), pp.7 & 71. e-edition at Canadian Libraries Collection www.archive.org.

16 McCulloch, N. C. C., 1888, reported in *American Charities*, Amos G. Warner, (Thomas Y. Crowell Co., New York, 1908), p.37. Document displayed by the Disability History Museum at www.disabilitymuseum.org doc 1648 para ref: 286. Quoted with slight variations (used here) in 'The Tribe of Ishmael', Arthur Estabrook, in *Eugenics, Genetics and the Family*, Vol.I (Williams & Wilkins Co., Baltimore, 1923), p.400. (Papers of the Second International Congress of Eugenics, New York, September 22–8, 1921.)

17 *Eugenics, Genetics and the Family*, p.401.

18 Ibid. p.402.

19 Ibid. pp.403–4.

20 For the full story of Perkins and his eugenics projects, see *Breeding Better Vermonters: The Eugenics Project in the Green Mountain State*, Nancy L. Gallagher (University Press of New England, 1999).

21 *Descent*, Charles Darwin, 2nd Edition (John Murray, 1882), p.124.

22 *The Hill Folk*, Florence H. Danielson & Charles B. Davenport, ERO Memoir No.1, Cold Spring Harbor, New York, 1912.

23 *Three Generations, No Imbeciles: Eugenics, the Supreme Court, and Buck V. Bell*, Paul A. Lombardo (Johns Hopkins University Press, 2008). Lombardo, Paul A., 'Carrie Buck's Pedigree', *The Journal of Laboratory and Clinical Medicine*, 138:278–82 (2001); Lombardo, Paul A., 'Involuntary Sterilization in Virginia: From Buck v. Bell to Poe v. Lynchburg', *Developments in Mental Health Law*, 3 (July–September 1983); Lombardo, Paul A., 'Taking Eugenics Seriously', *Florida State University Law Review*, Number, 30 (Winter 2003).

See also: 'The American Eugenics Movement and the Tyranny of Scientific Expertise', John G. West, Seattle Pacific University, a paper prepared for the Science and Democratic Culture Panel at the Southwestern Political Science Association Annual Meeting, March, 2005, New Orleans; and 'Carrie Buck's Daughter', Stephen Jay Gould,

*Natural History* 93 (July): 14–18 and in *The Flamingo's Smile*, Stephen Jay Gould, (W. W. Norton & Company, New York, 1985), pp.307–13.

24 'A Soldiers Faith', Oliver Wendell Holmes Jr., Memorial Day Address to the Graduating Class, Harvard University, 30 May 1895, in *The Essential Holmes: Selections from the Letters, Speeches, Judicial Opinions, and Other Writings of Oliver Wendell Holmes, Jr.*, Oliver Wendell Holmes, Richard A. Posner (University of Chicago Press, 1997), pp.87–93. For effect of Darwin on Holmes, see *Law without Values: The Life, Work, and Legacy of Justice Holmes*, Albert W. Alschuler (University of Chicago Press, 2000).

25 Quoted in *Law without Values*, Alschuler, 2000, pp.31–2. Gilmore's Storrs Lectures were subsequently expanded and published as *The Ages of American Law*, Grant Gilmore (Yale, 1977).

26 Letter from Holmes to Lewis Einstein, 19 August 1909 in *The Essential Holmes*, Introduction, pp.xxv–xxvi.

27 *Holmes–Laski Letters*, (ed.) Mark DeWolfe Howe (Harvard University Press, 1953). Searchable e-text version in Universal Library Collection at www.archive.com.

28 Quoted in *Feeble-Minded in Our Midst*, Steven Noll (UNC Press, 1996), p.73.

29 'Virginia Governor Apologizes For Eugenics', Dave Reynolds, *Inclusion Daily Express*, 06 May 2002 Disability Rights News: www.inclusiondaily.com/

30 *Relf v. Weinberger et al.*, U.S. District Court of D.C., 15 March 1974.

31 'Norplant: A New Contraceptive with the Potential for Abuse', ACLU, 1994. www.aclu.org/

CHAPTER FIVE

1 *Congressional Record*, 68th Congress, 1st Session, Vol.65, 5961–2, 9 April 1924, GPO, Washington DC, 1924.

2 *Time*, 20 May 1940.

3 The story of Hitler's letter to Grant is widely told and is said to have originated in the unpublished manuscript of an autobiography by the late Leon Fradley Whitney (1894–1973), an officer of the American Eugenics Society, who reportedly saw the original letter. I have not seen

Whitney's MS, which is held in the library of the American Philosophical Society under the reference B W613b.

4 *Descent* (1871), Vol.II, p.388. Darwin goes on to say: 'Nevertheless all the races agree in so many unimportant details of structure and in so many mental peculiarities, that these can be accounted for only through inheritance from a common progenitor; and a progenitor thus characterised would probably have deserved to rank as man.'

5 *Darwin's Sacred Cause: Race, Slavery and the Quest for Human Origins*, Adrian Desmond & James Moore (Allen Lane, 2009).

6 *Descent* (1871) Vol.I, p.166.

7 *Descent* (1882 edition), p.612.

8 *Descent* (1871), Vol.II, p.404.

9 *Voyages of the Adventure and Beagle: Narrative of the surveying voyages of His Majesty's Ships Adventure and Beagle between the years 1826 and 1836, describing their examination of the southern shores of South America, and the Beagle's circumnavigation of the globe. Journal and remarks. 1832–1836*, Charles Darwin (Henry Colburn, London, 1839), Vol.III, p.235.

10 *Descent* (1871), Vol.I, p.166.

11 Letter Darwin to Sulivan, 30 June 1870 in *Life and Letters of Charles Darwin*, Volume 2, Project Gutenberg e-text # 2088.

12 *The Passing of the Great Race*, Madison Grant (Charles Scribner & Co., New York, 1916), p.3.

13 Ibid., p.5–8.

14 *The Rising Tide of Color Against White World-Supremacy*, Lothrop Stoddard (Charles Scribner's Sons, New York, 1921), pp.261–2.

15 *Descent* (1871), Vol.I, p.179.

16 *The Rising Tide of Color Against White World-Supremacy*, p.252.

17 *The Passing of the Great Race*, p.81.

18 *Mankind: Racial Values and the Racial Prospect*, Seth K. Humphrey (Scribner, New York, 1917), reissued as *The Racial Prospect* (Scribner, 1920). E-edition at http://openlibrary.org

19 *The Passing of the Great Race*, pp.91, 263.

20 *Biological Aspects of Immigration*, Hearings Before the Committee on Immigration and Naturalization, House of Representatives, 66th Congress, Second Session, 16–17 April 1920, GPO, Washington DC, 1921.

21 'The Intelligence of Immigrants', Dr H. H. Goddard, *Journal of Heredity*,

1917; 8: 554–6. See also: 'Two Immigrants Out of Five Feebleminded', from *The Survey*, 15 September 1917 at Disability History Museum Library: www.disabilitymuseum.org/

22  *A Study of American Intelligence*, Carl Campbell Brigham (Princeton University Press, 1923), p.205.

23  Ibid. p.190.

24  Ibid, pp.208–10.

25  Reported in 'The Immigration Problem Today', Robert de C. Ward, *Journal of Heredity*, 1920; 11. p.323.

26  Quoted in *Defending the Master Race: Conservation, Eugenics, and the Legacy of Madison Grant*, Jonathan Peter Spiro, (UPNE, 2008), p.206.

27  Ibid., p.207.

28  Document collection of the American Presidency Project, University of California Santa Barbara: www.presidency.ucsb.edu/

29  *The Great Gatsby*, F. Scott Fitzgerald (Simon & Schuster Scribner Classics, reprint 1996). First published by Scribner, New York, 1925. Edition consulted here: *The Great Gatsby*, Francis Scott Fitzgerald, Ruth Prigozy (Oxford University Press, 1998), p.14.

## CHAPTER SIX

Quotation at head of chapter is from *Hitler: A Study in Tyranny*, Alan Bullock (Harper & Row, 1964), p.398.

1  See 'Eugenic Sterilization Laws', Paul Lombardo (University of Virginia), Eugenics Archive, Dolan DNA Learning Center, Cold Spring Harbor Laboratory: www.eugenicsarchive.org. The Eugenics Archive also holds the invitation to Laughlin from the University of Heidelberg to attend its 550th Jubilee. Laughlin was in esteemed company receiving his honorary degree in this anniversary year: among other non-Germans so honoured was the Finnish composer Jean Sibelius.

2  'Darwinism and Death: Devaluing Human Life in Germany 1859–1920', Richard Weikart, *Journal of the History of Ideas*, Johns Hopkins University Press, Volume 63, Number 2, April 2002, pp. 323–44. See also *From Darwin to Hitler*, Richard Weikart (Palgrave Macmillan, 2006).

3  'Don't Doubt It', David Klinghoffer, *National Review Online*, 18 April 2008.

4 *Charles Darwin's Notebooks*, (eds.) Barrett, Gautrey et al. (Cornell University Press, 1987). Notebook C, # 196-7.

5 *The Passing of the Great Race*, Madison Grant, p.45.

6 *Descent* (1871), pp.168-9.

7 'Skepticism and Freedom: A Modern Case for Classical Liberalism', Daniel J. Mahoney, *First Things*, January 2004.

8 *Autobiographies*, Charles Darwin, (eds.) Michael Neve & Sharon Messenger (Penguin Classics, 2002), p.54.

9 *Mein Kampf*, Adolf Hitler, Reynal & Hitchcock (Houghton Mifflin Co., Boston 1941). Searchable e-edition, Universal Digital Library call no. 35176, www.archive.com.

10 Ibid.

11 *Racial Hygiene: Medicine Under the Nazis*, Robert N. Proctor (Harvard University Press, 1988), p.193.

12 Adolf Hitler, op. cit.

13 *The Destruction of the European Jews*, Raul Hilberg (Holmes & Meier, 1985).

14 Letter from Charles Darwin to William Graham, 3 July 1881. Darwin Correspondence Project letter ref. #13230. www.darwinproject.ac.uk/

## CHAPTER SEVEN

1 *Racial Hygiene*, Robert N. Proctor (Harvard University Press, 1988), p.10.

2 'US Eugenist Hails Nazi Racial Policy', *New York Times*, 29 August 1935; *The Nazi Connection*, Stefan Kühl (OUP US, 2002), pp.33-4; 'The Cooperation of German Racial Hygienists and American Eugenicists Before and After 1933', Stefan Kühl, in *The Holocaust and History*, Michael Berenbaum, Abraham J. Peck, United States Holocaust Memorial Museum (Indiana University Press, 2002), pp.134-47; 'Eugenics and Population Control', Gabriele Liebig, *American Almanac*, 1994; 'Pioneer's Big Lie', Paul A. Lombardo, *Albany Law Review*, Vol.66, p.1137; 'Moral Courage', Stephen Metcalf, *Slate* 17 October 2005.

3 Kühl, *The Nazi Connection*, p.62.

4 Letter from Gates to Keith Briant, Marie Stopes papers at the British Library: BL-MCS 59848-6-7, 1962.

5 *Radiant Motherhood*, Marie Carmichael Stopes (Putnam, London, 1920), p.219.

6 *The Life of Marie Stopes*, Keith Briant (W. W. Norton, 1962), p.143.

7 *The Future of Human Heredity,* Frederick Osborn (Weybright & Talley, New York, 1968).

8 Frederick Osborn made these remarks in some unpublished notes he made relating to a draft of a paper entitled 'Paradigms or Public Relations: The Case of Social Biology' by the sociologists Gerald Markle and John Fox. Markle and Fox argued that the rebranding of eugenics as 'social biology' was essentially a public-relations exercise in response to the stigma resulting from eugenics' association with the Nazis and reactionary politics. Osborn disagreed, claiming the change reflected a genuine shift in understanding of the relationship between cultural factors and genetics. I have not seen *Notes on 'Paradigms or Public Relations: The Case of Social Biology'*, which is among the Frederick Henry Osborn Papers at the American Philosophical Society (MS. Coll.24). The contents are described by Edmund Ramsden in 'Confronting the Stigma of Perfection: Genetic Demography, Diversity and the Quest for a Democratic Eugenics in the Post-war United States', *Working Papers on the Nature of Evidence: How Well Do 'Facts' Travel?* No. 12/06, Department of Economic History, London School of Economics, 2006, p.42. The document is also quoted in *Margaret Sanger's Eugenic Legacy*, Angela Franks (McFarland, 2005), p.83; and in *The Politics of Heredity*, Diane B. Paul (SUNY Press, 1998), p.142. Osborn's notes are dated 25 January 1974 and relate to a draft of Markle and Fox's paper dated 8 December 1973. *Roe vs. Wade* was decided on 22 January 1973.

9 'Wrongful Deaths and Rightful Lives – Screening for Down Syndrome', Buckley F., Buckley S. J., *Down Syndrome Research and Practice*, Vol.12, Issue 2, October 2008, pp.79–86.

10 'In New Tests for Fetal Defects, Agonizing Choices', Amy Harmon, *New York Times*, 20 June 2004.

11 *Roe vs. Wade*, US Supreme Court, 22 January 1973.

12 Abortion Act 1967. The UK Statute Law Database: www.statutelaw.gov.uk/

13 *Hansard*, House of Lords, 16 March 2004, cols. 215–19.

14 'Abortion campaigners welcome MP's change of heart', Elizabeth Day, *Daily Telegraph (Online)*, 7 December 2003.

15 Shopping at the Genetic Supermarket', Peter Singer, in *Asian Bioethics in the 21st Century*, (eds.) S. Y. Song, Y. M. Koo & D. R. J. Macer (Tsukuba, 2003), pp.143–56.

16 *Practical Ethics*, Peter Singer (Cambridge, 1993), pp.175–217.

17 *Who Should Play God?* Ted Howard & Jeremy Rifkin (Dell, 1981), p.81.

18 Address delivered by Pope Benedict XVI to participants in a conference sponsored by the Pontifical Academy for Life on the theme 'New Frontiers of Genetics and the Danger of Eugenics'. Report with English translation at www.zenit.org/

## CHAPTER EIGHT

1 *guardian.co.uk* Science Blog, posted by Prof Michael Reiss, 11 September 2008. Link: www.guardian.co.uk/science/blog/2008/sep/11/michael.reiss.creationism

2 'Royal Society to be called to account for creationist view', Mark Henderson, *The Times*, 16 September 2008.

3 Ibid.

4 Letter from Sir Richard Roberts (writing also on behalf of Sir John Sulston and Sir Harold Kroto) to Lord Rees, President of the Royal Society, 13 September 2008. www.richarddawkins.net.

5 http://nobelprize.org/nobel_prizes/chemistry/laureates/1996/kroto-autobio.html

6 *Observer*, 14 September 2008.

7 'Royal Society Statement Regarding Professor Michael Reiss', RS Press Release, 16 September 2008.

8 *Guardian,* 16 September 2008; *The Times*, 17 September 2008.

9 *Guardian*, Science Blog posted by James Randerson, 12 September 2008. www.guardian.co.uk

10 www.cofe.anglican.org/darwin/malcolmbrown.html. See also: 'Church makes "ludicrous" apology to Charles Darwin', Jonathan Petre, *Daily Mail*, 13 September 2008.

11 See *Under God: Religion and American Politics*, Garry Wills (Simon & Schuster, 1990) and *Head and Heart: American Christianities*, Garry Wills (Penguin Press, 2007).

12  See *Treason*, Ann Coulter (Crown Forum, 2003).

13  *A Civic Biology: Presented in Problems*, George William Hunter (American Book Co., New York, 1914). See 'A Book for No Seasons: The Forgotten Aspects of John Scopes's Famous Biology Textbook', Garin Hovannisian, *Weekly Standard*, 12 July 2007.

14  *The World's Greatest Court Trial* (National Book Co., Cincinnati, 1925), p.332. Darrow had not been entirely a genetic determinist; he allowed for environmental determinism too. The full quotation reads: 'I know that one of two things happened to this boy; that this terrible crime was inherent in his organism, and came from some ancestor, or that it came through his education and his training after he was born.' Bryan quoted Darrow's words back at him during the Scopes trial.

15  'John Scopes', Douglas O. Linder (University of Missouri-Kansas City School of Law, 2004), www.law.umkc.edu

16  *The World's Greatest Court Trial*, pp.298–302.

17  *Epperson vs. Arkansas*, Supreme Court of the United States, decided 12 November 1968.

18  State of Arkansas, 73rd General Assembly, Regular Session 1981, Act 590.

19  McLean v. Arkansas Board of Education, 529 F. Supp. 1255, 1258–64.

20  *Kitzmiller vs. Dover Area School Board*, Memorandum of Opinion, Case 4:04-cv-02688-JEJ; Document 342; Filed 20 December 2005.

21  *USA TODAY*/Gallup Poll, conducted 1–3 June 2007; reported 7 June 2007.

## CHAPTER NINE

Quotation at head of chapter is from *Marriage and Morals*, Bertrand Russell (George Allen & Unwin, 1929), p.266.

1  Memo from Pat Buchanan to President Richard Nixon dated 26 August 1971, reprinted in *From the President: Richard Nixon's Secret Files*, (ed.) Bruce Oudes (HarperCollins,1990), p.311.

2  'Summers' remarks on women draw fire', Marcella Bombardieri, *Boston Globe*, 17 January 2005.

3  'What Larry Summers Said – and Didn't Say', Swarthmore College Bulletin, January 2009.

# NOTES

4 *Letters to a Young Conservative*, Dinesh D'Souza (Basic Books, 2002), p.103.

5 Remarks at NBER Conference on Diversifying the Science & Engineering Workforce (Lawrence H. Summers, January 14, 2005). See also: 'We're Different – Get Over It', Steve Sailer, *National Post*, Toronto, 24 February 2005.

6 *Boston Globe*, 17 January 2005.

7 'Gender Similarities Characterize Math Performance', Janet Hyde et al., *Science*, 25 July 2008 Vol.321. no.5888, pp.494–5.

8 *Independent*, 30 November 2006. See Irwing & Lynn, *British Journal of Psychology* 2005 Nov:96(Pt.4):505–24.

9 Darwin, *Autobiographies*, p.20.

10 *Descent* (2nd edition, 1882), p.68.

11 'Groups and Genes: The Lessons of the Ashkenazim', Steven Pinker, *New Republic Online*, Post date: 17 June 2006; Issue date: 26 June 2006.

12 'The Apportionment of Human Diversity', R. C. Lewontin, *Evolutionary Biology* 6: 381–98.

13 'A Family Tree in Every Gene', Armand Marie Leroi, *New York Times*, 14 March 2005.

14 'Black people "less intelligent" scientist claims', *Times Online*, 17 October 2007. (Watson subsequently retracted/denied this interpretation.)

15 'In America; Throwing a Curve', Bob Herbert, *New York Times,* 26 October 1994.

16 'The Inequality Taboo', Charles Murray, *Commentary*, September 2005.

17 *The Blank Slate*, Steven Pinker (Allen Lane, 2002), p.340.

18 'Faster Evolution Means More Ethnic Differences', Jonathan Haidt (World Question Center 2009), Edge, http://www.edge.org/

19 *g – a statistical myth* www.cscs.umich.edu/~crshalizi/weblog/523.html 18 October 2007.

20 *Yet More on the Heritability and Malleability of IQ* www.cscs.umich.edu/~crshalizi/weblog/520.html 27 September 2007.

21 'Towards a Racial Abyss: Eugenics, Wickliffe Draper and the Origins of the Pioneer Fund', Michael G. Kenny, *Journal of History of the Behavioral Sciences*, Vol.38(3), 259–283 Summer 2002. p.279.

22 *Race Crossing in Jamaica*, Charles B. Davenport & Morris Steggerda (Carnegie Institution, Washington), 1929.

23  Kenny, op. cit. p.261.

24  Henry Fairfield Osborn, Preface, *The Passing of the Great Race*, Madison Grant (Scribner, New York), 1916. p.vi.

25  *The Funding of Scientific Racism*, William H. Tucker (University of Illinois Press, 2002), p.92.

26  Ibid. p.91.

## CHAPTER TEN

Quotation at head of chapter is from 'Transhumanism' by Julian Huxley in *New Bottles for Old Wine*, Julian Huxley (Chatto & Windus, London, 1957), pp. 13-17.

1  Baylor College of Medicine News 13 April 2007: 'DNA sequence of Rhesus macaque has evolutionary, medical implications', www.bcm.edu/news/item.cfm?newsID=853

2  *New York Times*, 22 March 1998.

3  *Nature*, News, Meredith Wadman, 26 March 1998.

4  'The genius generation', David Plotz, *Guardian*, 15 April 2004.

5  *Redesigning Humans: Our Inevitable Genetic Future*, Gregory Stock (Houghton Mifflin Harcourt, 2002), p.2.

6  Ibid., p.104.

7  *Remaking Eden: Cloning and Beyond in a Brave New World*, Lee M. Silver (Avon Books, New York), 1997.

8  *Times Higher Education Supplement*, 14 March 1997.

9  http://lapa.princeton.edu/peopledetail.php?ID=332

10  *Our Posthuman Future: Consequences of the Biotechnology Revolution*, Francis Fukuyama (Profile Books 2002), p.218.

11  'Darwin's Influence On Modern Thought', Ernst Mayr, 23 September 1999; lecture delivered in Stockholm on receiving the Crafoord Prize from the Royal Swedish Academy of Science. www.biologie.uni-hamburg.de/b-online/e36_2/darwin_influence.htm

12  *The Counter-Revolution of Science: Studies On the Abuse of Reason*, F. A. Hayek, Liberty Fund, 1980, pp.17–165.

13  'The Shamans of Scientism', Michael Shermer, *Scientific American*, June 2002.

14  http://scienceblogs.com/pharyngula/2008/07/ the_great_desecration.php

15 http://richarddawkins.net/article,2848,PLEASE-WRITE-IN-
   SUPPORT-OF-PZ-MYERS,Richard-Dawkins-PZ-Myers-Pharyngula

16 'Viruses of the Mind', Richard Dawkins in *Dennett and His Critics:
   Demystifying Mind*, (ed.) Bo Dalhbom (Blackwell, 1993). 'Dawkins leads
   atheist revolt against "evil" church schools', *Independent*, 24 February
   2001.

17 Darwin, *Autobiographies*, p.84.

# Index

# INDEX

# INDEX

# INDEX

# INDEX

# INDEX

# INDEX

# picador.com

blog
videos
interviews
extracts